Anonymous

Judgment of the Judicial Committee of the Privy Council in the Manitoba School Case

With factums and other documents in connection therewith. Session 1893

Anonymous

Judgment of the Judicial Committee of the Privy Council in the Manitoba School Case
With factums and other documents in connection therewith. Session 1893

ISBN/EAN: 9783337301590

Printed in Europe, USA, Canada, Australia, Japan

Cover: Foto ©Suzi / pixelio.de

More available books at **www.hansebooks.com**

JUDGMENT

OF THE

JUDICIAL COMMITTEE OF THE PRIVY COUNCIL

IN THE

MANITOBA SCHOOL CASE

WITH FACTUMS AND OTHER DOCUMENTS IN CONNECTION THEREWITH

SESSION 1893

PRINTED BY ORDER OF PARLIAMENT

OTTAWA
PRINTED BY S. E. DAWSON, PRINTER TO THE QUEEN'S MOST EXCELLENT MAJESTY
1893

[No. 33*a* & 33*b*—1893.]

FURTHER PARTIAL RETURN

[33*a*]

To an ADDRESS of the HOUSE OF COMMONS dated the 6th February, 1893, for a copy of the judgment of the Judicial Committee of Her Majesty's Privy Council in the appealed case of Barrett *vs.* the City of Winnipeg, commonly known as the "Manitoba School Case"; also copy of factums, reports and other documents in connection therewith.

By order.

JOHN COSTIGAN,

Secretary of State.

OTTAWA, 14th February, 1893.

PRIVY COUNCIL.

***Present*:**

The Right Hon. Lord Watson,
The Right Hon. Lord Macnaghten,
The Right Hon. Lord Morris,
The Right Hon. Lord Hannen,
The Right Hon. Sir Richard Couch,
The Right Hon. Lord Shand.

CITY OF WINNIPEG,

Appellant,

and

BARRETT,

Respondent,

ON APPEAL FROM THE SUPREME COURT OF CANADA.

CITY OF WINNIPEG,

Appellant,

and

LOGAN,

Respondent,

ON APPEAL FROM THE COURT OF QUEEN'S BENCH FOR MANITOBA.

Law of Canada, Province of Manitoba.

Dominion Statute, 33 Vict., c. 3.

Manitoba Public Schools Act, 1890—Denominational Schools—Powers of Provincial legislature.

According to the construction of the Constitutional Act of Manitoba, 1870, 33 Vict., c. 3 (Dominion Statute), having regard to the state of things which existed in Manitoba at the date thereof, the legislature of that province did not exceed its powers in passing the Public Schools Act, 1890.

Section 22 of the act of 1870 authorizes the provincial legislature exclusively to make laws in relation to education, so as not to "prejudicially affect any right or privilege with respect to denominational schools which any class of persons have, by law or practice in the province, at the union."

Held, that the act of 1890, which abolished the denominational system of public education established by law since the union, but which did not compel the attendance of any child at a public school, or confer any advantage in respect of attendance other than that of free education, and at the same time left each denomination free to establish, maintain and conduct its own schools, did not contravene the above proviso; and that accordingly certain by-laws of a municipal corporation, which authorized assessments under the act, were valid.

Appeal in the first case from a judgment of the supreme court (Oct. 28, 1891), reversing one of the court of queen's bench for Manitoba (Feb. 2, 1891); in the second case from a judgment of the court of queen's bench (Dec. 19, 1891), which followed that of the supreme court.

The province of Manitoba joined the union in 1870, upon the terms of the Constitutional Act of Manitoba, 1870, 33 Vict., c. 3 (Dominion Statute.)

Section 22 is the material section, and is set out in their lordships' judgment. In 1890 the provincial legislature passed two statutes relating to education —chaps. 37 and 38—the latter of which is intituled "The Public Schools Act, 1890." Its validity was the subject of this appeal.

The facts are stated in the judgment of their lordships.

In the first case the application was for a summons to show cause why the by-laws in question, which were passed under the act for levying a rate for school and municipal purposes in the city of Winnipeg, should not be quashed for illegality on the ground that the amounts levied for protestant and Roman catholic schools were therein united, and that one rate was levied upon protestants and catholics alike for the whole sum, in a manner which but for the act of 1890 would have been invalid according to the education acts thereby repealed.

Killam, J., dismissed the summons, holding that the rights and privileges referred to in the Dominion statute were those of maintaining denominational schools, of having children educated in them, and of having inculcated in them the peculiar doctrine of the respective denominations.

He regarded the prejudice effected by the imposition of a tax upon catholics for schools to which they were conscientiously opposed as something so indirect and remote that it was not within the act.

The court of queen's bench affirmed this order.

Taylor, C. J., and Bain, J., held that "rights and privileges" included moral rights, and that whatever any class of persons was in the habit of doing in reference to denominational schools, should continue, and not be prejudicially affected by provincial legislation, but that none of those rights and privileges had been in any way affected by the act of 1890.

Dubree, J., dissented, holding that the right or privilege existing at the union was the right of each denomination to have its denominational schools, with such teaching as it might think fit, and the privilege of not being compelled to contribute to other schools of which members of such denomination could not in conscience avail themselves; and that the act of 1891 invaded such privilege, and was consequently *ultra vires.*

The supreme court reversed the order.

Ritchie, C. J., held that as catholics could not conscientiously continue to avail themselves of the public schools as carried on under the system established by the Public Schools Act, 1890, the effect of that act was to deprive them of any further beneficial use of the system of voluntary catholic schools which had been established before the union, and had thereafter been carried on under the state system introduced in 1871.

Patterson, J., pointed out that the words "injuriously affect" in section 22, sub-section 1, of the Manitoba Constitutional Act, would include any degree of interference with the rights or privileges in question, although falling short of the extinction of such rights or privileges. He held that the impediment cast in the way of obtaining contributions to voluntary catholic denominational schools by reason of the fact that all catholics would, under the act, be compulsorily assessed to another system of education amounted to an injurious affecting of their rights and privileges within the meaning of the sub-section.

Fournier, J., pointed out that the mere right of maintaining voluntary schools, if they chose to pay for them, and of causing their children to attend such schools, could not have been the right which it was intended to reserve to catholics or other classes of persons by the use of the word "practice," since such right was undoubtedly one enjoyed by every person or class of persons by law, and took a similar view to that taken by Patterson, J.

Taschereau, J., gave judgment in the same sense, holding that the contention of the appellants gave no effect to the word "practice" inserted in the section.

In the second case a similar application was made by the respondent Logan, and allowed in consequence of the supreme court's decision in Barrett's case.

Sir H. Davey, Q.C., McCarthy, Q.C., and Campbell, Q.C. (both of the Canadian bar), for the appellant, contended that the view taken by Killam, J., Taylor, C.J., and Bain, J., was correct.

The act of 1890 did not affect any right or privilege with respect to denominational schools which the respondent or any class of persons had by law or practice in the province prior to the union.

It established one system of public schools throughout the province, and abolished all the laws regarding public schools which had theretofore been passed and were then existing.

Sections 21 and 22, sub-sections 1, 2 and 3, of the Manitoba Act, 1870, were referred to, and the various affidavits which had been made in the case, and it was contended that the act of 1890 was not *ultra vires*. It enacted that all public schools in the province are to be free schools (section 5); that all religious exercises therein shall be conducted according to the regulation of the advisory board which is provided by section 6; but in case the guardian or parent of any pupil notifies the teacher that he does not wish such pupil to attend such religious exercises, then the pupil need not attend. All public schools are non-sectarian, and no religious exercises are allowed, except as provided by the act, which, moreover, is not compulsory.

With regard to the state of things, "law or practice" in Manitoba prior to the union, the law then in force was the law of England, as it existed at the date of the Hudson's Bay Company's charter, viz., the 2nd of May, 1670, in so far as applicable. Accordingly, the respondent had not, nor had the Roman catholics of the province, any right or privilege by law in relation to the Roman catholic denominational schools.

The only right and privilege on this subject which they possessed was, as shown by the affidavits, the privilege to establish and maintain private schools which were supported by fees paid by the parents or guardians of the children who attended them, supplemented, it may be, by those who belonged to the Roman catholic church.

The act of 1890 does not interfere with or prejudicially affect this right, for the respondent and Roman catholics are still entitled to establish and maintain denominational schools as before the union. Consequently it has not been shown that the act interferes with any rights and privileges which were locally enjoyed within the city.

Reference was made to *ex parte* Renaud (1); Fearon *vs.* Mitchell (1). In the other appeal, the respondent Logan represented members of the church of England, whose rights and privileges were similar to those of Barrett and his co-religionists.

Sir Richard Webster, A.G., Blake, Q.C., and Ewart, Q.C. (both of the Canadian bar), and Gore, for the respondent Barrett :—

The act of 1890 prejudicially affects the rights and privileges of Roman catholics in the province, as they existed by law or practice at the date of the union, with respect to denominational schools.

By its operation they are deprived of the system of Roman catholic denominational schools as they existed before the union.

The public schools constituted by the act are, or may be, protestant denominational schools, and catholic ratepayers are compelled to contribute thereto.

They cannot conscientiously permit their children to attend the schools established by the act, and, having regard to the compulsory rate levied upon them in support thereof, material impediments are cast in the way both of subscribing and of obtaining subscriptions in support of catholic denominational schools, and of setting up and maintaining the same. The rights and privileges of catholics are, accordingly, prejudicially affected.

At the date of the union there was not, and there never had been, any state system of education in Manitoba, nor was there any compulsory rate or state grant for purposes of education.

There was, however, an established and recognized system of voluntary denominational education, including Roman catholic schools supported in part by voluntary contributions from catholics and contributed by the Roman church.

In a similar way, the church of England and various protestant sects supported their own schools.

The provincial legislature established by the Dominion Statute of 1870, passed 34 Vict., c. 12, establishing a state system of education in the province. Subsequent acts were passed, and the whole were codified by 44 Vict., c. 4; and modification was made therein by 45 Vict., cc. 8 and 11; 46 & 47 Vict., c. 46; 47 Vict., cc. 37 and 54; 48 Vict., c. 27; 50 Vict., cc. 18 and 19; 51 Vict., c. 31; 52 Vict., cc. 5 and 21; all which acts show that useful education can be provided without disturbing rights and privileges as they existed in 1870. Then came the act complained of.

Besides the establishment of public schools, controlled as to religious teaching by an advisory board, section 179 abolished pre-existing catholic school districts, and provided that all the assets of such catholic schools should belong to, and all the liabilities thereof should be paid by, the public school districts established by the new act.

The right and privilege which had been prejudicially affected was the right to have a religious education conducted under the supervision of their church, administered in the schools which they were compelled to support; to have the immunity existing in 1870, from being compelled to support schools to which they objected.

Their interests were prejudiced in being compelled by the act to support one set of schools while, as a matter of religion and conscience, they would, at the same time, have to establish another set of schools to which alone they could send their children.

The new public schools, controlled ultimately by a majority of ratepayers, would be conducted for the benefit of protestant and presbyterian denominations, and catholics would thereby be prejudiced and injured.

It was contended that Fearon vs. Mitchell (1) had no bearing on the case.

See Musgrave *vs.* Inclosure Commissioners (2), and Barlow *vs.* Ross (3), where the existence of rights and privileges is discussed.

In *ex parte* Renaud (4), the head note is wrong.

It was not decided that no legal privilege existed in that case, but merely that it had not been infringed.

A. J. Ram, for the respondent, Logan. McCarthy, Q.C., replied.

The judgment of their lordships was delivered by Lord Macnaghten:—

These two appeals were heard together. In the one case the city of Winnipeg appeals from a judgment of the supreme court of Canada reversing a judgment of the court of queen's bench for Manitoba; in the other from a subsequent judgment of the court of queen's bench for Manitoba following the judgment of the supreme court.

The judgments under appeal quashed certain by-laws of the city of Winnipeg which authorized assessments for school purposes in pursuance of the Public Schools Act, 1890, a statute of Manitoba to which Roman catholics and members of the church of England alike take exception.

The views of the Roman catholic church were maintained by Mr. Barrett; the case of the church of England was put forward by Mr. Logan. Mr. Logan was content to rely on the arguments advanced on behalf of Mr. Barrett; while Mr. Barrett's advisers were not prepared to make common cause with Mr. Logan, and naturally would have been better pleased to stand alone.

The controversy which has given rise to the present litigation is, no doubt, beset with difficulties.

The result of the controversy is of serious moment to the province of Manitoba, and a matter apparently of deep interest throughout the Dominion.

But in its legal aspect the question lies in a very narrow compass.

The duty of this board is simply to determine as a matter of law whether, according to the true construction of the Manitoba Act, 1870, having regard to the state of things which existed in Manitoba at the time of the union, the provincial legislature has or has not exceeded its powers in passing the Public Schools Act, 1890.

Manitoba became one of the provinces of the dominion of Canada under the Manitoba Act, 1870, which was afterwards confirmed by an imperial statute known as the British North America Act, 1871.

Before the union it was not an independent province, with a constitution and a legislature of its own.

It formed part of the vast territories which belonged to the Hudson's Bay Company, and were administered by their officers or agents.

The Manitoba Act, 1870, declared that the provisions of the British North America Act, 1867, with certain exceptions not material to the present question, should be applicable to the province of Manitoba, as if Manitoba had been one of the provinces originally united by the act.

It established a legislature for Manitoba, consisting of a legislative council and a legislative assembly, and proceeded, in section 22, to re-enact, with some modifications, the provisions with regard to education which are to be found in section 93 of the British North America Act, 1867. Section 22 of the Manitoba Act, so far as it is material, is in the following terms:—

"In and for the province, the said legislature may exclusively make laws in relation to education, subject and according to the following provisions:

"(1.) Nothing in any such law shall prejudicially affect any right or privilege with respect to denominational schools which any class of persons have by law or practice in the province at the union."

Then follow two other sub-sections. Sub-section 2 gives an "appeal," as it is termed in the act, "to the governor-general in council from any act or decision of the legislature of the province, or of any provincial authority, affecting any right or privilege of the protestant or Roman catholic minority of the queen's subjects in relation to education."

Sub-section 3 reserves certain limited powers to the Dominion parliament, in the event of the provincial legislature failing to comply with the requirements of the section, or the decision of the governor-general in council.

At the commencement of argument a doubt was suggested as to the competency of the present appeal, in consequence of the so-called appeal to the governor-general in council, provided by the act. But their lordships are satisfied that the provisions of sub-sections 2 and 3 do not operate to withdraw such a question as that involved in the present case from the jurisdiction of the ordinary tribunals of the country.

Sub-sections 1, 2 and 3 of section 22 of the Manitoba Act, 1870, differ but slightly from the corresponding sub-sections of section 93 of the British North America Act, 1867.

The only important difference is that, in the Manitoba Act, in sub-section 1, the words "by law" are followed by the words "or practice," which do not occur in the corresponding passage in the British North America Act, 1867.

These words were no doubt introduced to meet the special case of a country which had not as yet enjoyed the security of laws properly so called.

It is not perhaps very easy to define precisely the meaning of such an expression as "having a right or privilege by practice." But the object of the enactment is tolerably clear.

Evidently the word "practice" is not to be construed as equivalent to "custom having the force of law."

Their lordships are convinced that it must have been the intention of the legislature to preserve every legal right or privilege, and every benefit or advantage in the nature of a right or privilege, with respect to denominational schools, which any class of persons practically enjoyed at the time of the union.

What then was the state of things when Manitoba was admitted to the union? On this point there is no dispute.

It is agreed that there was no law or regulation or ordinance with respect to education in force at the time.

There were, therefore, no rights or privileges with respect to denominational schools existing by law.

The practice which prevailed in Manitoba before the union is also a matter on which all parties are agreed.

The statement on the subject by Archbishop Taché, the Roman catholic archbishop of St. Boniface, who has given evidence in Barrett's case, has been accepted as accurate and complete.

"There existed," he says, "in the territory now constituting the province of Manitoba a number of effective schools for children.

"These schools were denominational schools, some of them being regulated and controlled by the Roman catholic church and others by various protestant denominations.

"The means necessary for the support of the Roman catholic schools were supplied to some extent by school fees paid by some of the parents of the children who attended the schools, and the rest was paid out of the funds of the church, contributed by its members.

"During the period referred to, Roman catholics had no interest in or control over the schools of the protestant denominations, and the members of the protestant denominations had no interest in or control over the schools of Roman catholics.

"There were no public schools in the sense of state schools.

"The members of the Roman catholic church supported the schools of their own church for the benefit of Roman catholic children, and were not under obligation to, and did not contribute to, the support of any other schools."

Now, if the state of things which the archbishop describes as existing before the union had been a system established by law, what would have been the rights and privileges of the Roman catholics with respect to denominational schools?

They would have had by law the right to establish schools at their own expense, to maintain their schools by school fees or voluntary contributions, and to conduct them in accordance with their own religious tenets.

Every other religious body, which was engaged in a similar work at the time of the union, would have had precisely the same right with respect to their denominational schools.

Possibly this right, if it had been defined or recognized by positive enactment, might have had attached to it, as a necessary or appropriate incident, the right of exemption from any contributions under any circumstances to schools of a different denomination.

But, in their lordships' opinion, it would be going much too far to hold that the establishment of a national system of education upon an unsectarian basis is so inconsistent with the right to set up and maintain denominational schools that the two things cannot exist together, or that the existence of the one necessarily implies or involves immunity from taxation for the purpose of the other.

It has been objected that if the rights of Roman catholics and of other religious bodies in respect of their denominational schools are to be so strictly measured and limited by the practice which actually prevailed at the time of the union, they will be reduced to the condition of a "natural right" which "does not want any legislation to protect it."

Such a right, it was said, cannot be called a privilege in any proper sense of the word. If that be so, the only result is that the protection which the act purports to extend to rights and privileges existing "by practice" has no more operation than the protection which it purports to afford to rights and privileges existing "by law."

It can hardly be contended that, in order to give a substantial operation and effect to a saving clause expressed in general terms, it is incumbent upon the court to discover privileges which are not apparent of themselves, or to ascribe distinctive and peculiar features to rights which seem to be of such a common type as not to deserve special notice or require special protection.

Manitoba having been constituted a province of the Dominion in 1870, the provincial legislature lost no time in dealing with the question of education.

In 1871 a law was passed which established a system of denominational education in the common schools, as they were then called.

A board of education was formed, which was to be divided into two sections, protestant and Roman catholic.

Each section was to have under its control and management the discipline of the schools of the section.

Under the Manitoba Act, the province had been divided into twenty-four electoral divisions, for the purpose of electing members to serve in the legislative assembly.

By the act of 1871 each electoral division was constituted a school district in the first instance. Twelve electoral divisions, "comprising mainly a protestant population," were to be considered protestant school districts, twelve, "comprising mainly a Roman catholic population," were to be considered Roman catholic school districts.

Without the special sanction of the section there was not to be more than one school in any school district.

The male inhabitants of each school district, assembled at an annual meeting, were to decide in what manner they should raise their contributions towards the support of the school in addition to what was derived from public funds.

It is perhaps not out of place to observe that one of the modes prescribed was "assessment on the property of the school district" which must have involved, in some cases at any rate, an assessment on Roman catholics for the support of a protestant school, and an assessment on protestants for the support of a Roman catholic school.

In the event of an assessment, there was no provision for exemption, except in the case of the father or guardian of a school child—a protestant in a Roman catholic school district, or a Roman catholic in a protestant school district, who might escape by sending the child to the school of the nearest district of the other section, and contributing to it an amount equal to what he would have paid if he had belonged to that district.

The laws relating to education were modified from time to time. But the system of denominational education was maintained in full vigour until 1890.

An act passed in 1881, following an act of 1875, provided, among other things, that the establishment of a school district of one denomination should not prevent the establishment of a school district of the other denomination in the same place, and that a protestant and a Roman catholic district might include the same territory in whole or in part.

From the year 1876 until 1890, enactments were in force declaring that in no case should a protestant ratepayer be obliged to pay for a Roman catholic school, or a Roman catholic ratepayer for a protestant school.

In 1890 the policy of the past nineteen years was reversed, the denominational system of public education was entirely swept away.

Two acts in relation to education were passed.

The first (53 Vict., c. 37) established a department of education, and a board consisting of seven members, known as the "Advisory Board." Four members of the board were to be appointed by the department of education, two were to be elected by the public and high school teachers, and the seventh member was to be appointed by the university council.

One of the powers of the advisory board was to prescribe the forms of religious exercises to be used in the schools.

The Public Schools Act, 1890 (53 Vict., c. 38), enacted that all protestant and Roman catholic school districts should be subject to the provisions of the act, and that all public schools should be free schools.

The provisions of the act with regard to religious exercises are as follows:—

"6. Religious exercises in the public schools shall be conducted according to the regulations of the advisory board.

"The time for such religious exercises shall be just before the closing hour in the afternoon.

"In case the parent or guardian of any pupil notifies the teacher that he does not wish such pupil to attend such religious exercises, then such pupil shall be dismissed before such religious exercises take place.

"7. Religious exercises shall be held in a public school entirely at the option of the school trustees for the district, and upon receiving written authority from the trustees it shall be the duty of the teachers to hold such religious exercises.

"8. The public schools shall be entirely non-sectarian, and no religious exercises shall be allowed therein except as above provided."

The act then provides for the formation, alteration, and union of school districts, for the election of school trustees, and for levying a rate on the taxable property in each school district for school purposes. In cities the municipal council is required to levy and collect upon taxable property within the municipality such sums as the school trustees may require for school purposes.

A portion of the legislative grant for educational purposes is allotted to public schools; but it is provided that any school not conducted according to all the provisions of the act, or any act in force for the time being, or the regulations of the department of education, or the advisory board, shall not be deemed a public school within the meaning of the law, and shall not participate in the legislative grant.

Section 141 provides that no teacher shall use or permit to be used as text books any books except such as are authorized by the advisory board, and that no portion of the legislative grant shall be paid to any school in which unauthorized books are used.

Then there are two sections (178 and 179) which call for a passing notice, because, owing apparently to some misapprehension, they are spoken of in one of the judgments under appeal as if their effect was to confiscate Roman catholic property.

They apply to cases where the same territory was covered by a protestant school district and by a Roman catholic district. In such a case Roman catholics were really placed in a better position than protestants.

Certain exemptions were to be made in their favour if the assets of their district exceeded its liabilities, or if the liabilities of the protestant school district exceeded its assets. But no corresponding exemptions were to be made in the case of protestants.

Such being the main provisions of the Public Schools Act, 1890, their lordships have to determine whether that act prejudicially affects any right or privilege with respect to denominational schools which any class of persons had by law or practice in the province at the union.

Notwithstanding the Public Schools Act, 1890, Roman catholics and members of every other religious body in Manitoba are free to establish schools throughout the province; they are free to maintain their schools by school fees or voluntary subscriptions; they are free to conduct their schools according to their own religious tenets without molestation or interference.

No child is compelled to attend a public school. No special advantage other than the advantage of a free education in schools conducted under public management is held out to those who do attend.

But then it is said that it is impossible for Roman catholics, or for members of the church of England (if their views are correctly represented by the bishop of Rupert's Land, who has given evidence in Logan's case), to send their children to public schools where the education is not superintended and directed by the authorities of their church. Roman catholics or members of the church of England who are taxed for public schools, and at the same time feel themselves compelled to support their own schools, are in a less favourable position than those who can take advantage of the free education provided by the act of 1890.

That may be so. But what right or privilege is violated or prejudicially affected by the law?

It is not the law that is in fault. It is owing to religious convictions which everybody must respect, and to the teaching of their church, that Roman catholics and members of the church of England find themselves unable to partake of advantages which the law offers to all alike.

Their lordships are sensible of the weight which must attach to the unanimous decision of the supreme court.

They have anxiously considered the able and elaborate judgments by which that decision has been supported.

But they are unable to agree with the opinion which the learned judges of the supreme court have expressed as to the rights and privileges of Roman catholics in Manitoba at the time of the union.

They doubt whether it is permissible to refer to the course of legislation between 1871 and 1890, as a means of throwing light on the previous practice, or on the construction of the saving clause in the Manitoba Act. They cannot assent to the view which seems to be indicated by one of the members of the supreme court, that public schools under the act of 1890 are in reality protestant schools.

The legislature has declared in so many words that "the public schools shall be entirely unsectarian," and that principle is carried out throughout the act.

With the policy of the act of 1890 their lordships are not concerned. But they cannot help observing that, if the views of the respondents were to prevail, it would be extremely difficult for the provincial legislature, which has been entrusted with the exclusive power of making laws relating to education to provide for the educational wants of the more sparsely inhabited districts of a country almost as large as Great Britain, and that the powers of the legislature, which on the face of the act appear so large, would be limited to the useful but somewhat humble office of making regulations for the sanitary conditions of school houses, imposing rates for the support of denominational schools, enforcing the compulsory attendance of scholars, and matters of that sort.

In the result their lordships will humbly advise her majesty that these appeals ought to be allowed with costs.

In the City of Winnipeg *v.* Barrett it will be proper to reverse the order of the supreme court with costs, and to restore the judgment of the court of queen's bench for Manitoba.

In the City of Winnipeg *v.* Logan the order will be to reverse the judgment of the court of queen's bench and to dismiss Mr. Logan's application, and discharge the *rule nisi* and the rule absolute with costs.

Solicitors for the City of Winnipeg,
FRESHFIELDS & WILLIAMS.

Solicitors for Barrett,
BOMPAS, BISCHOFF & CO.

Solicitors for Logan,
HARRISON & POWELL.

IN THE JUDICIAL COMMITTEE OF THE PRIVY COUNCIL.

COUNCIL CHAMBERS, WHITEHALL, Tuesday, 12th July, 1892.

Present :

The Rt. Hon. Lord Watson,
The Rt. Hon. Lord Macnaghten,
The Rt. Hon. Lord Morris,
The Rt. Hon. Lord Hannen,
The Rt. Hon. Lord Shand,
The Rt. Hon. Sir Richard Couch.

THE CITY OF WINNIPEG
vs.
BARRETT,
and
THE CITY OF WINNIPEG
vs.
LOGAN.

[Transcript of the shorthand notes of Messrs. Marten & Meredith, 13 New Inn, Strand, W.C.]

Counsel for the appellants:—Sir Horace Davey, Q.C., Mr. McCarthy, Q.C., and the Hon. Mr. Martin.

Counsel for the respondent Barrett:—The Attorney-General (Sir Richard Webster, Q.C., M.P.), Mr. Blake, Q.C., Mr. J. S. Ewart, Q.C., and Mr. Gore.

Counsel for the respondent Logan:—Mr. A. J. Ram.

Lord WATSON:—I presume the parties have arranged as to the two cases.

Sir HORACE DAVEY:—I shall only address your lordships once.

Lord WATSON:—There is only one point.

The ATTORNEY GENERAL:—I am not instructed in Logan's case, but speaking for myself in the case of the City of Winnipeg *vs.* Barrett, which is the first, I would certainly ask your lordships in any event to hear my learned friend Mr. Blake, the second counsel in the case, because it is a matter of extreme importance (I am speaking of Barrett's case in which he and I are instructed) and I should have asked your lordships under any circumstances that Mr. Blake should be heard for the respondents in the event of counsel being heard. I only mention that because some question may arise as to there being two cases, and only one counsel being heard in each, but I regard it as of extreme importance that Mr. Blake should be heard, and as we are here in this case, and I am not instructed in the Logan case, I should ask that that course should be pursued.

Mr. RAM:—I assent to that. I am for Logan, and I assent to that.

Sir HORACE DAVEY:—I do not think your lordships will find there is any substantial distinction between the two cases.

The ATTORNEY GENERAL:—That of course will get over any difficulty.

Sir HORACE DAVEY:—Because the Logan case was decided on the Barrett case, and if the Barrett case is right I think I should find it difficult to support the appeal in the Logan case. The only difference is that in the Barrett case the objector is a member of the Roman catholic church. In the Logan case he is a member of the episcopal church.

Mr. RAM:—Perhaps I may state that I am instructed on behalf of Mr. Logan, and on his part I assent to the suggestion made that the two cases should be taken together, and that counsel should be heard only in the case of Barrett.

Sir HORACE DAVEY:—I shall only use the Logan case for the purpose of illustrating the arguments. It is not a very powerful argument, I admit, of *reductio ad absurdum.* If the church of England is entitled to object, then the other communities are, and you are reduced to this, that there is a school for every two or three persons who call themselves a different denomination.

Your lordships will understand that in the observations I make I address myself to this book in the Barrett case and before I sit down I will just mention the Logan case. For the present I think it will be better to confine myself to the Barrett case, which is the first appeal on the list. It is an appeal from the judgment of the supreme court of Canada of the 28th October, 1891, in which the learned judges unanimously differed from a previous judgment of the court of queen's bench for the province of Manitoba, which itself confirmed a previous decision of a single judge, Mr. Justice Killam. My learned friend the attorney-general was quite warranted in saying that it is a matter of extreme importance to the colony of Manitoba because according to the view which I am instructed to present to your lordships if the judgment of the supreme court of Canada is upheld it practically paralyses and renders nugatory their power of legislating with regard to any public system of education. The formal question is this: Mr. Barrett took out a summons under procedure which is provided by the Manitoba code, which I need not trouble your lordships about, for the purpose of quashing two by-laws, which had been made by the city of Winnipeg, for illegality. The illegality alleged was that by the city by-laws the amounts to be levied for school purposes for the protestant and Roman catholic schools are united and the rate levied upon protestants and Roman catholics alike for the whole sum. The question of substance is this: It is not disputed that the by-law was correct and that the rate was properly made under the Public Schools Act of 1890, but it is alleged that the Public Schools Act of 1890 of the province of Manitoba was *ultra vires* and inoperative. The ground upon which that is alleged is this: because by the act of parliament confirmed by the imperial act which incorporated the province of Manitoba in the dominion of Canada there was a proviso that no law with regard to education should prejudicially affect the rights and privileges of any class of persons which they had either by law or practice before incorporation. Now, my lords, your lordships will at once see the importance of that. Let us now see what the province of Manitoba has done. I think your lordships have this book of the statutes. The Public Schools Act of 1890 is the last statute in that book at page 110. It repealed the previous Public Schools Act and it enacted on page 112, section 5:—

"All public schools shall be free schools and every person in rural municipalities between the age of five and sixteen years, and in cities, towns and villages between the age of six and sixteen, shall have the right to attend some school." Your lordships will observe that there is nothing in that which makes it compulsory upon any child to attend, or upon the parent or guardian to send him to the public schools. "Religious exercises in the public schools shall be conducted according to the regulations of the advisory board. The time for such religious exercises shall be just before the closing hour in the afternoon. In case the parent or guardian of any pupil notifies the teacher that he does not wish such pupil to attend such religious exercises, then such pupil shall be dismissed before such religious exercises take place. Religious exercises shall be held in a public school entirely at the option of the school trustee for the district, and upon receiving written authority from the trustees it shall be the duty of the teachers to hold such religious exercises."

Lord MACNAGHTEN:—It says "Trustee." Who is that?

Sir HORACE DAVEY:—There is no trustee previously mentioned. I think it must be "Trustees." I have a queen's printer's copy here. There it is "Trustees" in the queen's printer's copy. "Religious exercises shall be held in a public school entirely at the option of the school trustees for the district, and upon receiving written authority from the trustees it shall be the duty of the teachers to hold such religious exercises." Then, "The public schools shall be entirely non-sectarian, and no religious exercises shall be allowed therein except as above provided." Well then, section 9 provides for new school districts being formed; I do not know that I need trouble your lordships about that. Then section 10, "For each rural school district there shall be three trustees, each of whom, after the first election of trustees, shall hold office for three years, and until his successor has been elected. The trustees elected at a first school meeting in a rural school district shall respectively continue in office as follows"—and then it provides for that. Then section 12 is as to the qualifications of school trustees. Section 13, "Electors for rural school districts." Then follows a lot of detail as to the meetings and so forth, of the trustees.

Now, for the present, that is all that I desire to call attention to.

Lord SHAND:—Which is the clause which regulates the advisory board, as it is called?

Sir HORACE DAVEY:—That, I am told, is in a separate act, called "The Department of Education Act," which is at page 107. I ought to have drawn your lordships' attention to this first: "There shall be a department of education, which shall consist of the executive council," &c., (reading to the words, page 108, line 9:) "The department of education shall from time to time divide the province into two districts, so that the said teachers in each district may elect one member of the said board." "13. The seventh member of the said board shall be appointed by the university council," &c. (Reading to the words, bottom of page 108:) "To make regulations for the classification, organization, discipline and government of normal, model, high and public schools"; and then the rest is formal. So that your lordships see the aim of these two acts taken together was this: to establish a public system of non-sectarian schools throughout the province, and not to exclude religious exercises from the province, but to place the form of the religious exercises, and the mode in which they shall be conducted, under the regulation of the advisory board, subject to what is known as a conscience clause.

Lord SHAND:—May I ask whether in practice there have been religious exercises as a rule prescribed in those schools?

Sir HORACE DAVEY:—I was going to tell your lordships the system before this time, but I thought it convenient to mention the act first. I will draw your lordships' attention to that afterwards. Under section 108, sub-section 1, of this act of 1890, a legislative grant is provided. It provides that:—"The sum of seventy-five dollars shall be paid semi-annually for each teacher employed in each school district;" and then sub-section 3: "Any school not conducted according to all the provisions of this or any act in force for the time being or the regulations of the department of education or the advisory board shall not be deemed a public school within the meaning of the law, and such school shall not participate in the legislative grant." Then, in addition to the legislative grant, there is this power in section 89, page 129: "For the purpose of supplementing the legislative grant," &c., rea ding down to the words, sub-section 2: "Of the proportion thereof allotted to such district," and so forth. So that your lordships see that the system of public education was to be maintained. There were to be free schools, and they were to be maintained partly by a legislative grant from the legislature of the province and partly by an assessment or rate levied upon every taxable person within the rural municipality, without regard to the particular church, sect or denomination to which such person belonged.

Now, my lords, it is alleged that this is invalid and it is alleged that it infringes the terms upon which Manitoba was admitted into the Dominion. In the first place I ought to call your lordships' attention to the 92nd, 93rd and one other section of "The British North America Act" that is on page 14. The sections are very familiar to your lordships.

The second matter in section 92 is "In each province the legislature may exclusively make laws in relation to matters coming within the classes of subjects next hereinafter enumerated that is to say: (2) Direct taxation within the province in order to the raising of a revenue for provincial purposes." It is not suggested that this does not come within those words—It is direct taxation within the province for the purpose of raising a revenue for provincial purposes Then section 93 deals with the question of education with which we are more immediately concerned. Your lordships understand—forgive me if I mention things which are commonplace, but you will bear in mind that Manitoba was not included in the original Dominion. It only included the two Canadas which were Ontario and Quebec, and New Brunswick and Nova Scotia. "In and for each province the legislature may exclusively make laws in relation to education, subject and according to the following provisions"—That is, of course, a provincial legislature. "Nothing in any such law shall prejudicially affect any right or privilege with respect to denominational schools which any class of persons have by law in the province at the union." That was adopted with a variation, to which attention will be called when Manitoba was admitted within the union. "(2) All the powers, privileges and duties at the union by law conferred and imposed in Upper Canada on the separate schools and school trustees of the queen's Roman catholic subjects shall be and the same are hereby extended to the dissentient schools of the queen's protestant and Roman catholic subjects in Quebec." Your lordships see that that sub-section relates exclusively to the two Canadas, Ontario and Quebec, but it is used very much in the course of the arguments which are contained in the numerous judgments of the learned judges for the purpose, on the one hand, of showing that there was express provision of this character with regard to the denominational schools for Ontario and Quebec and contrasting that with the absence of any such express provision with regard to Manitoba. It is also used on the other side for the purpose of showing the policy, as it is called, of the law of this act. I ought to say that the system which prevailed in Upper Canada and Ontario at the date of the union was this. There were public schools for the community at large, but any Roman catholics certainly, and I do not know whether any other particular sect, might establish denominational schools of their own and if they did so they were exempt from payment of the school rate for the maintenance of the general public schools. They had a right to claim exemption from payment of school rate by saying that they were maintaining efficient denominational schools of their own. The effect of this sub-section 2 is to make that system, if I may call it so, applicable to the minority, who would be the protestants in Quebec, to give the protestant minority in Quebec the same privileges in maintaining denominational schools, thereby obtaining exemption from the general school rate which a Roman catholic minority had in Ontario.

Lord SHAND:—Was that an exemption by statute?

Sir HORACE DAVEY:—I think it was by statute in Upper and Lower Canada—in Upper Canada certainly and this extended it to Lower Canada:—"Where in any province a system of separate or dissentient schools exists by law at the union, or is thereafter established by the legislature of the province, an appeal shall lie to the governor-general in council from any act or decision of any provincial authority affecting any right or privilege of the protestant or Roman catholic minority of the queen's subjects in relation to education." That is where there exists by law a right to separate or dissentient schools, and any act or decision of any provincial authority affects such right or privilege, then there is an appeal to the governor-general in council. "In case any such provincial law as from time to time seems to the governor-general in council requisite for the due execution of the provisions of this section is not made, or in case any decision of the governor-general in council on any appeal under this section is not duly executed by the proper provincial authority in that behalf, then and in every such case and as far only as the circumstances of each case require, the parliament of Canada may make remedial laws for the due execution of the provisions of this section, and of any decision of the governor-general in council under this section," that is to say, if the provincial legislature does not make the proper laws for the purpose of carrying into effect any decision of the governor-general in council or passes any act infringing this act for the protection of the minority, in each case, whether catholic or protestant, then it gives a special power of legislation to the Dominion parliament to supplement the legislation which the province ought but refuses to effect for that purpose. Then your lordships know that the power to admit other colonies is in section 146 of this act, page 22:—"It shall be lawful for the queen by and with the advice of her majesty's most honourable privy council on addresses from the houses of parliament of Canada and from the houses of the respective legislatures of the colonies or provinces of Newfoundland, Prince Edward Island, and British Columbia, to admit those colonies or provinces or any of them into the union, and on address from the houses of the parliament of Canada to admit Rupert's Land and the North-Western Territory or either of them into the union"--Rupert's Land is what is now known as Manitoba. I do not think Manitoba comprises the whole of Rupert's Land, but Manitoba is comprised within Rupert's Land—"on such terms and conditions in each case as are in the addresses expressed and as the queen thinks fit to approve, subject to the provisions of this act, and the provisions of any order in council in that behalf shall have effect as if they had been enacted by the parliament of the united kingdom of Great Britain and Ireland." Then Manitoba was admitted in the year 1870. That was by an act of the Dominion, which is at page 33. There was a subsequent act of the imperial legislature confirming this. It provides for the admission of Manitoba by name and boundaries, and provides in section 2. [Reads section 2.] Then there are details about the representation in the house of commons and the legislative council and so forth, and I pass on to section 22, page 36. "In and for the province the said legislature may exclusively make laws in relation to education, subject and according to the following provisions:—(1.) Nothing in any such law shall prejudicially affect any right or privilege with respect to denominational schools which any class of persons have by law or practice in the province at the union." Your lordships will see that that textually repeats sub-section 1 of section 93 of the British North America Act with the addition of the words "or practice" after the word "law." "An appeal shall lie to the governor-general in council from any act or decision of the legislature of the province or of any provincial authority affecting any right or privilege of the protestant or Roman catholic minority of the queen's subjects in relation to education." That is not exactly the same as the provision in section 93. It resolves a doubt in the first place whether an act or decision of any provincial authority included an act of the legislature of the province by expressly putting in the words "legislature of the province," and secondly it is more general than the analogous provision in section 93.

Lord WATSON:—It is a little wider.

Sir HORACE DAVEY:—Yes, it resolves a doubt whether in section 93 of the British North America Act, any act or decision of the provincial authority includes the provincial legislature.

Lord WATSON:—What is the exact meaning of the phrase "dissentient schools?"

Sir HORACE DAVEY:—I understand it to mean this—denominational schools, which were established by any denomination; as a matter of fact, I believe in Ontario by Roman catholics, which, by law, so long as they provided efficient schools, exempted those who founded them from the payment of school rates. Then sub-section 3 is this. [Reads sub-section 3.] If your lordships would care to compare the different provisions, you will find at page 4 of the record in Barrett's appeal the sections set out side by side, on the one hand the British North America Act, and on the other hand the provisions of the Manitoba Act. Then section 25 provides. [Reads section 25.] I ought to mention this as to the customs duty. Section 27 provides. [Reads section 27.] Your lordships will remember that under the British North America Act there was no power for the provinces to levy indirect taxation, but all the customs and excise (I must not say stamps, because that raises a thorny question,) go to the consolidated revenue of Canada, and the treasury of Canada makes a grant to the different provinces, and that is the scheme which is continued by this Manitoba Act.

Now, my lords, it may be interesting and worth while to pause here for a moment to ask what was the previous condition of what is now the province of Manitoba before its incorporation in the Dominion? Manitoba formed part, at any rate, and perhaps a greater part, of what was known as Rupert's Land, and Rupert's Land was the territory granted in the reign of Charles II to the Hudson's Bay Company, in which Prince Rupert was one of the principal grantees. That territory of Rupert's Land was, of course, part of the territory of the crown; it formed part of the British empire, but it was governed, and laws were made for it, exclusively, by the Hudson's Bay Company. The Hudson's Bay Company appointed the governor. It had no elected representative legislature. The Hudson's Bay Company appointed certain gentlemen of position and others, in the territory of Rupert's Land, to form a legislative council, and that legislative council made ordinances. Of course it was all subject to the legislation of the imperial parliament, but the only provincial legislative authority was the legislative council who were the nominees of the Hudson's Bay Company, who were, I must not say the sovereign, because that would not be constitutionally accurate, but were the ruling authority, subject to the British crown, in Rupert's Land. There was a portion of Rupert's Land which had been purchased by Lord Selkirk, I believe, in the early part of the present century, which had been settled by him, and which was repurchased by the Hudson's Bay Company and formed the district of Assiniboia, a district on the Red river. That was the more settled part of the territory known as Rupert's Land.

At that time there was no legislation of any sort or kind with regard to education. There were Roman catholics in the province, and there were protestants of various denominations, chiefly belonging to the episcopal church in connection with the church of England, and with the presbyterian church of Scotland. There was no legislation of any sort or kind providing for a public or any other system of education throughout Rupert's Land. The different churches and denominations, the Roman catholic church and the episcopal church of England, and the presbyterian church, maintained their own schools where they had sufficient congregations for the purpose. The population was sparse, and the prevailing form of religion was one of those I have mentioned. No doubt many children of other forms of religion attended those schools, but they were purely voluntary schools, they were private schools which were maintained by the people themselves, partly by school fees paid by the scholars, and partly by the subscriptions of various persons belonging to the different churches and denominations.

Lord WATSON—The clause in the first sub-section, that nothing should prejudicially affect seems to be general, and apply to persons of any denomination.

Sir HORACE DAVEY—Yes, it does.

Lord WATSON—But when you come to the appeal given to the governor-general it is only catholics and protestants.

Sir HORACE DAVEY—Yes.

Lord SHAND—That embraced all denominational schools, I suppose.

Sir HORACE DAVEY—Yes; but they only regarded two denominations, one catholic and one protestant; whereas now we have a gentleman of the church of England, in Logan's appeal, appearing before your lordships, and saying:—"Nonsense about protestants: I am a member of the church of England, and I claim not to be taxed for any other denomination, including other protestant denominations."

That was the state of things, your lordships observe, that there was no law on the subject, nor by practice was there any right or privilege enjoyed by any denomination other than the right or privilege of maintaining their own private voluntary schools, and providing for them out of their own moneys, and admitting, of course, such persons as they thought fit to the benefits of those schools on making the prescribed or stipulated payment. That was the condition of things at the time when Manitoba was incorporated with the union.

Now, my lords, it is important that your lordships should be put into possession of the legislation with regard to schools prior to the Public Schools Act, 1890, because a great deal is said about it in the judgment, though I am unable myself to see, except by way of illustration, how what was done after incorporation can in any way affect the construction of a clause in an act of parliament by which Manitoba was admitted to the Dominion. Your lordships cannot follow the judgments unless you are put into possession of the scheme which was established first by an act of 1871, which was afterwards repealed, and together with certain amending acts incorporated in an act of 1881. The act of 1871 is printed at page 39 of this book. I can pass it over very lightly because it was very much enlarged, and to a certain extent modified, by the act of 1881. By section 1, page 39, it provided for a board of not less than ten or more than fourteen persons, to be a board of education for the province of Manitoba, of whom one-half should be protestants and the other half catholics. It says:—"The lieutenant governor may appoint one of the protestant members of the board to be superintendent of protestant schools, and one of the catholic members to be superintendent of the catholic schools, and the two superintendents shall be joint secretaries of the board." Then the rest is detail until we come to section 8, "each section of the board"—now, my lords, prior to this time, I do not think anything is said about sections and boards, but it obviously means either the protestant section or the catholic section.

The ATTORNEY GENERAL:—Read the 7th section.

Sir HORACE DAVEY:—My learned friend refers to the 7th section. "It shall be the duty of the board:—First—To make from time to time such regulations as they may think fit for the general organization of the common schools."

Lord WATSON:—I understand these were denominational schools?

Sir HORACE DAVEY:—Yes; the scheme was to establish denominational schools only. Your lordships observe that when I say denominational schools they contemplated the protestants as together constituting one denomination, so to speak, or one class, as distinguished from Roman catholics. Section 7, "To make from time to time," &c. (Reading to the end of section 8.) That appears to contemplate a protestant section and a Roman catholic section. Then section 9 "at the first meeting of each section," &c. (Reading to end of section 13.) Then it provides for the districts. "The following districts, comprising mainly a protestant population shall be considered protestant school districts: nos. 2, 3, 4, 8, 10, 18, 19, 20, 21, 22, 23, 24. The following districts, comprising mainly a catholic population, shall be considered catholic school districts: nos. 1, 5, 6, 7, 9, 11, 12, 13, 14, 15, 16 and 17. There shall not, without the special sanction of the section, be more than one school in any school district, and no school shall derive from the public funds a sum more than three times what is contributed by the people of the district."

Lord WATSON:—They appear to contemplate by this act what are commonly called state aided schools, subject to certain conditions. I see the word "licensed" is used. "No school that is not licensed by the board of education shall participate in the government grant."

Sir HORACE DAVEY:—Yes, they were to be of two classes, protestant schools and catholic schools.

Lord SHAND:—Would this practically have embraced all the schools in the province?

Sir HORACE DAVEY:—Yes.

Lord SHAND—Were there none that did not fall under the one class or the other?

Sir HORACE DAVEY:—Yes. "The moneys at the disposal of the section shall be appropriated among the schools of the section as the members of the section shall deem best for the promotion of education, having reference to the efficiency of the schools, the number of scholars in attendance, and the capacity and services of the teachers." Section 19, "In an exceptional case, where the people of a school district shall, in the judgment of the members of the section, be unable to contribute towards the support of the school, the section may declare the district a poor-school district, and give such aid as the circumstances may seem to justify." Your lordships see that the scheme under this act was to divide the province into districts, to provide that in each district there should be a school either managed by the catholic section or by the protestant section, according as the Roman catholics or the protestants were in the majority in that particular district, and what is of importance is that there could be no other school within that district under section 17 without the special sanction of the section, so that if there were a catholic school district there could be no protestant school within that district without the special sanction of the catholic section.

Lord WATSON:—Does it mean that there could be no state aided schools?

Sir HORACE DAVEY.—So I understand it. There may be a voluntary school, but it would not get state aid.

Lord SHAND:—There seems an equal division—twelve of each.

Sir HORACE DAVEY:—Yes. "They shall also decide in what manner they shall raise their contributions towards the support of the school, which may be either by subscription, by the collection of a rate per scholar, or by assessment on the property of the school district, as the meeting may determine." That is a meeting of the male inhabitants of each school district of the age of twenty-one years and upwards. So that your lordships see that under this scheme, as to which no complaint was made, a district in which the majority of the inhabitants were Roman catholic would be a catholic school district. There could be no protestant school within that district without the consent of the catholic section. But the inhabitants of the district might impose taxes on themselves for the maintenance of the catholic schools if it were a protestant district, or *vice versa*. The majority of the protestant inhabitants could exclude, or rather the protestant section could exclude any catholic schools, and might impose taxation upon the catholics for the purpose of maintaining the protestant schools. Of course, my lords, that may have been equally *ultra vires* with the act of 1890, and I do not pretend that it is a very strong argument upon the construction of the act of 1870, which after all is what we have to construe. But it is not without its importance, when one reads the eloquent denunciations of the infamy of taxing Roman catholics for the support of protestant schools that we meet with in the judgments in this case.

The ATTORNEY GENERAL:—I beg your pardon for interrupting you. Will you read section 27—the exemption from payment.

Sir HORACE DAVEY:—I ought to have read section 27. (Reads it.) If he has no children, and is a protestant, he is still bound to maintain the catholic schools or *vice versa*.

Now, my lords, the act of 1881, which was the ruling act, subject to immaterial amendments, which I will not trouble you with, at the time when the system of 1890 was established, your lordships will find at page 42. You will forgive me for reading it, perhaps repeating some of the provisions which were in the earlier act. (Reads section 1.) It is open, of course, to conjecture that the relative strength of the catholics and protestants had at this time, in the course of ten years, altered from what it was in the year 1871. "Four of the protestant members and three of the Roman catholic members shall retire and cease to hold office at the end of each year,' &c. "3. It shall be the duty of the board (a) to make from time to time such regulations," &c. (Reading to the words, end of section 5.) "To appoint inspectors, who shall hold office during the pleasure of the section appointing them." Then there are provisions for the appointment of superintendents, and then taking section 12 at page 44, it provides for the establishment and readjustment of school districts in a rather remarkable and minute manner. The scheme is that the districts shall be territorial, but at the same time the same area may form part of, or may constitute two districts, a catholic district and a protestant district, or in other words, there may be a catholic district and a protestant district in the same area. "It shall be the duty of the council of the municipalities to establish," &c. (Reading to the words, end of section 12) "shall have the same power with regard to catholics." Then section 13, sub-section *a*. (Reads same.) Then school assessment, section 25, page 47. "For the purpose of supplementing the legislative grant, it shall be the duty of the boards of trustees," &c. (Reads section 25.)

Then section 26 provides for the case where more municipalities are embraced than one in a school district and limits the school assessment to one cent in the dollar. Then section 27 provides this:—"The school assessment shall be laid equally according to valuation upon rateable real and personal property in the school district and shall be payable by and recoverable from the owner, occupier or possessor of the property liable to be rated, and shall, if not paid, be a special mortgage, and not requiring registration to preserve it on all real estate."

Now, my lords, section 28 is a remarkable section. The corporations are treated as having no religion:—"The corporations situated in a locality where different school districts are established and persons who are neither protestants nor catholics shall be assessed only for the school district of the majority; yet out of such assessment they shall give to the school district of the minority a part of such assessment in proportion to the number of children of school age, and the majority shall be determined by the number of protestant or catholic children of school age, as the case may be according to the census." Then there is an exception of certain real estate, and then section 30:—"The ratepayers of a school district, including religious, benevolent, or educational corporations shall pay their respective assessments to the schools of their respective denominations; and in no case shall a protestant ratepayer be obliged to pay for a catholic school, or a catholic ratepayer for a protestant school."

Then section 31 provides for the case of the owner being of one religion and the occupier of another. "When property owned by a protestant is occupied by a Roman catholic and *vice versa*, the tenant in such cases shall only be assessed for the amount of property he owns, whether real or personal, but the school taxes on said rented or leased property shall in all cases and whether or not the same has been or is stipulated in any deed, contract or lease whatever, be paid to the trustees of the section to which belongs the owner of the property so leased or rented, and to no other, subject to the exemptions aforesaid."

Then section 32:—"Whenever property is held jointly as tenants or as tenants in common, by two or more persons, the holders of such property being protestants and Roman catholics, they shall be assessed and held accountable to the two boards of school trustees for the amount of taxes, in proportion to their interest in the business, tenancy, or partnership respectively, and such taxes shall be paid to the school of the denomination to which they respectively belong."

Then there were to be school trustees, but I do not think anything turns on that. Then, I think, I may pass on to page 57, section 84, which provides for the apportionment of what we should call the school grant, that is the legislative grant. "The sum appropriated by the legislature for common school purposes shall be divided between the protestant and Roman catholic section of the board of education, in the manner hereinafter provided, in proportion to the number of children between the ages of five and fifteen inclusive, residing in the various protestant and Roman catholic school districts in the province where schools are in operation, as shown in the census returns."

Lord Watson:—The scheme that runs through these acts of 1871—if you will allow me to make the observation now—and 1881, appears to be this, that no ratepayer shall be taxed for contribution towards any school except one of his own denomination.

Sir Horace Davey:—Well, my lord, this scheme continued in operation until the new scheme which is now attacked and impeached as *ultra vires* was brought into operation by the act of 1890, subject to amendments which I do not think altered the substance of it as it existed. I will not trouble your lordships by referring to the amendment act, because my view is that the amendment act has nothing to do with it.

The ATTORNEY GENERAL :—Quite so.

Lord MORRIS :—The upshot of the whole legislation up to 1890 is that the produce of the rate or assessment was to be distributed on a denominational system, and, as I understand it, that of 1890 distributes it on a secular system.

Sir HORACE DAVEY :—That is to say, the public schools alone receive, and the public schools are non-sectarian.

Lord MORRIS :—Therefore the produce of the rate up to 1890 was applied on a denominational system. Now it is to be applied on a secular system.

Sir HORACE DAVEY.—Subject to this, that it made no distinction between different protestant denominations, and I do not know what Mr. Logan will say to that.

Lord MORRIS:—It was clearly under a denominational system as regards catholics and protestants, and the governing body was so divided.

Sir HORACE DAVEY :—Your lordship is quite right, if I may respectfully say so, but I wish to guard myself, because Mr. Logan introduces denominations within the protestant body.

Lord WATSON:—Section 30 of the act of 1881 is very explicit on that point—" and in no case shall a protestant ratepayer be obliged to pay for a catholic school, or a catholic ratepayer for a protestant school."

Sir HORACE DAVEY :—Still that would leave a member of the church of England open to pay rates for the support of a presbyterian school, and a presbyterian open to pay rates for the support of a church of England school.

Lord MORRIS :—Practically speaking the distinction was not so marked.

Sir HORACE DAVEY :—Yes, I quite follow; but I did not wish to pass by that. I did not dissent from what your lordship said, but I supplemented it.

Lord WATSON :—As far as the constitution of the governing body is concerned under the act of 1881, I see nothing to prevent the whole twelve protestant members being either episcopalians or presbyterians.

Sir HORACE DAVEY :—Nothing whatever.

Now, my lords, one is not surprised that the people of this province found this system to be cumbrous, inconvenient and unsuitable, and accordingly, in the exercise of the powers which they believe were imposed by law, in the legislature of the province of Manitoba, they repealed the act of 1881 and the amendment act, and provided an entirely new system. Now, my lords, what is the new system? It is contained in the act of 1890, and the general features of it I have pointed out to your lordships. It provides, so far as the rating is concerned, in section 89, on page 129: " For the purpose of supplementing the legislative grant, it shall be the duty of the council of each rural municipality to levy and collect each year by assessment upon the taxable property within the municipality, a sum equal to twenty dollars for each month for which school has been kept open in each school district in the municipality during the current year; and for each school district partially included within the municipality, they shall levy and collect in like manner a proportionate part of twenty dollars per month as fixed in the manner hereinafter provided. A school district which employs more than one teacher, shall receive said sum of twenty dollars per month for each teacher employed." Then sub-section 2: " From the moneys so levied and collected, the council shall, upon the 1st day of December following, pay over to each school district wholly or partially included in the municipality one-half the sum of twenty dollars per month, or the proportion thereof allotted to such district as hereinbefore provided," &c. Then there are details about the mode of taxing, and then the legislative grant is provided for in section 108. It provides for the payment of seventy-five dollars to each teacher semi-annually out of the legislative grant, and it provides in sub-section 3 that :—" Any school not conducted according to all the provisions of this or any act in force for the time being or the regulations of the department of education or the advisory board, shall not be deemed a public school within the meaning of the law, and such school shall not participate in the legislative grant."

Lord WATSON:—I presume there can be no complaint as to the terms on which the grant is distributed.

Sir HORACE DAVEY:—No.

Lord SHAND:—May I ask what is the bearing broadly of those intervening acts of 1871 and 1881 in construing the act of 1870?

Sir HORACE DAVEY:—I think they only alter it in detail. I do not think they alter the wide features of it.

Lord SHAND:—What I mean is, to return to page 36: you get the Manitoba Act of 1870.

Sir HORACE DAVEY:—I beg your lordship's pardon. I do not agree they have anything to do with it.

Lord SHAND:—What is the bearing of those intermediate acts?

Sir HORACE DAVEY:—It did not occur to me that for the purpose of construing the act of 1870 it was either useful or permissible to refer to what had been done under the intermediate legislation of 1871 and 1881. I do not admit that it is.

Lord WATSON:—One thing suggests itself. Possibly it may be said that the course of legislation indicated what had been the practice at the date of the union.

Lord SHAND:—The practice, I should think, must be ascertained as a matter of fact in the construction of the statute.

Sir HORACE DAVEY:—Yes.

Lord SHAND:—It may aid you in getting at the fact; but the question is, what was the law and practice when that statute passed, as a matter of fact?

Sir HORACE DAVEY:—Certainly. Now, my lords, each side appeals to the intermediate legislation of 1871 and 1881 and the amending acts as an *argumentum ad hominum*, but I will not trouble your lordships with much argument of that kind. I do not want to give up any point which is made in my favour in the judgments which it will be my duty to read to your lordships, but I desire to put it on the broad ground, and I will state at once, if your lordships will permit me, the broad ground on which I put it. I say that neither by law nor practice was there anything which existed before the incorporation of Manitoba with the Dominion which in any way restricted what would otherwise be the undoubted power of the Manitoba legislature to establish a system of common schools for the purpose of abolishing ignorance and improving the good government of Manitoba.

Lord WATSON:—The interpolation of the word "practice" in the act of 1870 rather suggests that practice was a matter regulating the case of Manitoba as was meant to regulate in the case of the provinces united by the act of 1867.

Sir HORACE DAVEY:—It is very well put in one of the judgments in words which, without reading the judgment, at the present moment I will adopt.

Lord WATSON—According to your statement of the existing law, before that date there was no law that that act applies to, nor any privilege.

Sir HORACE DAVEY—Then I answer what was the practice? On page 92, line 35, there is this passage:—"I take the meaning of the clause to be that rights and privileges in respect of denominational schools existing by statute, if any such there had been, and rights actually exercised in practice at the time of the union, were not to be prejudicially affected by provincial legislation." That is in one of the judgments against me, but I adopt that, and I think it is a very fair statement of the result. It is put as strongly as it possibly can be put against me. Now, my lords, I ask what was the practice? Why there was no school rate at all. Such a thing was unknown. There were no taxes or rates for the support of any schools at all. There were merely voluntary private schools which any person might, if he thought fit, maintain, and which persons of the Roman catholic faith, or of the episcopal or presbyterian faith did maintain partly by the fees paid by scholars, partly by contributions or subscriptions by charitable persons, probably, and mostly of their own accord, but not necessarily so—voluntary contributions made by charitable persons who desired to maintain a denominational form of education. That was the practice. If so, is there anything whatever in this legislation which in the least degree interferes with the practice? No. If the Manitoba legislature had enacted that every child should attend the public schools, I quite conceive that might have been said, because that would practically have taken away all the scholars from the voluntary schools; but there is nothing whatever in the legislation of 1890 which in the least degree interferes with the right and privilege which all persons and all classes of persons enjoyed at the date of incorporation, of having their own private voluntary schools maintained partly by the fees of the scholars, and partly from subscriptions from such persons as were willing to make voluntary contributions.

Lord SHAND—How do you show that the only right or privilege in practice which existed in Manitoba when the annexation act was passed was that of maintaining their own private voluntary schools?

Sir HORACE DAVEY—From the archbishop's affidavit?

Lord SHAND—That comes as a matter of evidence?

Sir HORACE DAVEY—Yes.

Lord SHAND—You say there was no other privilege in practice.

Sir HORACE DAVEY—None whatever. It is admitted there was no law and it is stated in the archbishop's affidavit, on which great reliance is placed, but which seems to me, with great respect to that very distinguished person, to give himself away, so to say.

Now, I would ask your lordships' particular attention to the particular words in this act of 1870: "Nothing in any such law"—that is, in any law relating to education; so we must read in that—"relating to education shall prejudicially affect any right or privilege with respect to denominational schools"—it is only a right or privilege with respect to denominational schools—"which any class of persons have"—it must be a right or privilege enjoyed by any class of persons; that is to say, enjoyed adversely to or exclusively by, or at any rate by that class of persons, and not by the community generally—"by law or practice in the province at the union." I am reading this from page 4, which is a convenient place to read it from. but it is at page 36 of the acts. Now, what is a right or a privilege? To say you have a right or privilege by practice is, of course, if you use the words "right or privilege" a contradiction in terms, because a right or privilege means something which you can enforce and which is protected by some law. Therefore, if it does not exist by law, it is not strictly a right or privilege. But I conceive that the words "right or privilege" must be construed in a larger sense and include that privilege which, although not secured to any class of persons by positive law, was yet acquiesced in and allowed to subsist.

Lord WATSON:—If there had been a law to the effect that no person who assisted in maintaining out of his own pocket the denominational schools should be liable to pay to the support of any other schools that would have been a privilege secured by law. Now when you come to the word "practice" what is the meaning of practice? At that time there was no law which would have enabled any person to take that money from him.

Sir HORACE DAVEY:—No, my lord.

Lord WATSON:—Is that practice, or is it not? It must mean some legal prescription by which you acquire immunity.

Sir HORACE DAVEY:—It is said that this prejudicially affects a right or privilege enjoyed by practice in two ways. In the first place it is said, and this is most strongly put forward, that at that time they enjoyed the right or privilege of not contributing towards the support of a denominational school.

Lord WATSON:—It may be a good deal of the population did not contribute at all.

Sir HORACE DAVEY:—That seems to me to carry them too far. There were no school rates then. There were no school rates at all, and you might equally say that a person who had no children, and therefore did not choose to contribute towards the school of his own church, enjoyed the right or privilege of not contributing to education at all unless he thought fit. Then if you tax a childless person for the education of other persons' children you are infringing a right or privilege which he enjoys with reference to denominational schools. You are calling on him to pay what otherwise he would not be liable to pay.

Lord MORRIS:—The childless men could hardly be considered a class of persons.

Sir HORACE DAVEY:—I do not know whether childless persons are not a very good class of persons.

Lord MORRIS:—I think not in the context.

Lord SHAND:—Having a right or privilege with respect to denominational schools.

Lord MORRIS:—"Nothing in any such law shall prejudicially affect any right or privilege with respect to denominational schools"—they are talking there about religious schools—"which any class of persons"—it must be any class of persons with relation to denominational schools and not any class of baldheaded people or childless people or otherwise.

Lord SHAND:—What right or privilege do you say was preserved by this which the common law would not have given?

Sir HORACE DAVEY:—The right or privilege which might very easily have been taken away, of maintaining private voluntary denominational schools. Supposing for instance the Public Schools Act had enacted that every child throughout the province should be bound to attend a public school. I think that would have been interfering with the right or privilege of having your children educated by a denominational school if you thought fit. Supposing the Public Schools Act had enacted that no person should be qualified to be a school teacher except he passed certain examinations, or to put an extreme case, that no person other than a member of one of the protestant religious communities should be qualified to be a school teacher. I am not putting an extreme case because your lordships know that up to within a very recent period in this country no unitarian could be a school teacher by law, so that I am not putting at all an extreme case. However, I will confine myself to saying if they had imposed a qualification of passing certain government examinations and obtaining a certificate before any person could act as a school teacher, I think that would have interfered with the right or privilege of a denomination to maintain their own schools with their own money, and through their own school masters and school teachers; but I am unable to see how there was any right or privilege enjoyed by the Roman catholics so far as contributing or not contributing to common schools which was not in the first place at least equally enjoyed by every other member of the community. It was not enjoyed by them as a class. It was not a *privilegium* of the Roman catholics not to contribute to public schools; in the first place because there were no public schools, and in the second place because it was equally a right of every other member of the community. It is not something which they enjoyed *qua* Roman catholics, but *qua* inhabitants of Rupert's Land, because there was no law which compelled them to; but they enjoyed nothing *qua* Roman catholics, except the right which also was common to the rest of her majesty's subjects in Rupert's Land of maintaining private voluntary schools if they thought fit to do so and out of such moneys as they could collect by contributions from their co-religionists.

Lord WATSON:—I suppose the ground of the judgment against you is simply this: That that matter is reserved to the legislature of the colony.

Sir HORACE DAVEY:—No, they do not say that. They give the go-by to that section altogether. There may be a point upon that, whether the proper course is not to appeal to the Canadian government.

Lord WATSON:—That would be relegating to the Dominion a particular subject of legislation under the act of 1867, section 91, page 14: "Such classes of subjects as are expressly excepted in the enumeration of the classes of subjects by this act assigned exclusively to the legislatures of the provinces."

Sir RICHARD COUCH:—Education is assigned.

Sir HORACE DAVEY:—Education is assigned expressly to the provinces, subject to this, that if the provinces pass acts, or at any rate the province of Manitoba passes an act, which infringes the conditions, then there is an appeal to the governor-general, and the Dominion legislature may override the provincial act.

Lord WATSON:—I rather think that whatever is shut out from provincial legislation goes to the Dominion.

Sir HORACE DAVEY:—The presumption is in favour of the Dominion parliament.

Lord WATSON:—It is quite different in that respect to the constitution of the states.

Lord SHAND:—If this decision stands, is there a power to introduce what may be called a system of secular education anywhere?

Sir HORACE DAVEY:—My lord, I object to the expression "secular"—non-sectarian.

Lord SHAND:—Well, non-sectarian. I was putting it for shortness, but call it non-sectarian.

Sir HORACE DAVEY:—It is giving a dog a bad name. I call it non-sectarian.

Lord SHAND:—Is there a power that could introduce such a scheme as you have mentioned.

Sir HORACE DAVEY:—I do not think so.

Lord SHAND:—I fancy not, from a perusal of the papers. If lost it excludes anything of the kind for all time.

Sir HORACE DAVEY:—Yes. All that the Dominion legislature could do is to introduce legislation after there has been an appeal to the Dominion government, that is the governor-general in council; and the governor-general in council has given his decision that an act does infringe the provision of the corresponding section of the Manitoba Act. Then the Dominion legislature may introduce and pass an act for the purpose of doing that which the governor-general awards ought to have been done by the provincial legislature. That is, I consider, the limit within which they can legislate.

Lord SHAND:—So that in that case the country must for all time remain under such a provision as you have under the act of 1881, with all these details. That seems to have been accepted by both catholics and protestants as satisfactory. It operated for a number of years.

Sir HORACE DAVEY:—For twenty years, but it was hopelessly bad, according to Mr. Logan's contention and according to the archbishop, and acquiescence cannot make it *intra vires* if it was originally *ultra vires*.

Lord MORRIS:—This Manitoba Act is an act of the provincial legislature, and nothing can be intended except what is given to it. But why does it follow that the Dominion parliament would not have the power of passing any act they liked if they assented?

Sir HORACE DAVEY:—Because education is one of the subjects.

Lord MORRIS:—That is begging the question.

Sir HORACE DAVEY:—If your lordship will forgive me for looking at the words themselves:—"In and for the province the said legislature may exclusively make laws in relation to education subject and according to the following provisions" and then there are the provisions. It is not necessary for me to express any opinion, but I should be very loath, if I were asked to do so, to advise the Dominion government that they had the power to pass legislation on education at all for the province except in accordance with those conditions. However it is not necessary for me to express an opinion upon that.

Now, my lords, the other thing that is said is that if persons are compelled to pay school rates it diminishes their ability to be generous and to subscribe largely to the support of denominational schools. That may be true or it may not be, but certainly that is rather an indirect mode by which the right and privileges of persons are indirectly affected. The same may of course be said of any other tax which may be imposed. The more taxes a person has to pay the less his ability to be generous, and I do not think your lordships would entertain that consideration as coming within the words, prejudicially affect the rights and privileges of persons. Their right and privilege to subscribe to voluntary schools remains exactly where it was, although it may be that, owing to the larger municipal taxation they have to pay, their means of subscribing towards the denominational schools may be crippled.

Then, my lords, it is said that the public schools are in competition with the denominational schools. Of course they are and intended to be, but I am not aware of anything either in law or practice which prevented any person in the world in Rupert's Land, before it became the province of Manitoba, from setting up such schools as he thought fit either in competition with any existing schools or otherwise. So that there is really nothing in that. Your lordships will understand that I can give full force and effect to this section with which we are dealing—the words "have by law or practice." My lords, in the first place in the very undefined state in which law stood in Rupert's Land, which was governed by a private trading company subject of course to the crown—it was not a crown colony and had no legislative assembly or anything of that kind—it may well have been conceived that law, strictly speaking, and entitled to be called law on the strict construction that might be applied, did not exist, and therefore they used the words "or practice" to cover any rights or privileges which had grown up in the course of the government of the Hudson's Bay Company, though they were not strictly speaking law. But, my lords, I can go further, and I can suggest many cases which would satisfy those words "right or privilege by practice." My lords, it would prevent the legislature from extinguishing the voluntary schools by taking all the scholars away. Your lordships remember that you are now dealing with legislation in a very sparsely inhabited country, and if the legislature had said we will oblige every child to attend a public school; we will not allow it to go to work until it has had a certificate of competency from a public school, that would then have practically closed the denominational schools, because it would have made it necessary for every child and for every parent or guardian of a child to send the child to one of the public state schools. Or if it had imposed, as I said before, a particular qualification, religious or otherwise, on the teachers in any school it would have interfered; or if it had put children who had attended voluntary schools under any disqualification as regards public employment or otherwise afterwards. There are numerous cases in which those words "right or privilege existing by law or practice" might be satisfied. But, my lords, I confess I go further and say there was no right or privilege of exemption from public taxation for school purposes because there was no public taxation for school purposes. Such a thing was unknown and did not exist. There was no exemption known to the law. There can be no exemption from a thing which does not exist and if there was no public tax imposed on the ratepayers and taxpayers of the province of Rupert's Land for the purpose of education there could be no exemption.

Lord WATSON:—I think the case can be put a little higher than that against you. I think it would be more correct to state that there is no law or statute under which they could have been called upon to make such a payment.

Sir HORACE DAVEY:—That is quite true, and therefore there could have been no exemption. There was no law or statute by which they could have been called on to make a payment towards this denominational education. It is equally *ultra vires* to tax Roman catholics for Roman catholic schools.

Lord WATSON:—That being the state of the law, do you say when the law is altered it is not altered to their prejudice?

Sir HORACE DAVEY:—Of course, whenever a new tax is imposed it is to the prejudice of the taxpayer who has to pay it.

Lord WATSON:—I am not prepared to say, where there is no law before, a new statute may not alter the law to the prejudice of some people.

Lord HANNEN:—That would exempt them from taxation forever.

Lord SHAND:—The words of the clause are that nothing shall prejudically affect a right or privilege with respect to denominational schools.

Sir HORACE DAVEY:—What was the right or privilege of Roman catholics with respect to the denominational schools?

Lord SHAND:—It must be the right or privilege that attaches to a denominational school. That is the thing that is saved.

Sir HORACE DAVEY:—But which right or privilege of Roman catholics with respect to those denominational schools? I will put it as I think fairly, and the highest that can be put against myself. They had a right to maintain exclusively Roman catholic schools, that is to say schools the teachers of which were appointed by the authorities of the church, and in which the Roman catholic tenets, doctrines and worship were rigidly enforced on the scholars.

Lord MORRIS:—How was that a right?

Sir HORACE DAVEY:—By practice.

Lord MORRIS:—What does sub-section 1 refer to at all? What do you say sub-section 1 was meant to preserve?

Sir HORACE DAVEY:—It was meant to preserve rights—rights they are not strictly—but such rights, using that word in a large sense, as they enjoyed by practice.

Lord MORRIS:—They had no rights, as I understand your argument, except the rights of true-born subjects of the queen.

Sir HORACE DAVEY:—Which may be seriously interfered with by legislation. I do not know that it is an abstract right of people to hold a school. Certainly, in no period of our history till quite modern times—if it is so now—has there been any such right throughout the British dominions. Nc unitarian could maintain a school in England until a very recent period, and I am speaking subject to correction, but I believe it is only within a recent period that a Roman catholic could teach in schools in Ireland.

Lord MORRIS:—That has not been so for the last hundred years.

Sir HORACE DAVEY:—Be it so. A great deal has happened since those days, but it is within historical times that that has been so. It is not by any means an abstract right, and it is quite conceivable and something more than conceivable.

Lord SHAND:—Supposing the legislature had gone the length of saying that every child was to attend the government schools.

Sir HORACE DAVEY:—Yes?

Lord SHAND:—Then that would have been clearly infringing the privilege which existed before.

Sir HORACE DAVEY:—That I agree—which existed by practice.

Lord SHAND:—That is the primary illustration you give?

Sir HORACE DAVEY: —Yes.

Lord SHAND:—That would meet what Lord Morris has put.

Sir HORACE DAVEY:—Saying that they must, or imposing a disqualification or disability on them.

Lord SHAND:—That would be the same thing.

Sir HORACE DAVEY:—As regards obtaining public appointments. For example, supposing they said no person shall be employed as a clerk in public offices unless he produces a certificate of competency from a public school.

Lord WATSON:—I should have thought that in the earlier history of England, before the reformation, the Roman catholics and Roman catholic clergy and benevolent persons had an absolute right to establish as many denominational schools as they chose. There was a period when they were proscribed, but that time has long since passed.

Sir HORACE DAVEY:—Yes, but I think it would be difficult to say that it is an absolute right of every British subject to maintain a private school without any restriction at all. I think that would be going a great deal too far.

Lord WATSON:—Does not that exist?

Lord MORRIS:—What is there to the contrary of that? Why should not anybody, if there is no statute to prevent it, open a school?

Sir HORACE DAVEY:—Certainly, but I say that it prevents the province of Manitoba from passing statutes. The province of Manitoba might pass a statute which would interfere with that right and it prevents their doing it.

LORD MORRIS:—That seems very peculiar that in the year of grace 1870 they contemplated doing it.

Sir HORACE DAVEY:—Pardon me, I do not think that it is so at all. It is to me quite conceivable.

Lord SHAND:—I understand that Sir Horace puts this case that supposing this legislature had passed a statute declaring that no subject in that district would be able to obtain an appointment under the government if he attended one of these denominational schools that would be struck out.

Sir HORACE DAVEY:—Or even if they said no child shall go to work till he obtains a certificate from a public school that he has passed a certain standard.

Lord MORRIS:—This is a privilege with respect to denominational schools or practice which they had at the time. What privilege had any class of persons in Manitoba with respect to denominational schools by practice in the year 1870?

Sir HORACE DAVEY:—If you look at what the practice was all you can say is that they maintained schools at their own expense, which they supported or not as they thought fit—the support of which was thoroughly voluntary, and it was within their competency either to subscribe to, or to drop, or to maintain or not as they thought fit.

Lord MORRIS:—And that is preserved.

Sir HORACE DAVEY:—Yes, that is preserved.

Lord MORRIS:—Then the question is, does taxing them to pay for another school injuriously affect that practice?

Sir HORACE DAVEY:—I ask how? and I am trying to analyse that. That is exactly what I am directing my mind to, and that is the point to which, if I may say so, I respectfully say your lordships will have to direct your minds. There are very powerful arguments in the judgments, and perhaps it would be as well if I were to take an early opportunity of reading the judgments, because the whole of the arguments are in them. I think there are eight judgments in which the arguments are thrashed out.

Lord SHAND:—Was the judgment of the last court unanimous against you?

Sir HORACE DAVEY:—Yes.

Lord SHAND:—And what in the courts below?

Sir HORACE DAVEY:—Both in my favour. There was one, Mr. Justice Dubuc, who was against me. What I was proceeding to point out was this. If you say that it was a right and privilege not to be taxed for the support of other schools, it was equally a right and privilege not to be taxed for the support of their own schools, and the right and privilege is of exactly the same quality and exactly the same stamp. Their right and privilege with regard to denominational schools was to support them or not as they thought fit; to contribute such sums as they thought fit; to pay such fees as the school charged for any children they sent there; but it was a right and privilege of the Roman catholics to say we will not support this particular Roman catholic school at all unless we think fit. It was a right and privilege of the protestants to say we will not contribute one single dollar or one single cent towards the support of this school. So that any taxation for the support of any denominational school clearly prejudicially affects the right and privilege of not being compelled to pay towards its support. What I mean is that the obligation to support schools of another denomination was of exactly the same quality, depending on exactly the same choice and voluntary character as the obligation to support their own schools. There was no obligation on a Roman catholic or on a presbyterian or a member of the church of England to support any denominational school unless he thought fit to do so. That is his right and privilege. His right and privilege is to pay such sums as he thinks fit to such school as he thinks fit and no other.

Lord MORRIS:—It is not his right and privilege but the privilege and right of a class.

Sir HORACE DAVEY:—Well, a class of persons. Take the presbyterians as a class, or take any other. I will take Roman catholics if your lordships desire. The right and privilege of the Roman catholics as a class was to contribute such sums as the individual members of that class thought fit to the support of such schools as they thought fit, and anything which puts a compulsion on them to contribute a certain sum whether they like it or not either to a school of their own denomination or to any other school——

LORD SHAND:—Do you mean by that he had a right or privilege of refraining from contributing to one school or another—to any school?

Sir HORACE DAVEY:—Yes.

LORD SHAND:—And that the right or privilege is as broad in one case as the other.

Sir HORACE DAVEY:—Quite so, and exactly the same quality. Of course I am aware that there are charitable persons of every denomination and public minded persons of every denomination who would think it right to contribute according to their means and would probably prefer contributing towards the schools of their own church. Indeed some public minded persons, if the Roman catholic school was efficient and the only school within a sparsely inhabited district, would think it right, though not Roman catholics, to contribute according to their means to that school. Is that a right and privilege that is preserved?

LORD MORRIS:—You say the right and privilege of a class. There may be idiosyncracies of individuals in a class but surely what the statute is aiming at is the class that supported each of these denominational schools.

Sir HORACE DAVEY:—I say so.

LORD MORRIS:—And the class would be subscribers.

Sir HORACE DAVEY:—I want to know what is the right and privilege of the class? The right and privilege of the class—they use that word over and over again—is not to contribute a single dollar or cent unless they think fit towards any school or any particular school.

LORD MORRIS:—That could not have been the practice.

Sir HORACE DAVEY:—But it was the practice. The archbishop tells us so.

LORD MORRIS:—Not to subscribe to their own schools?

Sir HORACE DAVEY:—No.

LORD MORRIS:—For the moment you were putting to us the case that it was just as strong in the case of the class of Roman catholics or presbyterians, that they would be affected as much if they were called on to subscribe to their own denominational schools. That is how I understood you. But then it says "practice," and surely the practice of Roman catholics at the time and presbyterians and everybody —of the class—was to subscribe to their own schools.

Sir HORACE DAVEY:—Not at all. Where there were general schools, for instance, in a sparsely inhabited district, you could not maintain three schools. There would be only one. It would be the school of the majority. At any rate the right and privilege is merely to do as they thought fit—of the class of persons to do as they thought fit. That was their right and privilege. I can find no right and privilege, either by law or practice, which would compel them. It is the archbishop's affidavit on which reliance is placed, and I will refer your lordship's at once to that on page 13 of the record. He says: "I have been a resident continuously of this country since 1845, as a priest in the Roman catholic church, and as bishop thereof since the year 1850, and now am the archbishop and metropolitan of the said church"—that is the Roman catholic church—"and I am personally aware of the truth of the matters herein alleged. Prior to the passage of the act of the dominion of Canada, passed in the 33rd year of the reign of her majesty Queen Victoria, chap. 3, known as the Manitoba Act, and prior to the order in council issued in pursuance thereof, there existed in the territory now constituting the province of Manitoba a number of effective schools for children. These schools were denominational schools, some of them being regulated and controlled by the Roman catholic church, and others by various protestant denominations. The means necessary for the support of the Roman catholic schools were supplied to some extent by school fees paid by some of the parents of the children who attended the schools, and the rest was paid out of the funds of the church, contributed by its members. During the period referred to Roman catholics had no interest in, or control over, the schools of the protestant denominations, and the members of the protestant denominations had no interest in, or control over, the schools of Roman catholics. There were no public schools, in the sense of state schools. The members of the Roman catholic church supported the schools of their own church, for the benefit of Roman catholic children, and were not under obligation to, and did not contribute to, the support of any other schools. In the matter of education, therefore, during the period referred to, Roman catholics were, as a matter of custom and practice, separate from the rest of the community, and their schools were all conducted according to the distinctive views and beliefs of Roman catholics as herein set forth. Roman catholic schools have always formed an integral part of the work of the Roman catholic church. That church has always considered the education of the children of Roman catholic parents as coming peculiarly within its jurisdiction.

The school in the view of the Roman catholics is in a large measure the children's church, and wholly incomplete and and largely abortive if religious exercises be excluded from it. The church has always insisted upon its children receiving their education in schools conducted under the supervision of the church, and upon their being trained in the doctrines and faith of the church. In education the Roman catholic church attaches very great importance to the spiritual culture of the child, and regards all education unaccompanied by instruction in its religious aspects as possibly detrimental and not beneficial to children. With this regard the church requires that all teachers of children shall not only be members of the church but shall be thoroughly imbued with its principles and faith; shall recognize its spiritual authority and conform to its directions. It also requires that such books be used in schools with regard to certain subjects, as shall combine religious instruction with those subjects, and this applies peculiarly to all history and philosophy. The church regards the schools, provided for by the Public Schools Act and being cap. 38 of the statutes passed in the reign of her majesty Queen Victoria in the 33rd year of her reign, as unfit for the purpose of educating their children, and the children of Roman catholic parents will not attend such schools." Now there is this sentence: "Rather than countenance such schools, Roman catholics will revert to the system in operation previous to the Manitoba Act, and will establish, support and maintain schools in accordance with their principles and faith as aforementioned." Now, my lords, that is exactly what I say they are at liberty to do—exactly. It appears to me the archbishop expresses it and says: if you maintain this Public Schools Act, I will do——what? I will resume the exercise of those rights and privileges with regard to denominational education which I enjoyed by practice before the Manitoba Act. "Protestants are satisfied with the system of education provided for by the said act—the 'Public Schools Act,' and are perfectly willing to send their children to the schools established and provided for by the said act"—except, I understand Mr. Logan—"Such schools are in fact similar in all respects to the schools maintained by the protestants under the legislation in force immediately prior to the passing of the said act," &c. [Reads the remainder of archbishop Taché's affidavit.] Now, my lords, with the greatest respect to this very eminent person, I venture to point out that the archbishop (to use a vernacular expression) gives himself away. What does he threaten, himself? He threatens us with reverting to the position in which he stood before the Manitoba Act came into force, and what he seems to dread is the competition of a free school. Supposing he is right—supposing it is a school supported only by the rates of presbyterians—leave out the Roman catholics—leave them free exactly as they were; relieve them from taxation for the presbyterians, and let it be a denominational system of education. They will still have to compete with the free presbyterian or church of England or protestant schools. The real truth is that the competition does not enter into the right or privilege at all, because if it were a right or privilege at all of the Roman catholics as a body, it was equally a right or privilege of every other religious body or denomination throughout.

Lord SHAND:—The statute of 1890 says something about religious instruction being given in accordance with some consultory board.

Sir HORACE DAVEY:—That was in 1871.

Lord SHAND:—What was dealt with in 1890?

Sir HORACE DAVEY:—In accordance not with the advisory board, but the board of education.

Lord SHAND:—I think it is the advisory board.

Sir HORACE DAVEY:—I beg pardon, my lord, it is in this act.

Lord SHAND:—I was going to ask with regard to that, if you could tell us what has been the practice under that, or do you happen to know whether in point of fact there is religious instruction given in the public schools?

Sir HORACE DAVEY:—Yes.

Lord SHAND:—If so, what is its character?

Sir HORACE DAVEY:—Portions of scripture are read.

Lord SHAND:—I see there is the privilege of withdrawing the child. I wanted to know in point of fact what is done?

Sir HORACE DAVEY:—In point of fact portions of scripture are read either from the English version or from the Douay version.

Mr. MCCARTHY:—That was in New Brunswick.

Sir HORACE DAVEY:—Portions of scripture are read without note or comment and some simple prayer such as the Lord's prayer is said on opening the school in the morning. Your lordships will see on page 13 of the record in Logan's case at the beginning there is the advisory board which I had forgotten.

Lord SHAND:—I see, "Regulations."

Sir HORACE DAVEY:—"The reading, without note or comment, of the following selections from the authorized version of the Bible or the Douay version of the Bible. The use of the following forms of prayer," and then some readings, historical parts and from the Gospel, and then there is a form of prayer on page 17 which your lordships will read. My lords, it may be useful to read the affidavit of Professor Bryce, of course, more or less argumentative, on page 20, in reply to the archbishop's affidavit. Professor Bryce, who is a professor in Manitoba college says on page 18:—"That I have been a resident in the province of Manitoba since the year 1871." [Reading down to the words on page 19 line 6.] "I think it is our firm belief that this system joined with the public school system has produced and will produce a moral, religious, and intelligent people."

Lord WATSON:—There appears to have been a good deal more about the evidence taken on the Manitoba commission.

Sir HORACE DAVEY:—I prefaced it by saying it was more or less argumentative.

Lord SHAND:—I think the same remark may be made to some extent to this one, but the previous one does go to this—as to the state of matters existing in fact in 1870. This gentleman does not really touch that.

Lord MORRIS:—He has put it as his individual opinion that the belief of the Roman catholics ought to be different from what it is.

Sir HORACE DAVEY:—I do not think he says that.

Lord MORRIS:—"I cannot see that there should be any conscientious objection on the part of the Roman catholics."

Sir HORACE DAVEY:—Then I won't say it was not. I said it was rather argumentative. I desire to argue this question as a perfectly impartial person and having no proclivities, and argue it simply upon what I have seen. It must be argued upon the construction of the acts. Your lordships will forgive this gentleman who no doubt thinks it is a matter of importance to himself in expressing his views in the form of an affidavit.

Lord SHAND:—Was there any affidavit put in by you in reference to the state of matters in 1870 as to the facts?

Sir HORACE DAVEY:—There is an affidavit of Sutherland, my lord. There is Polson's affidavit on page 17: "For a period of fifty years I have been a resident in the province of Manitoba. That schools which existed prior to the province of Manitoba entering confederation were, so far as the people were concerned, purely private schools, and were not in any way subject to public control, nor did they in any way receive public support." He is the health inspector for the city of Winnipeg. "No school taxes were collected by any authority prior to the province of Manitoba entering confederation, and there were no means by which any person could be forced by law to support any of said private schools. I think the only public revenue of any kind then collected was the customs duty of 4 per cent." Then John Sutherland says: "For the period of fifty-three years I have been a resident in the province of Manitoba."

Lord SHAND:—It is *verbatim*—the same.

Sir HORACE DAVEY:—Now, my lords, with regard to that customs duty, your lordships see they surrender them to the Dominion government, and the Dominion government regrant a certain portion out of the consolidated fund of Canada to this province, but a portion of the provincial revenue is applied—the legislative grant. Whatever considerations applied they would say no public moneys ought to be applied to the maintenance of non-sectarian schools. I cannot see any difference between the legislative grant out of the public money which is raised by customs duty upon the people and the school rate. In each case public money is being applied towards the support of a denominational school. If the Roman catholics have their way, the protestants may say: you shall not apply any part of the public moneys towards the maintenance of denominational schools. There was no such application before incorporation, and each religious body had a right to object to any portion of the taxes which were paid going to the support of any denominational school. It seems to me that argument is equally sound, and if that prevails, then it comes to this that there can be no state-aided schools at all, because each denomination will object to any legislative grant being made out of public moneys to any school which is a denominational school of some other denomination. The Roman catholics will object to any public moneys being applied for the maintenance of any protestant school, and the church of England will object to any public moneys being applied to the maintenance of Roman catholic or presbyterian schools.

Lord SHAND:—I suppose the objection would apply to an industrial school which is established for the purpose of teaching some industry?

Sir HORACE DAVEY:—Yes, if it is not non-sectarian.

Lord SHAND:—Apart from religion altogether?

Lord WATSON:—Was not there the application of public money under the act of 1881?

Sir HORACE DAVEY:—Yes, my lord, it is quite true, there was no objection made, but it is quite open to the same objection.

Lord SHAND:—It was a compromise, I suppose, the act of 1881? The parties chose to accept it, because each party got something?

Sir HORACE DAVEY:—As a matter of strict argument, it is just as much open to the objection, because if the objection is sound, it goes to the application of any single dollar or cent of public money to the maintenance of any schools for either non-sectarian teaching or denominational, because they say we were not liable to contribute towards the non-sectarian school, because each religious body might say we were not liable before the act to contribute to the maintenance of the schools of another denomination. So it comes to this that no single dollar of public money can be applied towards the maintenance of either denominational or non-sectarian schools.

Lord MORRIS:—How would the right of the non-sectarian class be reserved by sub-section 1 of the act—the non-sectarian class of persons?

Sir HORACE DAVEY:—I do not say they would.

Lord MORRIS:—But then, sub-section 1 wants to reserve the rights of denominational schools—of a denominational class.

Sir HORACE DAVEY:—You do not quite follow me. I say, if you apply public money to the support of non-sectarian schools, then the Roman catholics and the members of the church of England rise in arms and say you are applying moneys which are partly contributed by us towards the support of schools other than those of our own denominations.

Lord MORRIS:—The contention is that they are not to pay for anything but their own schools.

Sir HORACE DAVEY:—Quite so. I say, public moneys which are raised by customs duties on the provinces generally and public money belonging to the province are applied in support of the non-sectarian schools, then so far forth as those Roman catholics are taxed for the purpose of raising these moneys or from being taxed for the support of schools not of their own denomination, and, on the other hand, if you apply public moneys to the support of schools which are raised by the general taxation of the country—to the support of denominational schools, then the church of England will say: "No; you must not apply those moneys which we contribute, and which are raised partly by taxing us, to support presbyterian schools or to the support of Roman catholic schools," and the Roman catholics will say "you must not apply moneys which are raised partly by taxing us towards the support of church of England schools or presbyterian schools, or any other sect or denomination."

Lord MORRIS:—How would that prejudicially affect if both got a share of it?

Sir HORACE DAVEY:—I quite agree.

Lord MORRIS:—As I understand it, Logan's case and Barrett's case is, they would not get any share of the public money under this act of 1890 unless they put their schools on a system which they do not think they can put them on.

Sir HORACE DAVEY:—No, unless they send their children to the public schools.

Lord MORRIS:—To the schools they can send them to. That is unjustly and prejudicially affecting them, surely.

Sir HORACE DAVEY:—No; why? It does not affect the person, but it would affect a privilege which they had in respect of denominational schools. It does not prejudicially affect the persons, and you will see so throughout the judgments.

Lord MORRIS:—I have not read the judgments.

Sir HORACE DAVEY:—You will see the fallacy running throughout. It is treated as prejudicially affecting the person, but it is only affecting some right or privilege which they had. I think the argument is so fully contained in the judgment that I had better at once go to the judgment.

Lord SHAND:—I see there was a power of appeal in this matter to the governor in council.

Sir HORACE DAVEY:—No, it is the other side would do that; and that may be a point I desire to have your lordships' opinion upon.

The ATTORNEY GENERAL.—Steps were taken.

Lord SHAND:—As I understand they hold that this act is bad. Then they get their remedy in that way. They do not require to go to the governor in council upon any appeal.

The ATTORNEY GENERAL:—Yes; the governor refused to interfere.

Lord MORRIS:—Is there any contention that the proper course would have been to have gone to the governor general.

Sir HORACE DAVEY:—I think there would be a great deal in that contention but my instructions are, as your lordships might expect, to lay the case on its merits before this court, and to invite your lordships' decision unfettered by any technicality.

Lord MORRIS:—Do you call that a technicality if the act of parliament avoids a mode of plea--is that a technicality?

Sir HORACE DAVEY:—If your lordships say it is not a technicality I withdraw the word. My desire and my friend's desire I think is to have the opinion of this court upon the constitutional aspect.

Lord MORRIS:—That would be so if this board assisted as an academical reviewer, but I should have thought that *primâ facie* if an act of parliament creates a liability of a rate it must give the mode for levying that rate.

Sir HORACE DAVEY:—If your lordship presses me to express an opinion I think that is a very strong argument, but your lordship's experience, although it is very remote at the bar, reminds one that one is not desired to press arguments which one may desire

Lord WATSON:—There is at least some possibility of this that in the first instance it lies on the governor general to say how far the act does harm.

Sir HORACE DAVEY—Then if the act does and the provincial legislature decline to alter their legislation, then the intermediate legislature may intervene.

Lord SHAND:—They may have something to say for this that the courts of law are the first persons of authority to interpret an act on appeal from any decision or act affecting a right or privilege, but if the court declare there was no such right or privilege then the governor general would not be let in, whereas if the decision were referred you would have a right.

Lord WATSON:—Supposing they had referred the matter to go to the governor general and he had decided the right was infringed, what could a court of law have done?

Sir HORACE DAVEY:—Nothing.

Lord SHAND:—Do I understand, Mr. Attorney, the governor general refused to interfere, or did he think it did not affect any right.

Mr. RAM:—The appeal was to the governor to veto the act There was no appeal as against the validity of the act.

Lord SHAND:—Under another clause

Mr. McCarthy:—Both appeals were put in.

Sir Horace Davey:—As your lordships have invited me to do so, I feel my hands are free. I should like to place the point before your lordships, your lordships understanding that my clients do not shrink from asking your lordships' opinion on the merits. There are counsel at your lordships' bar, and I have no right to ask your lordships to express an opinion which may afterwards be overruled by the governor-general, without placing the whole facts before your lordships.

Lord Watson:—As to the act of 1867, as to the veto by the governor-general in the case of provincial legislation.

Sir Horace Davey:—If your lordship will look at page 4, in our record, you will see the two sets of clauses printed side by side. I think you will be of opinion that the Manitoba clauses have replaced the clauses in the British North America Act.

Lord Watson:—Yes, but I was speaking of the other. I was dealing with reference to the appeal to the governor-general. I think there are provisions for the governor-general interposing his veto.

Sir Horace Davey:—Yes.

Lord Watson:—Under the act of 1867 you must attempt to explain what is meant by the veto.

Sir Horace Davey:—The veto is quite a different thing, my lord.

The Attorney General:—Your lordships will find it in sections 55 and 56, page 8.

Sir Horace Davey:—What is called the veto is quite a different thing. There is no such thing as a veto except it is a royal assent.

Lord Watson:—The queen's assent is given in the Dominion parliament by the governor-general, in the provincial parliament by the lieutenant-governor.

Sir Horace Davey:—Unless he can reserve it.

Lord Watson:—That would not affect the right of appeal.

Lord Macnaghten:—Is there any other section in the act dealing with that?

Sir Horace Davey:—I believe that is the only section in which an appeal is given from a subordinate legislature—your lordship knows—I must not say your lordship knows, because I believe it is *sub judice* at the present moment before your lordship; but the general opinion is that the provincial legislatures are not subordinate to the Dominion—that each is a *quasi-sovereign* within its own sphere. This is the only instance, I believe, in the scheme of the British North America Act where the Dominion parliament is expressly given power to over-ride the legislation.

Lord Macnaghten:—Not the Dominion parliament.

Sir Horace Davey:—Yes, because they intervene supposing the provincial parliament does not comply with the governor-general.

Lord Watson:—There is a remedial power given in the other. It seems to be part of the duty of the governor-general to see that the provincial legislature carries out the provisions.

Sir Horace Davey:—If it does not, then the intermediate tribunal can intervene.

Lord Watson:—They do not oppose what he considers to be a proper measure, and there seems to be power to declare that they have passed improper measures.

Sir Horace Davey:—The Dominion parliament carries into effect the award of the governor-general. The section which regulates a royal assent to bills in the provincial legislature, in section 90, "The following provisions of this act respecting the parliament of Canada, namely," &c., &c. (Reads down to the words), "And of the province for Canada." So that you must read sections 55 and 56 with this substitution, "Where a bill passed by the provincial house is presented to the lieutenant-governor for the queen's assent he shall declare according to his discretion, and subject to the provisions of this act and to the governor-general's instructions, either that he assents thereunder in the queen's name, or that he withholds the queen's assent, or that he reserves the bill for the signification of," I suppose "the governor-general," then "where the lieutenant-governor assents to a bill in the governor-general's name, he shall by the first convenient opportunity send an authentic copy of the Act to" I suppose "the governor-general, and if the governor-general within two years after receipt thereof thinks fit to disallow the act."

Lord MORRIS:—Is not this the way the case came on? There is some power by a municipal act of having by-laws made by the municipality to carry out this school act of the legislature.

Sir HORACE DAVEY:—Yes.

Lord MORRIS:—And by-laws for a rate, properly speaking anybody dissatisfied could apply to the court of queen's bench, I presume in that country as they would here.

Sir HORACE DAVEY:—There is express statutory power.

Lord MORRIS:—That is to set aside those by-laws; but, as I understand it, then the by-laws are all right on the assumption that the school is all right, but the court goes behind the by-laws which are right and says that there was no power of the legislature to pass that act of parliament. Now what gave authority to that court to enter into that question.

Sir HORACE DAVEY:—Well, that is a very old question, my lord. It was at first agitated very soon after the British North America Act was passed, and it has been decided in numerous cases, many of which have come up before your lordships court, that where a question arises *inter partes* which involves substantially the question whether the Dominion legislature has exceeded its powers, the court must necessarily construe that act and the constitution act, and if it finds that the act in question is not within the purview of the constitution act, if necessary,—

Lord SHAND:—The language of section 22 makes that pretty clear because it is "In and for the province," and one of the limits is this, "Nothing in any such law shall prejudicially affect any right" &c. (Reading the section.) Then the statute goes on to name to whom you are to appeal, if an appeal lie to the governor-general, from any act of the legislature.

Lord WATSON:—We should feel a good deal more satisfied if you could assure us we have cleared everything, for this reason, supposing the governor-general be dissatisfied with the terms of the act of 1871 and had got the Dominion parliament to pass a statute in the terms of the act of 1890 on what ground could that have been assailed?

Sir HORACE DAVEY:—My hands are perfectly free. I think there are very grave doubts whether your lordships have any jurisdiction at all, because, if you look at the section of the Manitoba act, and I think I am bound to say so, if you look at the section of the Manitoba act, I presume that the statutory "authority," if I may use that expression, created for the purpose of saying whether or no an education act is confined to education and exceeds the power of the provincial legislature, is the governor-general.

Lord WATSON:—Suppose there had been an appeal in this case to the governor-general in council and the governor-general in council had held that their legislative powers had been rightly exercised in the terms of the Act of 1870, what interference could we have?

Sir HORACE DAVEY:—Your lordships have only the jurisdiction of a single judge of the queen's bench in this matter, you are only saying what a judge of the queen's bench ought to have done.

Lord WATSON:—We cannot entertain anything here that was not properly brought before the other court.

Sir HORACE DAVEY:—Not a single judge of the queen's bench in the province of Canada has over-ruled the statutory decision given in pursuance of the statutory power of the governor-general, who is the person to whom the appeal lies.

Lord SHAND:—But this board could not have entertained anything that was not brought before that court at all.

Sir HORACE DAVEY:—Yes, in this particular case, because observe what the act says after the first section, that "nothing in any such law shall prejudicially affect."

The ATTORNEY-GENERAL:—No point has ever been raised either in the courts below or by my friend.

Lord SHAND:—You may take it it is raised by the court.

Sir HORACE DAVEY:—I stated to your lordships my client would desire to have your lordships' opinion on the merits, but I am bound, in answer to your lordship, to say that it is a point which has occurred outside this court.

Lord MACNAGHTEN:—To take a different view from the governor-general in Canada.

. Sir HORACE DAVEY:—After saying "that nothing shall prejudicially affect," etc., it goes on to say "an appeal shall lie to the governor-general in council from any act of the legislature of the province, or of any provincial authority affecting any right or privilege of the protestant or Roman catholic minority of the queen's subjects."

Lord WATSON:—I understood you stated that the act of 1870 was confirmed by a subsequent act.

Sir HORACE DAVEY:—Yes, there was an order in council and then there was an act removing doubts. Your lordships will see it on page 31.

Lord WATSON:—Except so far as reserved by the act of 1870, the Dominion legislature's powers seem to be ousted. It is a very peculiarly worded clause. It tends to show, except in so far as the governor-general has a right to interfere, there is no power of legislating in educational matters reserved to the Dominion parliament.

Sir HORACE DAVEY:—That is so. It is familiar law to all of us, which does not require supporting by authority, that where a new right is created by statute, and by the same statute, or by another statute *in pari materia*, a particular means of interfering with the right is given, then the mode of enforcement is confined to the particular means which are given by the statute which creates the right. Now here the exclusive right to make laws in relation to education is vested in the provincial legislature, but there are certain restrictions imposed on the provincial legislature. Then an appeal is given to the governor-general in council to say where or how far any act of the provincial legislature, which is expressly mentioned in the Manitoba Act, getting rid of the ambiguity in the general act—the former act—how far any act in the provincial legislature of Manitoba does or does not infringe the rights reserved and the privileges of the Roman catholic or protestant minority as the case may be. Well, if that is so, it is obvious that this being a right or privilege which is reserved by the act itself, to the Roman catholic minority, and in case it is infringed an appeal being given—the act has provided within its own four corners a remedy for an infringement of the right or privilege which it has created by the act itself, and therefore, it would seem that this act of parliament, being an act relating to education—exclusively relating to education—is an act which *prima facie* falls within the jurisdiction of the Manitoba legislature, but then the question whether it has complied with those provisos and restrictions which are imposed upon the right to legislate arises, and that is the question as to which the statute which imposed those provisos and restrictions has given an appeal to the governor-general.

Lord SHAND:—Are there any authorities upon cases such as this, of an appeal to the governor-general, before this board that you remember?

Sir HORACE DAVEY:—I do not think this has ever come before it.

Lord SHAND:—Anything of this kind?

Sir HORACE DAVEY:—I think I may undertake to say it has not. I think I have probably argued the majority of them, and I think I am acquainted with nearly all the cases.

Lord WATSON:—Do you think any question has arisen on the act of 1867?

Sir HORACE DAVEY:—No, that is what I mean. It could not on the Manitoba Act.

The ATTORNEY-GENERAL:—I do not think there is any case in which this education section has been considered, or the corresponding section, 93.

Sir HORACE DAVEY:—There is one case, Renaud's case, but that is not reported.

Lord WATSON:—Renaud's case was from New Brunswick. The following note of the privy council is taken from the *Times* of 18th July, 1874: "Judgment is not given in the regular reports. Lord Justice James, after conferring with the other members of the committee, gave judgment without calling on the respondents.

Their lordships concurred in the opinion of the court below, and would advise her majesty the appeal be dismissed with costs."

Sir HORACE DAVEY:—Was a judgment given?

The ATTORNEY-GENERAL:—There was no judgment reported.

Lord SHAND:—Was there in that case a power of appealing?

Sir HORACE DAVEY:—It was under this section, under the section of the British North America Act.

Lord SHAND:—Yes, the corresponding one to this.

Sir HORACE DAVEY:—The question was whether the rights and privileges of certain Roman catholics had been infringed, because the practice was before incorporation to read from the Douay version of the Bible, and they held that that was only practice and not the privilege secured by law, which were the words within the British North America Act.

Lord MACNAGHTEN:—What is the date of that?

Sir HORACE DAVEY:—1874. That is the only appeal which has come before your lordships' board on the corresponding section 93, the education section. Frequently your lordships have had to consider in later cases—Hodge *vs.* Russell, and another case which refers to Lord Lansdowne—the constitutionality of the liquor legislation of the province of Ontario, and then your lordships in Dobie? had to consider there the constitutionality of an act for amalgamating presbyterian endowments to the province of Ontario. There are numerous cases in which you have had to express an opinion, and you have had similar questions come from Australia, I suppose.

Lord SHAND:—The appeal lies to the governor-general.

The ATTORNEY-GENERAL:—Except in Renaud's case.

Lord SHAND:—Of course there must be an appeal to a court of appeal, if there was no such clause as this.

Sir HORACE DAVEY:—It follows from the very conception of a subordinate legislature—it must necessarily follow, because an act of parliament is put forward by way of defence. But you say: "Is there such an act of parliament? Let us look at the authority under which it was passed."

Lord MORRIS—Then there was a *certorari* so that the court of queen's bench should have a right to intervene, although there was an appeal given.

Sir HORACE DAVEY—No, there was not to be a *certorari*, my lord. I do not want to get into other subjects, but necessarily if a legislature is in the same position as a county council, if it passes an act, and if it derives its authority to make acts from an act of the imperial legislature, and it purports to pass an act which is in excess of the authority conferred upon it—

Lord MORRIS—The courts of queen's bench still hold that although the statute expressly takes away—

Sir HORACE DAVEY—Then on the other hand, my lord, it is this: this act is *prima facie* within the exclusive jurisdiction of the Manitoba legislature, because it relates to legislation, and the only question is whether it has complied with the provisos and restrictions. If you look at the third sub-section that sets out the appeal: "In case any such provincial law as from time to time seems to the governor-general in council requisite for the due execution of the provisions of this section is not made, or in case any decision of the governor-general in council on any appeal under this section is not duly executed by the proper provincial authority in that behalf, then, and in every such case, and as far only as the circumstances of each case may require, the parliament of Canada may make remedial laws for the due execution of the provisions of this section, and of any decision of the governor-general in council under this section." That gives jurisdiction to the parliament of Canada, based upon the decision of the governor-general in council.

Lord SHAND—Supposing the governor-general were to decide on appeal that this was a competent act of parliament, I do not think section 3 could have any application.

Sir HORACE DAVEY—No, my lord; then it would not be done.

Lord SHAND—Equally, if he held it was incompetent. I do not think there was an appeal under that section.

Sir HORACE DAVEY:—Yes.

Lord SHAND:—Which clause.

Sir HORACE DAVEY:—"Then and in every such case."

Lord SHAND:—I do not think you get that case.

Sir HORACE DAVEY:—"In case any such provincial law as from time to time seems to the governor-general in council requisite for the due execution of the provisions of this section is not made."

Lord SHAND:—It would not be that case.

Sir HORACE DAVEY:—"Or in case any decision of the governor-general."

Lord SHAND:—"Is not duly executed."

Sir HORACE DAVEY:—That is to say, if the provincial legislature is to have an opportunity of amending its legislation and bringing it within the section.

Lord SHAND:—I think if the governor-general on appeal confirms something, but it has not been properly carried out; then there will be an appeal, but I do not think there will be any appeal.

Sir HORACE DAVEY:—Surely, my lord, the appeal is to lie to the governor-general from any act of the provincial legislature affecting any right or privilege.

Lord SHAND:—Then two cases are provided for in the next.

Sir HORACE DAVEY:—Then the governor-general gives his decision; then the provincial legislature, if they think fit, amend their act.

Lord SHAND:—There is no such suggestion as amending.

Lord WATSON:—The first part of the sub-section seems to imply the function of the governor-general is to watch the progress of legislation on educational subjects.

Sir HORACE DAVEY:—Yes, that is so.

Lord WATSON:—It may be to suggest to them that they shall amend their law if he thinks that law does not comply with the general feeling.

Sir HORACE DAVEY:—The legislature might comply with the requisition, decision or award of the governor-general, but if they do not, then I submit——

Lord SHAND:—There would be no mandamus if the governor-general were to hold that this is an act which does affect the Roman catholic minority.

Sir HORACE DAVEY:—Then they appeal on it.

Lord SHAND:—I do not see there is any appeal, it would be final on this matter.

Sir HORACE DAVEY:—The provincial legislature would then have to repeal the act.

Lord SHAND:—Would not deliverance of judgment by the governor-general be a repeal of the act.

Sir HORACE DAVEY:—I do not suppose your lordships' decision would repeal the act, it remains in the statute book.

Lord SHAND:—Yes, it would be a bad act.

Lord MACNAGHTEN:—Does the Dominion parliament have to comply? Supposing the governor-general directed remedial legislation, are the Dominion legislators bound to comply with it?

Sir HORACE DAVEY:—I do not know my lord.

Lord WATSON:—The governor-general has power to set in motion. There is an end of it.

Lord MORRIS:—Are they bound to do it?

Sir HORACE DAVEY:—We are getting within the apices of constitutional law. I do not see any obligation, of course there is no obligation on a legislature to pass a particular act or not.

Lord MORRIS:—They would not if the opinion of the majority was different from the decision that the governor-general came to, of course they would not pass an act. What would happen then?

Sir HORACE DAVEY:—It is easy of course to put an illustration, but supposing your lordships came to the conclusion either that this legislation was beyond the powers of the Manitoba legislature and wanted amending to bring it within its power, and the governor-general came to the conclusion in council, that it was within their powers then it is easy to suggest the difficulty in which people would be placed: Of course your lordships' decision is only a decision in the particular circumstances that that particular by-law is bad. That is all your lordships decision will be, and then an expression of opinion from your lordships is usually considered as sufficient, but it would remain that your lordships had declared the by-law bad because the Public Schools Act exceeded the jurisdiction of parliament and the governor-general may have determined that the by-law is good, because in his opinion it does not exceed the powers. It appears to me that there are good grounds, or at any rate very serious grounds to be considered for saying that under this particular section the intention was to invest in the governor-general and the Dominion parliament the protection of the rights of the minority, which were intended to be given by means of the section, and that the act in question, being within the general description of acts which are exclusively within the jurisdiction of the provincial legislature, has provided the means in this particular case for confining the act to an educational act and making it subject to the restrictions and provisions in question and that therefore on general principles there is no appeal. There can be no appeal and the act must be considered a good act until the particular tribunal provided by the act, namely, the governor-general, has pronounced upon its unconstitutionality. I have stated the point to your lordships, and I confess, if I am at liberty to express my own opinion, that it seems a point deserving of grave consideration. But I have also said to your lordships that this question being a question which greatly agitates the province—in fact the educational system of the province is paralyzed during this discussion—it being a matter of great public importance my clients do not shrink from submitting the case to your lordships on the merits, but at the same time, as the point has been raised and suggested by the court itself, I am bound to say what I have pointed out.

Now, having said that, I will now ask your lordships to let me read the judgments in the case, and I think, when I have read the judgments in the case, your lordships will be in possession of every thing that is to be said, either on one side or on the other.

Lord WATSON:—[Addressing the attorney-general] Their lordships desire to know whether you will consider this point of jurisdiction or whether you are prepared to argue it out now.

The ATTORNEY-GENERAL:—As it has been mentioned by Sir Horace Davey I am quite prepared to say a word or two upon it. I do not say I am bound to deal with the point, but I am quite prepared to do so, if your lordships will indicate that I should further argue the point. If your lordships were going to stop the case I would argue the point.

Lord WATSON:—We will hear you after lunch.

[Adjourned for a short time.]

The ATTORNEY-GENERAL:—Your lordships were good enough to indicate that you would wish to know whether I had any observations to make upon the question which was raised by your lordships as to the competence of this appeal, having regard to the provisions of section 22 of the Manitoba Act of 1870. Of course, I do not understand your lordships to be expressing any opinion at all upon the general merits of the appeal, because it is most important that it should be understood that we are dealing with this only as a preliminary question.

Lord MACNAGHTEN:—Will you tell us what has been done in the matter?

The ATTORNEY-GENERAL:—I was about to tell your lordships that, in the first place, the statute having been passed, by-laws were made, and it was attempted to charge the respondent, Barrett, with a rate made under those by-laws, whereupon he applied to the queen's bench division for an order to quash the application made to him for rates, on the ground that the by-laws were not binding upon him, because the statute under which they were made was, in his contention, *ultra vires*. I humbly submit that, apart from any provision of the 22nd section, that would clearly have been a perfectly legitimate and proper proceeding. In fact I do not think my learned friend, Sir Horace Davey, or those with him, would contend to the contrary. Mr. Justice Killam decided that the by-laws were good—the majority of the court on appeal, this point not having been taken in any of the courts—the majority of the court on appeal decided that the by-laws were good. The supreme court by an unanimous judgment decided that the by-laws were bad, on the ground that the statute was *ultra vires*. At no stage of these proceedings, as I am informed, was any objection taken to the action by application to the court of queen's bench to quash the by-laws as being bad, and I will submit presently that the outside that could be suggested would be that there would be two remedies and not one only. I am going to take a point different from that when I come to the merits. At some time a petition was presented, as I am informed, by Mr. Ewart to the governor-general under sub-section 2, and he simply postponed acting upon that petition until the final decision had been given by the court of law, as to whether the statute or the Manitoba Act of 1890 was, or was not, *ultra vires*. Those are my instructions, but with regard to those proceedings your lordships must kindly not take it from me, but be good enough to take it from one of my learned friends from Canada, who have instructed me as to what happened in regard to this matter.

Lord SHAND:—Do I understand there is no written deliverance, or anything that can be produced to show how the governor-general acted?

Mr. McCARTHY:—Oh, yes, it is here.

The ATTORNEY-GENERAL:—The point that is taken is not that the appeal does not lie to your lordships from the supreme court, but that the proceedings are ill-founded from the commencement. As your lordship pointed out you can only make the order which the judge of first instance could have made, and, therefore, the objection must be that they were not properly constituted proceedings; that the application to the court of queen's bench was ill founded.

Lord SHAND:—I suppose an application could have been made to the queen's bench in this way: Suppose there had been an appeal to the governor, and the person who appealed put in an application to stop the proceedings, in which the governor gave his deliverance, that would be a good proceeding.

The ATTORNEY-GENERAL:—It is a little difficult to answer that question until I have considered what the real language of the section is. Of course there are many cases in which the court has discretion to stop proceedings until a decision has been given. We know the application on the ground of what is called *lis alibi pendens*, or any other proceeding of the same kind in which the question is being raised. I am submitting that the proceedings were perfectly right. Assume the first sub-section stood alone. I humbly submit no question could be raised. "Nothing in any such law shall prejudicially affect any right or privilege with respect to denominational schools which any class of persons have by law or practice in the province at the union." If the law did purport to affect prejudicially the right of any class an order made under it would be bad and could be quashed, and your lordships have decided more than once that the courts of Canada and other colonial courts have the right and must examine to see whether the parliament with a limited mandate has, or has not, exceed its mandate. And that proposition my learned friends do not dispute. Then it is said that the second sub-section renders application to the queen's bench under the first sub-section bad, because there is another remedy. In the first place I do not admit that the existence of the other remedy would have rendered the application bad, the *certiorari* or those proceedings in no way being taken away; but I am about to point out that the second sub-section does not cover the whole ground. I understand and I submit that the second sub-section is to give the governor a discretion in dealing with a case that may be *intra vires*, and does not of necessity attach until there is a question of an *ultra vires* proceeding by the provincial legislature. "An appeal shall lie to the governor-general in council from any act or decision of the legislature of the province, or of any provincial authority, affecting any right or privilege of the protestant or Roman catholic minority of the queen's subjects in relation to education." It is wider in many ways, and narrower in other ways. In the first place it is with relation to education; it is not with respect to denominational schools. In that respect it is far wider. I am referring to page 4 of the record. It is printed in parallel columns. Further than that it is only in the case of the right or privilege of the protestant or Roman catholic minority being affected. The earlier sub-section, as we shall contend when we deal with the merits, deals with the question of the right or privilege of any class of persons, whether they be minority, majority or equality; and our respectful contention will be that under sub-section 1 there is a prohibition upon the legislature of the province interfering, as they have interfered, having regard to their limited powers given them by section 22.

Lord WATSON:—The framers of the act assumed that the majority are those whose representatives passed the act.

The ATTORNEY-GENERAL:—It is quite possible, but I am respectfully pointing out that the governor-general under sub-section 2, as we submit, has to do with more than the question of prejudicial affection. It is not prejudicially affected. It need not prejudicially affect.

Lord MACNAGHTEN:—It is very much wider. Do you say it does not include no. 1?

The ATTORNEY-GENERAL:—I say it does not in the sense of saying that the *ultra vires* question must go to the governor-general. My point with regard to sub-section 2 is, it was intended that there should be an appeal in all education matters at the instance of the protestant or Roman catholic minority to the governor general in council; that on that appeal he could give a decision which would vary, or might indicate that he thought that the act of the legislature of the province ought to be varied, even though there was no prejudicial affection.

Lord SHAND:—Do those words, "affecting any right or privilege" not mean "affecting prejudicially any right or privilege?"

The ATTORNEY-GENERAL:—I say not of necessity. For instance I can imagine there being a suggestion made that the benefit given was not sufficient. Take the case that the act of the provincial legislature had given an equal amount of grant, or had imposed an equal amount of rating upon inhabitants, and then it had been said that is unfair to the minority, because the minority ought to have a larger share. I can imagine a benefit given to the minority, so that their rights and interests were not prejudicially affected within the meaning of sub-section 1, still affording ground for an application by way of appeal to the governor-general in council. Then if your lordships will kindly refer to sub-section 3, I submit that that view is further carried out by the provisions made. "In case any such provincial law, as from time to time seems to the governor general in council requisite for the due execution of the provisions of this section, is not made, or in case any decision of the governor-general in council on any appeal under this section is not duly executed by the proper provincial authority in that behalf, then, and in every such case, and as far only as the circumstances of each case require, the parliament of Canada may make remedial laws for the due execution of the provisions of this section." If the question had been put to me that was put by Lord Macnaghten to Sir Horace Davey, I should have said that it was not compulsory, that the parliament of Canada were not bound to pass the law, or to implement or give effect to the view of the governor-general, that it was intended that they should have a legislative discretion as to what acts they would pass, having regard to the view expressed by the governor-general on the appeal. Therefore, I humbly submit that the whole framework of sub-sections 2 and 3 of this section 22 contemplates what I may call parallel legislative powers given to the governor-general and the Dominion legislature in the event of the judgment of the governor-general being in fact under sub-section 2.

Lord SHAND:—How could it be parallel? Suppose that the court were to hold that the legislature had gone too far.

The ATTORNEY-GENERAL:—Which court?

Lord SHAND:—This court or the court in Canada.

The ATTORNEY-GENERAL:—Then the law is bad without the necessity of going to the governor general. I am afraid I have not made my meaning clear.

Lord SHAND:—You would hold the governor-general bound by that decision then—because he may take a different view.

The ATTORNEY-GENERAL:—I say it would not go to the governor-general at all.

Lord SHAND:—Do you mean that it is an alternative appeal.

The ATTORNEY-GENERAL:—I do not say that it is an alternative appeal at all. I am not saying that things will not overlap at times. I say it is an alternative procedure, but your lordships must not impute to me by the word "alternative" that it simply covers exactly the same ground. What I suggest to your lordships is this: that the question of *ultra vires*, having regard to sub-section 1 of section 22, having regard, in fact, to the powers given to the legislature, must be decided by the court of queen's bench, and by your lordships' board, in exactly the same way as though sub-sections 2 and 3 had not been there. Sub-section 2 and sub-section 3, though they are clear, are not intended to take the place of the power of the court to consider whether or not the legislation is or is not *intra vires*, or in other words it is not a condition precedent to the action of the court that there should have been any appeal to the governor-general, who is to decide the view. It is obvious that the governor-general's decision is not in the position of that of the court, because the governor-general's decision is in itself inoperative. I think Sir Horace Davey, if I may say so, put it perfectly correctly when he said the statute will not be removed; it will remain an act of the provincial legislature; the only effect of it will be to found the right of action by the legislature of the Dominion to implement or fulfil the direction that is given by the governor-general having regard to his decision. I would point out with great respect that the same kind of question might have arisen under the British North America Act, which is in the left-hand column. Supposing that a law had been made prejudicially affecting any right or privilege which any class of persons have by law in the province. Take Ontario and Quebec, which are typical cases. In Ontario and Quebec, Upper and Lower Canada, by statutes of the two provinces, Roman catholics could not be called upon to contribute to protestant schools, and protestants could not be called upon to contribute to Roman catholics. Now, supposing a law had been made by the provincial legislature, prejudicially affecting those *quasi* statutory—I use the word "statutory" as referring to the provincial legislature of course—the *quasi* statutory rights by law of the classes of persons therein referred to, namely, Roman catholics on the one side and protestants on the other. Could it be contended that the queen's bench in Canada must give effect to those laws—that they must allow an action to be maintained upon that statute, because there is sub-section 3 in that section: "Where in any province a system of separate or dissentient schools exists by law at the union, or is thereafter established by the legislature of the province, an appeal shall lie to the governor-general in council from an act or decision of any provincial authority, affecting any right or privilege of the protestant or Roman catholic minority of the queen's subjects in relation to education?" There again, I submit a far larger jurisdiction is given to the governor-general under sub-section 3 than under sub-section 1. I do not wonder that this point has not been raised in any of the courts below, because it seems to me that it could not be seriously contended that the court of queen's bench must give effect to a statute admittedly *ultra vires* on the ground that an appeal with reference to an analogous matter, not an alternative appeal (if your lordships permit me to draw the distinction) had been provided by sub-section 3 and sub-section 4, exactly the same machinery being provided in subsection 4 for allowing the parliament of Canada to make remedial laws to give effect to the decision of the governor-general. It is scarcely possible that if this point had been what I may call a substantial point, it would not have been referred to in any of these proceedings. Of course, it was an answer to the whole application. It was never taken in the court below. It was not put on the ground there that they wished for your lordships' opinion. There they were resisting it on the merits, but they did not take that point before Mr. Justice Killam, nor before the supreme court, nor do they take it in their case before your lordships. On this point the decision of your lordships' board in *exparte* Renaud is distinctly analogous. In *exparte* Renaud proceedings had been taken, I think, by *certiorari*.

Lord SHAND:—I understand that in that case there was no other appeal.

The ATTORNEY-GENERAL:—Oh, yes, exactly the same appeal. It was under sub-section 1 of the British North America Act, section 93. The only distinction is that the words "or practice" occur in our section: "law" occurs in that section. The decision upon the merits was that there was no law entitling the then appellant, Renaud, to the protection which he desired in the matter of the Douay Bible.

Upon the merits the decision was against Mr. Renaud. But with regard to this point of practice it is a distinct authority in my favour. There was a *certiorari* to quash an assessment for school purposes in the county of Kent, in the parish of Richibucto, on the ground that the Common School Act, 1871, was beyond the powers of the local legislature, and consequently void, and of no effect, a rule *nisi* having been obtained in Michaelmas term, 1870. That was an assessment for school purposes, the province having established by the legislature certain schools under the British North America Act. That went to the court of queen's bench. The judgment of the court of queen's bench was there the judgment of some of the judges who have given judgment in this case. There they decided upon the merits against the *certiorari*, and that came to your lordships' board, and judgment was given by the then members of the privy council affirming the decision. It is unfortunate that in those days Mr. Reeve did not always have copies given of the judgments.

Lord MORRIS:—They did not preserve copies then.

The ATTORNEY-GENERAL:—Quite so. The practice arose some years afterwards; but in 1874 they were not in the habit of doing what your lordships do now, of printing the judgment which was kept on record.

Sir RICHARD COUCH:—In all the Indian cases they did it long before.

The ATTORNEY-GENERAL:—I am speaking of the other appeals. I am not speaking without information on the point. It was not till a year or two afterwards. It does not follow, because there is no written record that no oral judgment was delivered. Unfortunately there is no record either in the *Times* or in any contemporaneous reports of what judgment was delivered. Something more was said than appears in the official record. My point is that that was a case in which the privy council entertained upon the merits a case of exactly the same character as that which is now before your lordships. I should humbly submit to your lordships it would require express language to oust the jurisdiction of the court. I only apply the principle of Scott *vs.* Avory, and those cases. The court of queen's bench has ample and full jurisdiction. Unless it is said that no action shall be brought or no proceeding taken—I think Lord Watson in earlier days would have called it to reduce—that no action of the kind shall be brought unless there has been a preliminary enquiry before the governor-general or before some other tribunal, I should humbly submit that the superior court of the particular part of the Dominion or of the empire would be all-powerful to deal with the case. Of course, there are many cases where it has been decided that no action shall be brought having regard to contracts until an arbitrator has awarded certain amounts. There are numbers of cases in which either by statute or agreement, conditions precedent have to be fulfilled before actions can be entertained or applications made. For this purpose I am entitled to assume that this is an *ultra vires* law, and assuming that, I humbly submit that it is not only the right of the court of queen's bench, but the duty of the court of queen's bench upon the application to quash the by-laws and application for rates made upon Mr. Barrett; it was their duty to entertain that proceeding, and that assuming it to be alternative in the strictest sense of the term, the jurisdiction of the queen's bench would not be ousted. But I humbly submit it is not alternative. I submit it is wider in one respect and narrower in another. It is an appeal to Cæsar, so to speak, in the person of the governor-general, asking for different legislation, and his decision when given, if in favour of the appellants, is to be carried into effect by subsequent legislation. I therefore submit to your lordships it has no bearing upon the question of whether or not the court of queen's bench is entitled to consider upon the merits this application to quash.

Lord SHAND:—Perhaps you can give us the deliverance of the governor-general if it is in print. He may say expressly he desires to have the assistance of the court.

The ATTORNEY-GENERAL:—I was instructed to say that the governor-general had suspended dealing with the matter until the final opinion of the privy council had been given. This is what is given to me, and it is signed by the minister of justice. "The appeal has been presented, and the case is now before the supreme court of Canada, where it will in all probability be heard in the course of next month. If the appeal should be successful, these acts will be annulled by judicial decision. The Roman catholic minority in Manitoba will receive protection and redress. The acts purporting to be repealed will remain in operation, and those whose views have been represented by a majority of the legislature cannot but recognize that the matter has been disposed of with due regard to the constitutional rights of the province. If the legal controversy should result in the decision of the court of queen's bench being maintained, the time will come for your excellency to consider the petitions which have been presented by and on behalf of the Roman catholics of Manitoba for redress under sub-section 2 and sub-section 3 of section 22 of the Manitoba act." That is at page 5. That is exactly the information which is given to me. The governor-general has taken the view of subsections 2 and 3 which I submit to your lordships is the right view, namely, that he has the right of entertaining the appeal and considering the application upon the merits, and that when the application has been considered by him upon the merits, it will be for the Dominion parliament to decide whether they will give effect to any alteration.

Lord MORRIS:—That is that, although the action of the provincial legislature might be legal, still it might be so oppressive that the governor would redress it.

The ATTORNEY-GENERAL:—Yes. I contend that sub-sections 2 and 3 do not depend on *ultra vires* at all. Sub-sections 2 and 3 depend upon the protestant or catholic minority being able to make a case before the governor-general on petition that other legislation is required.

Lord WATSON:—Observations rather suggest themselves to my mind in this matter in your favour, and they are these:—Section 22 of the Manitoba Act of 1870 does not merely stand upon a Dominion act, but it stands upon an imperial statute.

The ATTORNEY-GENERAL:—It was a Dominion act assented to.

Lord WATSON:—It has the same effect as an act of the British legislature. Then when you come to subsection 3 the governor-general has made a determination, and suppose he induces the parliament of Canada to make a remedial law in that direction, that remedial law is to be for the due execution of the provisions of this action. The Dominion parliament can only come in to make remedial laws for the due execution of this very section. Would it not be open to challenge?

The ATTORNEY-GENERAL:—Quite possibly open to challenge; but my point is that if I can show it is *ultra vires* for this purpose I am entitled to assume that there is nothing to make valid an *ultra vires* provincial act of parliament.

Lord WATSON:—The right to determine whether the province has exceeded its powers or not is one thing; but undoubtedly what is contemplated here is not cases of excess of power by the provincial legislature; but cases where acting within their power they have not done what the minority thought justice.

The ATTORNEY-GENERAL:—That was why I thought unintentionally my learned friend had overlooked the distinction between the language of sub-section 1 and sub-section 2. The word "Appeal" is misleading; it is an appeal in the nature of asking for other legislation; for asking for Dominion legislation; for asking the Dominion parliament on the direction of the governor-general to do something which the legislature of the province have not done. But, my lords, there is nothing to say that that is either to take away the constitutional right of the courts to declare that an act of parliament passed by a legislature with limited powers is *ultra vires*, and that that legislature has exceeded its rights. Unless my learned friend can show that the two things were alternative, in the sense in which Lord Shand, I think, used the word a little time ago, the argument does not press me at all. I humbly submit that under sub-section 1, under the powers given to the legislature of Manitoba we have to consider whether what they have done is *intra vires* or *ultra vires*. And I must humbly further submit to your lordships that identically the same question would arise on the British North America Act. My learned friend, Sir Horace Davey, is infinitely more experienced than I. He says that except Renaud's case he does not think section 93 of the British North America Act has come before your lordships' board.

Lord SHAND:—It seems to be perfectly clear that the minister of justice in Canada has advised the governor general that he ought to wait to see the result, because in his report to the governor he puts the alternative, if the case is decided one way you will do so and so, and then he says, "If the legal controversy should result in the decision of the queen's bench being sustained the time will come to consider the petitions which have been presented under these sections, which are analogous to the provisions of the British North America Act."

The ATTORNEY-GENERAL :—" If it should at any time become necessary that the federal power should be resorted to for the protection of protestant and Roman catholic minorities against any act or decision of the legislature of the province, or of any provincial authority affecting any right or privilege" that might be *intra vires.* It does not suggest that the act which the governor is going to consider is an *ultra vires* act. It may be perfectly legitimate and lawful, passed by the provincial legislature within its narrowest powers. If there is a case to be made on the representation of the Roman catholic or protestant minority, then, as the governor points out, they have got the power to intervene and to pass other legislation. I submit to your lordships that upon the point which your lordships suggested, of course not having this matter fully present to your minds, there is no preliminary objection to these proceedings, and that this point will not prevent the case being gone into on the merits. Of course I do not address your lordships any further on any other point which has been urged by my learned friend.

Sir HORACE DAVEY :—My lords, the difference between my learned friend's, the attorney-general's view, and the view which I presented to your lordships, appears to me to turn upon the construction and effect which he puts upon subsections 2 and 3. Now there at once I must take issue with him. I do not agree that sub-section 2 does relate to anything but what is *ultra vires.*

The ATTORNEY-GENERAL :—May I point this out. I had missed the words "any provincial authority" in sub-section 2, which clearly would allow application to be made to the governor in a matter which was not by the legislation of the provincial legislature.

Sir HORACE DAVEY :—It is quite true that the words are different, but they are in substance the same. If anything, I should be disposed to say that the rights reserved by the 1st sub section are larger than the rights purporting to be dealt with by subsection 2, because the rights reserved by the 1st sub-section are "any right or privilege with respect to denominational schools," which not only any minority of protestants or a Roman catholic minority had, but "which any class of persons have by law or practice in the province at the union ;" and then sub-section 2, following upon it, provides for an appeal for the protection of any right or privilege of the protestant or Roman catholic minority who are at least included in any class of persons in relation to education. It is quite true that the word "denominational"—" with respect to denominational schools," is not there repeated, probably because it was considered that the only question which could arise with regard to education would be one with respect to denominational schools; but I am at a loss to conceive how there could be any difference between rights and privileges with respect to denominational schools, and rights and privileges in relation to education, having regard to the nature of the subject matter; and therefore, my lords, I venture to submit that subsection 2 does cover and include all cases which may arise under sub-section 1, and indeed from one point of view the rights referred to in sub-section 1 are larger because they are the rights of any class of persons, and not exclusively of a protestant or Roman catholic minority of the queen's subjects. That being so, and finding those sections follow one upon another, the inference is irresistible that it is intended that an appeal should be given for the protection of——

Lord WATSON :—My suggestion was sub-section 1 deals with that which prejudicially affects, and that the other leaves out the words, "prejudicially affecting."

Sir HORACE DAVEY :—Well, if it is not prejudicially affected there could not be an appeal. There cannot be an appeal unless you are hurt. It is usually so considered. If it affects them not prejudicially but beneficially, it is hardly to be contended that an appeal was intended to be given.

Lord SHAND :—There is another view which I think might reconcile everything, and that is to treat the court of law as the proper court to settle whether there has or has not been an interference with the right, and then, that being done, this appeal is for administrative purposes, not an appeal for a judgment, but an appeal in order that he may set in motion all that follows in the subsequent clauses.

Sir HORACE DAVEY:—Suppose there is no appeal to the court of law, can it be pretended that the appellants could not go direct to the governor-general, if they thought fit, and say, "Here is an act which affects us, and we want you to hear our appeal"?

Lord SHAND:—Then I think the governor-general might say: "*Prima facie* the act is passed, get a court of justice to hold that it is destitute of right, and then I will interfere."

Sir HORACE DAVEY:—There is nothing in the act which says so.

Lord SHAND:—It all depends upon whether that word "appeal" means more than an appeal for administrative aid.

Sir HORACE DAVEY:—It is the appeal shall lie, not only from any act of the legislature, but as the learned attorney-general has pointed out, from any decision, for instance, of the advisory board which affects, which must mean prejudicially affects, any right or privilege which I read to be a right or privilege which is intended to be preserved in favour of the catholic or protestant.

Lord WATSON:—Sub-section 2 would suggest this: that the Dominion legislature were under the impression that there might be provisions within the power of the provincial legislature which would affect the rights of these persons without affecting them prejudicially in the sense of sub-section 1, so as to make them *ultra vires*.

Sir HORACE DAVEY:—With the greatest respect to everything which your lordship says, I can hardly follow that. My mind cannot follow it. If it does not affect them prejudicially it cannot reasonably be suggested, as it was intended to be, the subject of an appeal. Either it affects them, or it does not. And if it affects them it is either beneficially or prejudicially. If it affects them beneficially it cannot be intended to have been the subject of an appeal. It must be something, therefore, which affects them prejudicially. If it affects them prejudicially it does affect them prejudicially, and then it comes within sub-section 1. If it comes within sub-section 1 it will be *ultra vires*. I cannot for myself frame the proposition which would lead to the inference that sub-section 2 was intended to deal with cases which were *intra vires*, and I beg leave to observe that it would be contrary to the whole scope and spirit of this legislation to provide for parliament intervening, not where the provincial parliament has acted beyond its powers—that I could conceive—that I could follow—there would be nothing inconsistent with the general course of legislation in that—but to allow the Dominion parliament to intervene, not to correct mistakes where the provincial legislature had gone wrong, and exceeded their powers——

Lord WATSON:—The difficulty arises from this: According to a very well-known canon of construction I feel constrained to hold that the legislature intentionally omitted the word "prejudicially" before "affected" in sub-section 2. What it meant by it is a different question.

Lord MACNAGHTEN:—It is enough to say that they conceived themselves prejudicially affected.

Lord WATSON:—It might be enough to say that another way of doing it would be more for their interests, without saying that the other was prejudicial.

Lord MACNAGHTEN:—Supposing some rights were created after the union, and then legislation had taken those rights away.

Sir HORACE DAVEY:—I can conceive this, that power should be given to the advisory board, as there was in the act of 1881, to compel the attendance of children at the board school. There was that in the act of 1881, and it continued simply as a power. You would say: Well that is not necessarily *ultra vires*, because you cannot say, whether they may exercise it or not, the exercise of it may be *ultra vires*, though the power itself might not. Then the advisory board passed a resolution compelling the attendance of every child at the board schools—the non-sectarian schools. But then the governor-general might say that exercise of the power is *ultra vires*. It may be it is a discretionary power which may be exercised in such a way as to be unlawful, but which would not be held to be unlawful, although the particular exercise of it might. Still it all comes back to the same point, that the protestant and catholic minority have a right to come with a grievance to the governor-general. What is that grievance? Why, that they are deprived of some right or privilege which they ought to have, and are entitled to enjoy. If they are not entitled by law to enjoy it they are not deprived of anything, and it would be an extraordinary system of legislation, having regard to the nature of this act, to say that the Dominion parliament has in certain cases to sit by way of a court of appeal from the provincial parliament, not to correct mistakes where the provincial parliament has erroneously legislated on matters not within its jurisdiction, but on matters of policy, to say it is quite true that the provincial legislature has legislated within its powers, it is quite true that there is nothing in the act which we can impugn as exceeding the power which the imperial parliament has conferred upon it; but we take a different point, we think it is inexpedient; we think that it is harsh; I will not say unjust, because nothing is unjust that the law allows—but that it is harsh; it is oppressive towards the Roman catholic minority to tax them for board schools. Therefore we, differing from the policy of that act, and differing from the views of those who are the majority who passed the act, say we will alter and repeal that legislation. If that be the effect to be given to these sub-sections, I venture to submit to your lordships that it will have rather startling consequences, and it will for the first time make the legislature of the Dominion parliament a court of appeal, or give them an appeal from the exercise of the discretion of the provincial parliament, or, in other words, it will place the provincial parliament in the position that it will be liable to have its decisions over-ruled by the Dominion parliament, and therefore in a position of inferiority.

Lord MACNAGHTEN:—At the instance of the governor-general.

Sir HORACE DAVEY:—Yes.

Lord WATSON:—What do you say to that view? I doubt whether the Dominion parliament has any more legislative power as against section 1 than the provincial legislature itself.

Sir HORACE DAVEY:—I doubt it also. What they are to do is to make remedial laws for the due execution of the provisions of this section.

Lord WATSON:—This is a higher authority than the governor-general who makes the recommendation, and it is a statutory provision. It makes its law in accordance with these provisions. If not it is *ultra vires*.

Lord MACNAGHTEN:—Then you come to the words, "and of any decision of the governor-general in council under this section."

Sir HORACE DAVEY:—These latter words seem to corroborate the view which I put forward, namely: that sub-sections 2 and 3 are correlative to sub-section 1, and intended to carry out the means of giving effect to sub-section 1. "Parliament may make remedial laws for the due execution of the provisions of this section." That is sub-section 1.

Lord MACNAGHTEN:—It goes on.

Sir HORACE DAVEY:—"And of any decision of the governor-general in council under this section."

Lord WATSON:—A remedial measure is to enable that decision to be put in force.

Lord SHAND:—It was that clause that induced me to say it appeared to me if you did not succeed in this appeal, then it necessarily followed that there could be no system of non-sectarian education introduced by the legislature in Canada, I rather think that must be so.

Sir HORACE DAVEY.—If we fail in this appeal, I agree that that is so. On the other hand, supposing that I succeed in this appeal—I am entitled to put the hypothesis of course—and induce your lordships to take the same view as was taken in the queen's bench, then, I am not prepared to admit—and at the proper time—at least I cannot undertake to say what may be done by the advisers of the Manitoba government in the colony—but so far as I am concerned, I should be prepared—well, I had better not express any opinion, perhaps.

Lord MACNAGHTEN:—The governor-general will have no power?

Sir HORACE DAVEY:—No. I must not be understood for a moment to admit that the governor-general would have the slightest jurisdiction to entertain the appeal of the archbishop which is in Lord Shand's hands.

Lord SHAND:—That shows that the one appeal excludes the other.

Sir HORACE DAVEY:—Yes.

Lord MACNAGHTEN:—Supposing he did, you could not stop him in any way, or if they pass a law on his recommendation, would you say that it was *ultra vires?* Supposing this board decided that this law of 1890 was *intra vires*—

Sir HORACE DAVY:—I am thinking in what form of procedure it could be done. No doubt some form of procedure could be devised. You could patch up some sort of action to try it in, but if you could try it I should say, undoubtedly,—

Lord MACNAGHTEN:—How could you prevent the governor-general making a recommendation to parliament?

Sir HORACE DAVEY:—And the Dominion parliament from passing an act? Supposing the Dominion parliament passes an act, then I should say that act of the Dominion parliament is *ultra vires.*

Sir RICHARD COUCH:—Unless it is authorized by this provision it would be *ultra vires.*

Sir HORACE DAVEY:—The other view which may be maintained against me would be this—and I do not know that I should disagree in that—saying that all the decisions of the queen's bench and of the supreme court and, I must add, of your lordships were all *ultra vires* and went for nothing, because the only tribunal that had any jurisdiction in the matter was the governor general.

Lord SHAND:—What do you say to the fact that the governor general through the minister of justice has said this:—"It became apparent at the outset that these questions required a decision of the judicial tribunals more especially as an investigation of facts was necessary for their determination?" Therefore his view is that before he can do anything, or be called upon to look at anything, this investigation must take place and he must have a decision of a judicial tribunal.

Sir HORACE DAVEY:—I have great respect for the opinion of the minister of justice, but I am not bound—

Lord SHAND:—Followed by the acting of the governor-general. He says:—"I am going to wait until I see the decisions of the courts."

Sir HORACE DAVEY:—It has been my duty to say before now that decisions of ministers of justice and other ministers are not always in accordance with purest wisdom.

Lord SHAND:—It looks very much as if he means to abide by what this court decides.

Sir HORACE DAVEY:—I should be more influenced by that if it were not a fact, as appears upon these papers, that the Dominion parliament are my opponents on the present occasion.

Lord WATSON:—I am afraid an opinion of theirs cannot be taken.

Sir HORACE DAVEY:—Really and truly, I have been led into arguing a point which, although it presented itself to my mind, was not a point I was instructed to argue. At the same time, I think your lordships probably would not entertain the appeal or rather you would not if you saw that it would bring you into conflict—

Lord MORRIS:—The matter appears to have been raised in Renaud's case. Did not the same point arise in Renaud's case?

Sir HORACE DAVEY:—I think it was.

Lord WATSON:—Renaud's case came from New Brunswick, I think.

Lord MACNAGHTEN:—The language is very much the same.

Sir HORACE DAVEY:—I am not sure it could arise. It would not arise under sub-section 2, nor would it arise under sub-section 3, because there was no system of separate or dissentient schools existing by law at the union in New Brunswick.

The ATTORNEY GENERAL:—It did not arise under sub-section 2.

Sir HORACE DAVEY:—Sub-section 2 only applied to Ontario and Quebec, and it did not arise under sub-section 3, because there was no system of separate or dissentient schools existing by law.

The ATTORNEY GENERAL:—But there was if you look at Renaud.

Sir HORACE DAVEY:—No, they were public schools or common schools. This is what the chief justice says:—"Assuming then that it is not only the right but the bounden duty of this court to deal with questions of this nature, when legitimately presented for its consideration, we must endeavour to ascertain whether there is such a repugnancy in this case as will constrain us to declare the Common Schools Act of 1871 void in part or in whole. It is contended that the rights and privileges of the Roman catholic inhabitants of this province, as a class of persons, have been prejudicially affected by the Common Schools Act of 1871 contrary to the provisions of subsection 1 of section 93 of the British North America Act. We have now to determine whether any class of persons had by law in this province any right or privilege with respect to denominational schools at the union which are prejudicially affected by the Common Schools Act of 1871."

Lord MORRIS:—If you were right in your contention would not the answer in that case have been given to the governor-general.

Sir HORACE DAVEY:—No, because it would only be under sub-section 3. What Renaud contended was that inasmuch as there was an option to read either the Douay version or the English version in school, abolishing the option to read the Douay version was an interference with the privileges.

Lord WATSON:—If you find it convenient, if you have any more to say on this point we will hear you. If not, we invite you to renew the discussion of the merits of the appeal.

Sir HORACE DAVEY:—Then the mode in which I was going to renew it was by reading the judgments, which will take some considerable time, and I may ask your lordships' indulgence to allow my learned friend to assist me. My lords, the first judgment is the judgment of Mr. Justice Killam, before whom the application to quash came. It contains a long statement of the facts and, unless my learned friends or any of your lordships desire me to do so, I do not think it necessary to read that. I will begin on page 26 at the 37th line:—"It is shown that on and prior to the 30th April last a school district, which had some years before been established, existed in the city of Winnipeg, &c." [Reads to the words page 27, line 34.] "I have referred to the old acts as shortly as possible rather in order to explain the form of the objection taken in the summons and as illustrative of one system which the applicant contends to have been within the powers of the legislature to establish, than because I can conceive that the adoption at one time of such a system could limit the authority of the legislature thereafter." Then his lordship reads certain sections of the British North America Act and the important section 22 of the Manitoba Act and continues at page 28, line 35:—"Now it is obvious that if there were merely the authority to legislate in relation to education without the limitations imposed by these sub-sections it would be quite competent for the provincial legislature to enact such a statute as the Public Schools Act, &c. [Reads a further passage to the words page 30, line 33.] "When, however, we come to Manitoba we are met at the outset by the difficulty that there was no public school system supported by public funds or by any mode of taxation. The existence of such in the other provinces served to determine whether there was a right to immunity from such taxation or not. Here that indication is wholly wanting." Then the learned judge reads the affidavit of the archbishop, which I need not trouble your lordships with again, and the two other affidavits which were filed—Polson's and Sutherland's. "While then these supplement to some extent the affidavit of his grace they are in no way inconsistent with it, &c." [Reads a further passage to the words] "and that if the reading into the act of any portion of the original 93rd section would involve either an extension or a limitation of the powers of the provincial legislature, beyond those fixed by the terms of this 22nd section, there would be an inconsistency with the Manitoba Act which is excluded by the express terms of its second section." I have not troubled your lordships with that argument. I think it is quite clear, saying so only as counsel of course, or that it is reasonably clear that the provisions of the 22nd section do override and prevent the application of the provisions of the 93rd section of the British North America Act. I should think that is reasonably clear. It does not matter very much. "The course of the legislation and the meaning of the first statute are of the greatest importance in interpreting the second, but I cannot consider any portion of the 93rd section of the former to be incorporated into the second act. The first question naturally arising is as to whether the Public Schools Act itself creates a system of denominational schools, or assumes to compel any class to support denominational schools other than their own. Upon the face of the statute it does not. The affidavit of his grace the archbishop, however, appears to be intended to lay a foundation for an argument that what are called in this act "Public Schools" are really schools of a protestant denominational character, although the act upon its face declares that they are to be unsectarian."

My lords, I must here observe that in some of the judgments against me there appears to be some confusion when they speak of schools to which catholics cannot send their children. Of course catholics are the best judges for themselves whether they will or will not send their children to a particular school. Of course they are entitled to their own opinions upon that, but when they say they cannot, there is a fallacy in that. The legislature has provided a school to which every citizen may send his child, if he thinks fit to do so. Then the learned judge refers further to the archbishop's affidavit, and to the affidavit of the Rev. Dr. Bryce. I do not think I need trouble your lordships with that again. Then he proceeds, at line 38:—"Here, however, I cannot conceive myself to be bound by, or confined to affidavit evidence. I am intrepreting statutes, and in doing so I am at liberty to take judicial notice of the circumstances with respect to which they are to be construed. I do not say this because I conceive that there is anything really untrue or intended to mislead or to give a false colouring to beliefs in any of the affidavits. Indeed they appear to me to offer, in most respects, a very fair view of the relative attitudes of most protestants on the one side, and most Roman catholics and the Roman catholic church as a body on the other side. I am not, however, convinced that there is any such distinctive difference between protestants generally and Roman catholics generally upon this question, as to constitute a mark of denominational division and to make what would ordinarily be termed non-denominational schools, really 'denominational' within the meaning of the Manitoba act as between protestants and Roman catholics. From my experience I would say that very many protestants have as strong opinions upon the importance of combining religious with secular instruction as any Roman catholics. In support of this view, I need only refer to the report of the royal commission," and so forth. I do not think I need read this part to your lordships but I will go on at line 21.

Lord SHAND:—That rather relates to the policy also.

The ATTORNEY-GENERAL:—I should think you might go to the bottom of the page.

Sir HORACE DAVEY:—Yes I think so. The judgments are very long anyhow and I do not want to trouble your lordships with too much. At the bottom of page 23 the judgment continues:—"Now, the rights and privileges protected by the first sub-section are those with respect to denominational schools which some class or classes of persons had before the union," etc. [Reading down to the words at line 43.] "The circumstances existing in the older provinces, and the general nature of the school systems in America suggest at once that it must have been contemplated in the enactment of the Manitoba act that the legislature of Manitoba should be at liberty to establish a system of free non-denominational public schools, and provide for their support by grant of provincial funds or direct taxation or by both methods." That is to say the learned judge, I suppose, means that the possibility of their doing so must have been in contemplation, because that was the usual method of providing schools on that continent. Then:—"Under the powers given, it would be open to the legislature to make laws to encourage or restrict education," etc. [Reading to the words at page 35, line 30.] "The effect is so indirect and remote that I cannot take it to be within the act, and it is precisely the same effect that would be produced by taxation for other purposes within the powers of the legislature."

Lord SHAND:—The learned judge does not seem to exhaust the considerations presented by the other side when he says that the two things that are objected to are the competition and the taking away of funds. I understand one of the leading arguments is that they are now compelled to contribute to denominational schools.

Sir HORACE DAVEY:—I think he intended to deal with that in the earlier part of the judgment, in asking whether they had any right or privilege or whether there was any right or privilege, and then he argues at great length, as your lordships remember, that the argument really comes to this,—I agree it wants a little development—that they have a right of immunity or of exemption from taxation for this particular purpose.

Lord WATSON:—The main feature of it was that they were keeping up their schools.

Sir HORACE DAVEY:—That is to say, they claim immunity or exemption from taxation for the purpose of maintaining common schools. That is what they claim.

Lord SHAND:—Might I point out here that on page 34 he seems to limit the two points on which he says there is an invasion of rights or privileges by these passages from line 25 to line 30, but perhaps you are right in saying he had anticipated it.

Sir HORACE DAVEY:—I think he had intended to deal with it under the heading of whether they had any right or privilege which entitled them to immunity from taxation for the common schools. Then he discusses the position of the two Canadas, and shows they had such a privilege by law, because any person who maintained a denominational school with efficiency had a right to immunity from taxation for common schools, and then he shows there could not be such an exemption or immunity because there was in fact no taxation for common schools and no system of common schools in Manitoba. Perhaps it would have been well if the learned judge had gone a little further. "It is, however, urged that, even though the natural meaning of the language of the statutes would lead to such conclusions as these, the history of the controversy respecting separate or denominational schools in the other provinces and elsewhere, and the mode in which it was settled for the other provinces by the original confederation act and the changes made in the wording of the Manitoba act, show that it was intended that a more enlarged view of the protected rights and privileges should be taken," &c. (Reads the remainder of Mr. Justice Killam's judgment.) Then he quotes some very sensible general observations of the chief justice of New Brunswick. I take it that comes to this: That it is within the provincial authority to legislate for education, and by means of direct taxation to provide the means of carrying its legislation into effect; those who claim an immunity from taxation must show their title to it; before the union there could be no such immunity because there was no such taxation; and what is intended to be preserved is *cum privilegium*, that is something to which some class of persons is entitled either adversely to or differing from the rest of her majesty's subjects. If it is only something which they enjoyed with the rest of her majesty's subjects, then it is not a right or privilege enjoyed by a class of persons. Every person in Manitoba before the union had an immunity from paying taxes for the support of public education. There were no school rates or school taxes at all. Therefore, every one of her majesty's subjects within that province enjoyed that immunity. It was not, therefore, a privilege enjoyed by a class of persons, because it was a right which they enjoyed.

Lord MORRIS:—They had it in point of law. They had not an immunity in point of practice.

Sir HORACE DAVEY:—Yes, from being taxed.

Lord MORRIS:—No, because, as I understand, there is no affidavit to say that these schools were not supported.

Sir HORACE DAVEY:—Nobody was bound to pay; it was voluntary.

Lord MORRIS:—That is the very reason: because it was only the practice.

Sir HORACE DAVEY:—Let us look what the practice is. The practice is to pay as much as you think fit.

Lord MORRIS:—That was not the practice.

Sir HORACE DAVEY:—Yes, surely.

Lord SHAND:—In 1870 the only schools, I understand, were voluntary schools; nobody need contribute unless he liked.

Sir HORACE DAVEY:—No, and they were supported by means of the fees charged to scholars or to the parents of the scholars, and by such voluntary contributions as charitable-minded persons were disposed to make.

Lord WATSON:—It is not disputed that in point of fact any persons who chose to set up a school to teach their own children according to their own denominational view could do so without being called on to contribute to any other. The issue comes to be, what is the meaning of "practice?"

Sir HORACE DAVEY:—There is another question, what is the meaning of right or privilege? That was not a privilege enjoyed by any class of persons.

Lord WATSON:—Is it simply the extent of the right enjoyed, or is it enjoying a right in such a way that they could not be deprived of it?

Sir HORACE DAVEY:—It was not a *privilegium* or right enjoyed by any class of persons, but it was something which the whole of her majesty's subjects enjoyed. Will your lordships allow me to read you some words of Lord Chief Justice Cockburn in that case of Fearon *vs.* Mitchell, which is reported in the law reports 7th, queen's bench, page 690? There the question was this: In a market act there was a proviso that "no market shall be established in pursuance of this section so as to interfere with any rights, powers or privileges enjoyed within the district by any person without his consent." There was a gentleman who had an auctioneer's shop or butcher's shop, and was carrying it on before the market was established, and he maintained that he had a right still to continue to do so, and he said he was within the saving because he had a right, power or privilege enjoyed within the district by him. The chief justice says:—"This right which the respondent was enjoying at the time when this market place was built, was not, I think, a right within the meaning of the section. It was a right which he enjoyed only in common with the rest of her majesty's subjects. He had no exclusive right to carry on this business, and he had no greater right than anybody else with suitable premises for setting up and carrying on a similar business. The word 'rights,' especially, when taken in conjunction with the words, 'powers or privileges' must mean rights acquired adversely to the rest of the world and peculiar to the individual. Such a right having been acquired, it is but just that the statute should say that any powers exercised by the local authority under the section in setting up a market should not interfere with it; but it could never have been meant that the powers given for the benefit of the inhabitants of the particular district in setting up a market should not be exercised in consequence of some private individual or company having a business of the same description."

Lord SHAND:—There the learned judge is dealing with the privilege of an individual. Of course this must be something similar, if this is a privilege of a class —that the class must represent the individual. For example, if Roman catholics or protestants as a class could say that we had a certain privilege that no one else had that might be kept.

Sir HORACE DAVEY:—To illustrate what I mean: In the state of Upper Canada, as described to us in this learned judge's judgment, there was a distinct privilege attaching to the protestant minority.

Lord WATSON:—Immunity from contributing to any other school was a privilege in this sense, that it could not be taken from them except by an enactment equivalent to legislation—the act of the governor.

Sir HORACE DAVEY:—It was not an immunity.

Lord SHAND:—That would apply to every tax and for every purpose. The thing did not exist.

Sir HORACE DAVEY:—The tax did not exist.

Lord SHAND:—Immunity implies a right to be clear of it.

Sir HORACE DAVEY:—I will give an illustration of what I mean, which appears to me to be a very apt one. Look at the state of things described to us in this learned judge's judgment as existing in Upper Canada.

Lord WATSON:—A privilege, created by statute, is open to the very same observation. It may be taken away by statute.

Sir HORACE DAVEY:—But it is something peculiar to that class.

Lord SHAND:—It is guarded, and it is said you shall not take it away.

Sir HORACE DAVEY:—The protestant minority had the right, by establishing denominational schools of their own, to gain exemption from taxation for the common schools. That was a privilege or right attaching to the class of persons, because it was something which they either had, or had a means of acquiring adversely, to the rest of their fellow citizens.

Lord WATSON:—There are so many different kinds of privileges. A great many kinds of privileges are taken away by statute, which may be said to be privileges in the ordinary sense of the word.

Sir HORACE DAVEY:—All I can say is, if they intended to say that for all time in Manitoba the provincial legislature shall never raise by taxation, nor apply any part of the public funds under its control for the support of a non-sectarian school, they have gone the oddest way about, to say so, that anybody ever saw.

Lord WATSON:—In this country one is apt to use the word "privilege" as meaning the possession of something beyond the rest of the citizens. In fact it becomes a right of property—a right which the legislature seldom takes away without compensation.

Sir HORACE DAVEY:—There is no doubt that in the proper sense privileges are something you enjoy.

Lord HANNEN:—It is not necessary to say to the detriment of others, but something which the others do not enjoy.

Lord MACNAGHTEN:—Which you enjoy exclusively.

Sir HORACE DAVEY:—I do not think it is necessary to say to the detriment.

Lord SHAND:—"Nothing in any such law shall prejudicially affect any right or privilege with respect to denominational schools, which any class of persons have by law or practice." Is that some right, acquired by law or practice, different to what other people have?

Sir HORACE DAVEY:—It would look so.

Lord SHAND:—That is the question. You say it is not a right that all the community had, and all the community were exactly on the same footing about this matter.

Lord WATSON:—You could not get the act unless you embraced the whole population.

Lord MORRIS:—Instead of saying "by law or practice," if it had said "which they now enjoy," how would that be?

Lord SHAND:—That would be exactly the same.

Lord WATSON:—They deal with the population, in that act, as consisting of denominationalists, and all the privileges of all these denominationalists, which practically included the whole population, were to be preserved. The denominationalists were divisible, but they all held the same.

Sir HORACE DAVEY:—According to the contention of my learned friends on the other side, it is that not a single cent can be raised for the purpose of education by general taxation.

Lord MORRIS:—It would be necessary to go further and say that every cent raised by taxation should be redivided out.

Sir HORACE DAVEY:—No, to each denomination—every denomination according to them.

The ATTORNEY-GENERAL:—Nothing of the kind; you cannot say so.

Sir HORACE DAVEY:—But I do say so, because they are a different class of persons.

Lord MORRIS:—They do not speak of denominations, and perhaps it was a case of *de minimis non curat lex.*

Sir HORACE DAVEY:—That is Logan's case.

The ATTORNEY-GENERAL:—I have nothing to do with Logan's case.

Sir HORACE DAVEY:—It is all very well for my friends to say they have nothing to do with Logan. Your lordships have something to do with Logan, and you cannot decide Barrett's appeal without deciding Logan's.

Lord SHAND:—Lord Morris is suggesting the ground on which Logan may be disposed of.

Lord MORRIS:—There might have been a Jews' school there for what I know, but there does not appear to have been. That is the fact.

Sir HORACE DAVEY:—It may have been said there was only one Jew in Scotland and he did not get a living.

Lord MORRIS:—He lost it.

Sir HORACE DAVEY:—I do not know whether there are any Jews in Canada. There may be for all I know. They certainly would be a class of persons. Then I go to the judgment of Chief Justice Taylor, and he says that it raises an important question. Then he states the grounds.

Lord SHAND:—Is he of the same way of thinking?

Sir HORACE DAVEY:—Yes. Then he says that the statute may be moulded, and deals with how the view of the legislature may be ascertained, and he refers to Lord Wensleydale's golden rule.

Lord SHAND:—I think the top of page 46 is where he first deals with the question.

Sir HORACE DAVEY:—On page 44, he says this:—"The argument was pressed that, by section 22 of the Manitoba Act, parliament, in view of the controversy," etc. [Reading to the words at line 22.] "Surely had it been intended to secure to Roman catholics, or to any other class of persons in Manitoba, the same right of having separate schools as is provided for in the province of Ontario, parliament would have said so."

Lord SHAND:—He means by that the same right of having separate schools without a public rate in support of it.

Sir HORACE DAVEY:—Yes. Then he says:—"Parliament had before it the express provisions of the British North America Act on this subject," etc. [Reading to the words at line 35.] "What the court has to deal with is, did any such right or privilege exist, and, if so, has such right or privilege been prejudicially affected by the public schools act?" Then after noticing section 22 he says:—"It may be remarked here that when the court in New Brunswick dealt in *re* Renaud, 1 Pugs. N.B.R., 273, with the same words in section 93 of the British North America Act, they held that they were not intended to distinguish between protestants and Roman catholics. It was held in the judgment delivered by the learned chief justice, now chief justice of the supreme court of Canada, that sub-section 1 meant just what it expresses, that 'any,' that is every 'class of persons' having any right or privilege with respect to denominational schools, whether such class should be one of the numerous denominations of protestants or Roman catholics, should be protected in such rights. As the judgment of the court in New Brunswick was affirmed on appeal by the judicial committee of the privy council, approving of the reasons given in the court below, it must be assumed that this was regarded by the ultimate court of appeal as the true construction of the sub-section." That is the construction, I may add, which has been adopted in Logan's case. Then:—"Are then the members of the Roman catholic church in Manitoba a class of persons who had at the time of the union, by law or practice, any right or privilege with respect to denominational schools? And if so, does the Public Schools Act prejudicially affect any such right or privilege? Happily there is no dispute as to the facts, as to the state of affairs with reference to education, existing at the time of the union, and upon which the claim to possess certain rights and privileges is based." Then his lordship reads the archbishop's affidavit and continues at the top of page 46:—"Had Roman catholics, as a class of persons, what can be considered or called rights and privileges within the ordinary meaning of these words as used in the act? There were schools established and carried on, the expense of which was defrayed by Roman catholics. Episcopalians and presbyterians had the same right, and also carried on and defrayed the expense of schools. Every other protestant denomination had the same right, and so had every private individual. Any man could establish and carry on a school at his own expense if he chose to do so. It seems to me the utmost the Roman catholics can be said to have had was what may be called a moral right. Had the words right or privilege, stood alone in the act it could not, I think, be said they had any which is prejudicially affected by the Public Schools Act." Then he refers to the definition of a "right" in the Imperial Dictionary, and to Bouvier's Law Dictionary, Brown's Law Dictionary and Wharton. Then he refers to the definition of privilege as "a right, immunity, benefit or advantage enjoyed by a person or body of persons beyond the common advantages of other individuals, the enjoyment of some desirable right, or an exemption from some evil or burden; a private or personal favour enjoyed; a peculiar advantage." Then he refers to the definition by Webster "a right or immunity not enjoyed by others or by all." Then, in Bacon's Abridgment, privilege is said to be "an exemption from some duty, burden or attendance with which certain persons are indulged. A particular disposition of the law which grants special prerogatives to some persons contrary to common right." Then he quotes from Comyns' Digest:—"*Privilegium est jus singulare, seu lex privata, quæ uni homini vel loco conceditur.*" Then he refers to Mackeldy's Roman Law and also to the case of Campbell *vs.* Spottiswoode and at page 47, line 5, he says:—"It seems then that rights and privileges, as used in the statute, must mean something special and peculiar, something not common to all the community, etc." [Reading to the words at page 48, line 20.] "From the circumstance that as education was then carried on, they had, in common with every other denomination, a right to establish and maintain schools, and in consequence of their doing so they were in fact separate from the rest of the community, but that was not because they had a positive right to be so, it was merely an incident to their right to have schools."

[Adjourned to to-morrow at half-past ten.]

IN THE JUDICIAL COMMITTEE OF THE PRIVY COUNCIL.

COUNCIL CHAMBER, WHITEHALL, Wednesday, 13th July, 1892.

Present:

The Rt. Hon. Lord Watson,
The Rt. Hon. Lord Macnaghten,
The Rt. Hon. Lord Morris,
The Rt. Hon. Lord Hannen
The Rt. Hon. Lord Shand,
The Rt. Hon. Sir Richard Couch.

THE CITY OF WINNIPEG

vs

BARRETT,

and

THE CITY OF WINNIPEG.

vs.

LOGAN.

[Transcript of the shorthand notes of Messrs. Marten & Meredith, 13 New Inn, Strand, W. C.]

Counsel for the appellants:—Sir Horace Davey, Q.C., Mr. McCarthy, Q.C., and the Hon. Mr. Martin.

Counsel for the respondent Barrett:—The Attorney-General (Sir Richard Webster, Q.C., M.P.), Mr. Blake, Q.C., Mr. J. S. Ewart, Q.C., and Mr. Gore.

Counsel for the respondent Logan:—Mr. A. J. Ram.

Second Day.

Sir HORACE DAVEY:—My lords, I was reading yesterday afternoon, when your lordships rose, the judgment of the chief justice in the queen's bench on page 48 at line 28. "Now any right the Roman catholics had, at the time of the union," etc. [Reading to the words page 49, line 10.] "How can it be said that in this respect they are prejudicially affected?" That is, prejudicially affected as a class of persons? "It is however argued that by the Public Schools Act a system of free schools," etc. [Reading to the page 52, line 5.] "The Public Schools Act, the validity of which is impeached, is an act dealing with the general educational system of this province." My lords, I am informed that "separate or dissentient schools" has acquired almost a technical meaning in Canada and in that clause in the British North America Act which was referred to, it refers to what many of these learned judges state from their knowledge to have been the practice in Canada, that, there being a general system of education, any denomination which set up separate or dissentient schools could exempt itself from the general taxation for the purpose. "The 22nd section of the Manitoba Act must receive the same construction. The Public Schools Act, the validity of which is impeached, is an act dealing with the general educational system of this province. It does not deal with denominational, separate, or dissentient schools. Its object is to provide for the general education of the people, to provide public non-sectarian schools, open to all the people of the province who choose to take advantage of them for the education of their children. I cannot see that any rights or privileges that Roman catholics enjoyed at the time of the union as to denominational schools are dealt with or in any way prejudicially affected by the act. It must, in my opinion, be held that the appeal fails."

My lords, may I sum up in one sentence what I think is the answer given by the learned chief justice to the argument about contributing to the schools? Really and truly, if it was a right or privilege it was a right or privilege not to be taxed, to be compelled to contribute to schools at all.

Lord WATSON :—My present impression is, looking to the statements of the judges and the condition of education in the different provinces, that the intention of the clause inserted in the act of 1867 was to enable dissentient and denominational parents to set up their own schools without paying the general rate. One object was to enable dissentient schools to exempt themselves from religious education.

Sir HORACE DAVEY :—In Upper and Lower Canada, yes, that is so.

Lord WATSON :—What do you conceive was the object of the other act ?

Sir HORACE DAVEY :—Of the Manitoba Act ? To put it shortly, it was to secure absolute religious equality.

Lord WATSON :—Was it to place the schools in the same position in Manitoba that they occupied elsewhere.

Sir HORACE DAVEY :—No, if that had been the intention they would have said so. My view is that it was to secure absolute religious equality between all the different religious denominations, Christian and otherwise which existed in the province.

Lord WATSON :—It is curious language if that is what is meant.

Sir HORACE DAVEY :—But leaving the province to make such laws regarding education and to impose such taxation for the maintenance of schools as it thought fit, provided it does not infringe in any way the absolute religious equality which then existed.

Lord MORRIS :—What privilege was it that existed which was certainly intended to be reserved.

Sir HORACE DAVEY :—I am afraid I shall repeat myself if I answer that again, but I will with pleasure: the privilege of each denomination of maintaining its own schools for its own scholars and teaching its own particular tenets unfettered by legislation.

Lord WATSON :—I do not think it goes that length—I do not think that is the point. The question is prejudice. On the face of that act of Manitoba taking it with the other I should say there was power in the state to prescribe a system, power to demand that children shall be educated, power to prescribe the education which it must pass as a citizen. They might impose disabilities on the child if it did not attain a proper standard. I think they had great power of modifying the general system. With the remark of the learned chief justice I agree. I do not think that is in any sense prejudicial. I think the legislature must have thought it was the interest of the parents to have their children well taught. If enactments were introduced for that purpose only, I should say they would prevent the child getting the effect of education.

Lord SHAND :—As it strikes my mind now, the act of 1867 and the act of 1870 may operate with totally different results because each of those acts severally refers to the privileges existing in the particular territory with which they deal at the date when the act was passed. If accordingly in the territory of British North America, dealt with in the act of 1867, there were certain privileges clearly established by law—they were by statute—then I think those are preserved, even though they are wider than Manitoba, but if there were no such privileges in Manitoba when the Manitoba Act passed I do not see how you can by the language of the Manitoba Act reserve the same privileges as in British North America. Then I should like to add this. I think the learned chief justice has developed an argument which strikes me as having very great force in this case, which Mr. Justice Killam has not done, and I am not sure, if I may venture to say so, that you have pressed it in the same way as the rest of the case, and that is that he denies and disputes that this is an act of parliament—I mean the schools act—which affects any right or privilege of denominational schools and he does so on this which appears to me to be a very formidable ground. He says this is not an act which touches religion at all or religious education. It will not do for one or two sects either protestant or catholic to come and say this is an act which affects denominational schools if in substance it does not. If it professes to be a non-sectarian act and if the court looking at it sees plainly that it is a non-sectarian act, then it does not affect the privilege; and it strikes me that that is a very forcible part of the opinion you have just read and requires very great consideration. I should like to put the illustration I did yesterday. Suppose the government were saying:—"We are of opinion that industrial schools for teaching them the elements of trades are necessary, or we think schools for writing and arithmetic and mathematics are of the utmost consequence, and one party comes forward and says: oh, we must have an appeal to religious considerations in every branch of education, could that be listened to as being a denominational act? I should say not; and I think one of the first things that this board will have to do is to say whether they can affirm, even because this is called an act which affects the denominational schools, that in any reasonable sense it does.

Lord WATSON:—The important words we have to consider are "or practice" in the Act of Manitoba. I think it comes to a very narrow point. I think they bear that the intention of that was to adopt the clause of the act of 1867, which as it stood was inapplicable to Manitoba, to the necessities and requirements of Manitoba, to give them the benefit of the same legislation. I am clearly of opinion that the Act of 1867 was as far as possible intended, as regards all civil rights, including educational matters, to place all the provinces of the Dominion as nearly as possible on the same footing as circumstances permitted. As I said before, I am not indicating an opinion. The language may tie you down, but I think it was intended to establish that uniformity, and I think it will be necessary to consider the suggestion whether it was the intention of the legislature with regard to denominational schools in Manitoba to handicap them in a way that they are not handicapped elsewhere.

Sir Horace DAVEY:—I do not think it can be said that there is anything in the British North America Act which indicates the intention to establish the same educational system in all the provinces of the Dominion. Sub-section 1 of section 93 preserves any right or privilege which any class of persons had in any particular province. The provinces might, and did in fact, differ in their educational arrangements.

Lord WATSON:—They may make different rights.

Sir Horace DAVEY:—Sub-section 2 applies only to Upper and Lower Canada—to Ontario and Quebec. Sub-section 3 gives the appeal which I have mentioned. I do not think it can be said that there is anything in the British North America Act which indicates an intention to introduce a uniform system of educational arrangements throughout the Dominion.

Lord WATSON:—Educational arrangements—no, that is a different matter.

Sir HORACE DAVEY:—I mean educational rights.

Lord WATSON:—Civil rights with relation to education is the matter we are dealing with.

Sir HORACE DAVEY:—I think your lordship understood me, though I did not select the best word.

LORD WATSON:—They appear to me to be totally different things. I think in the one uniformity was contemplated, in the other not. Because there is a provision in the act of 1867 that provides for interference, if they choose.

Sir HORACE DAVEY:—The only uniformity contemplated was to preserve existing rights and privileges.

Lord SHAND:—It is not put "which any class of persons have by law or practice in this or any of the other provinces." The right is measured out by that first sub-section, apparently to preserve the right according to law and practice in that province. Of course the word "practice" will undoubtedly cover whatever was going on, and being done.

Sir HORACE DAVEY:—Very likely I did not select the best words for expressing my meaning, but what I mean is that what was intended was to preserve whatever were existing rights and privileges with respect to the denominational schools in any province, not to create the same civil rights or privileges in each province over the whole Dominion. That is what we rather intended, and I think it is reasonably clear.

Sir RICHARD COUCH:—The British North America Act did not affect the system of education in New Brunswick at all?

Sir HORACE DAVEY:—No, it left it as it was, provided that the existing rights and privileges were preserved which they had by law; and in the same way it seems to have been contemplated in Manitoba by the introduction of the words "by law or practice." The words "or practice" may have been introduced because there was no positive law, because the law was of an uncertain hazy kind in Manitoba consisting merely of ordinances of the Hudson's Bay Company, and at any rate it makes it necessary for the court still to enquire what were the rights and privileges which they had by practice, and it seems to me impossible to say that it was a right or privilege which gave them immunity from taxation which did not exist.

Lord MORRIS:—This act contemplates that some right or privilege did exist in the year of grace 1870, in the province of Manitoba, to some class of persons in regard to denominational schools. I have in vain endeavoured to find what you say is that privilege. As I understand, you only say that there was no privilege, that it was a common law right of a true born Briton.

Sir HORACE DAVEY:—I do not think it was strictly privilege because it belonged to every class of persons. According to my view it belonged to every class of persons.

Lord MORRIS:—What in the year 1870 do you say as a matter of fact existed.

Sir HORACE DAVEY:—I take it the right of maintaining denominational schools under their own management for the education of such children whose parents chose to send them there.

Lord HANNEN:—And you may add and not to pay to other denominational schools.

Sir HORACE DAVEY:—Yes, and if you please, not to be taxed at all for other denominational schools.

Lord HANNEN:—The question is whether they have been taxed for other denominational schools.

Sir HORACE DAVEY:—I say if immunity from taxation is the right or privilege—I have said it more than once and I am afraid I have occupied a deal of your lordships' time—if immunity from taxation is the right or privilege it was immunity from being compelled to pay for any education at all, certainly for any denominational education.

Lord SHAND:—Will you allow me to interrupt you once more? I should like to say, with reference to what Lord Watson said, that I feel with him that it is a very important consideration that it may make a difference between the two provinces, and I go further and I would say this, that if the language at all clearly showed that the legislature did make it the same in the provinces I should expect it would be so: but then I have a difficulty in thinking that the language has done that. I quite feel what Lord Watson says very strongly that one would naturally expect everything to be put on the same footing, but because one expects that I think we must not come to that conclusion, unless the language does it, and I do not think we find that language.

Sir HORACE DAVEY:—Now I am going to read the judgment which is against me and, with the greatest respect to the judges in the court of appeal, which is the most powerful judgment against me—that of Mr. Justice Dubuc. It begins by a statement of the facts and some elementary propositions with regard to the mode of construing statutes, which probably your lordships will excuse me from reading. I will begin at page 57, line 26. "If the words 'or practice,' inserted in the Manitoba Act, were as clear and unambiguous as to admit of but one construction, the above rule would have to be applied, and there be no use for prosecuting the inquiry any further. But such is not the case. They are said to mean that the Roman catholics, while compelled to contribute to the support of public schools, are by said words allowed to have and maintain their denominational schools as private schools; this is the narrower construction. They are also alleged to secure to catholics the privilege of being exempted from compulsory attendance at the public schools; another and more liberal construction is that denominational schools existing as a matter of fact at the time of the union, were given by these words a legal status, so that they could not afterwards be interfered with by the provincial legislature." I am not at all disposed to dissent from that. I think they were given a legal status and could not be interfered with. My point is that they have not been interfered with. "As seen by these different interpretations, the words 'or practice' are susceptible of more than one construction; another rule then has to be applied. An old rule of construction says that a thing which is within the letter of the statute is not within the statute unless it be also within the meaning of the legislature." Then he refers to Lord Coke and what Lord Blackburn said in the River Wear Commissioners *vs.* Adamson, and what was said in Graham *vs.* The Bishop of Exeter, and other cases. I do not think it is necessary to read that. Going on to page 59, he says "In the light of those authorities it become necessary in trying to determine the true meaning of the words, &c." [Reading to the words, line 41] "But the said schools were not recognized by law as such denominational schools and the catholics had no right or privilege by law in respect of denominational schools." That is to say, I presume, that where the community was in the bulk catholic the public schools were tacitly allowed to be conducted by catholics as catholic schools. "In framing the British North America Act, the fathers of confederation," &c. [Reading from line 44, page 59, down to the words, line 40 page 60, of the record.] "The judgment of the court might have been different." It may be so. But observe that in New Brunswick there were public schools.

Lord Shand:—Did I understand also that in New Brunwick by practice they were exempt from paying except for their own schools?

Sir Horace Davey:—No, that was only in the two Canadas. In New Brunswick, as has been stated in more than one of these judgments, the system was a system of public schools, and in those public schools the religious exercises were determined apparently by the wishes of the trustees of the particular school. But that was not a privilege which was secured by law. As a matter of fact, some of the schools were catholic and some were protestant, according to the religious belief.

Lord Watson:—They had a Parish Schools Act in New Brunswick.

Sir Horace Davey:—Yes, and they were rated for a public schools act, and then the New Brunswickers when the new act came in making all schools non-sectarian said:—"This is an infringement of our right and privilege secured to us by law at the time of the union." They said no, it was not secured to you by law. As a matter of fact some of the schools were catholic, and some protestant, but that was not anything provided by law, but had grown up by usage. In the same way if there had been a public schools act in Manitoba, and some of the schools supported by public rating and public taxation had been catholic and some had been protestant it is possible that those words "or by practice" might have preserved to the catholics the right, although it was not contained in the legislation, of continuing that system, having some public schools protestant and some catholic. But nothing of the kind existed in Manitoba. "As to the point raised on the argument by Mr. Ewart, of counsel for the applicant, that the words 'or practice' were likely inserted in the Manitoba Act to remedy the defect which caused the difficulties in New Brunswick, which point was answered by the attorney-general that such could not be the case, because the New Brunswick Common Schools Act, was passed only in 1871, one year after the Manitoba Act"—in other words the Manitoba Act was before the decision in *exparte* Renaud, which is said to have given rise to it—"this at least may be said: It appears from the journals," &c. [Reading to the words, line 10, page 61.] "That bill provided that it was not to come into operation for one year after the passage thereof." But still the point was a perfectly good one. These words "or practice" cannot have been introduced in consequence of the decision in *exparte* Renaud, because the decision in *exparte* Renaud was a year later. "The Manitoba Act passed by the Dominion parliament," etc. [Reading to the words, line 24.] "Presumptions are constantly used in determining the real intent and meaning of statutes." My lords, I venture, with great deference to the learned judge, to express a feeling that your lordships will not be very much guided by those considerations in construing the section. "We have the fact that when the Manitoba Act was passed there were denominational schools," &c. [Reading down to the words, line 24, page 62.] "That accounts for the insertion of the two words 'or practice' in the Manitoba Act."

Lord SHAND:—Can you tell me what was the effect then of Columbia and Prince Edward Island coming in? They joined the confederation under the Act of 1871.

Sir HORACE DAVEY:—Yes. Whatever educational rights or privileges were secured to any denomination by the existing law in Prince Edward Island and British Columbia, were retained, but what those rights and privileges were I am not in a position to say. Perhaps one of my learned friends from across the Atlantic will be able to answer your lordship's question.

Mr. MCCARTHY.—Yes, I shall be able to answer that.

Lord SHAND.—Their privileges might be so clear and distinct that those words are quite sufficient for the purpose.

Sir HORACE DAVEY.—Yes. "Before examining more fully what is the true and real purport of the words 'or practice,' &c. [Reading down to line 45.] "The object in view." I observe you can only get the object in view from the words themselves. "In Jessem *vs.* Wright," &c. [Reading down to line 42, page 63.] "Those words were therefore inserted advisedly to secure to those interested the permanency of denominational schools enjoyed at the time by practice, but not recognized by law." I do not dissent from that. "The adverse contention is," &c. [Reading down to line 15, page 64.] "The right of any persons or class of persons to have and support private schools is a primordial right, as the right to breathe air or eat bread." I am not quite sure that that is not too strongly stated. "Supposing the legislature of a province," &c. [Reading down to line 21.] "So to have and conduct a private school in his own premises." Surely that is a rather strained argument. It would prevent persons holding schools to which parents were expected to send their children. "Nothing even would prevent him from having his neighbour's children attending such teaching," &c. [Reading down to line 35.] "That surely could not have been anticipated, and the enactment could not have been intended to prevent such imaginary mischief." I confess it does not appear to me, knowing something about educational legislation both in this country and in other countries, that it is by any means an imaginary mischief that you should make a compulsory clause compelling all children to attend the public schools, and thereby, of course, kill the private schools. "In R. *vs.* Skeen," &c. [Reading down to line 7, page 65.] "Why was there no provision made to protect them against such contingencies?" I am not aware that a provincial legislature can establish a state church. It is not within the object of section 92. "The reason is obvious," &c. [Reading down to line 12.] "The broad and equitable principles prevailing in modern British and other civilized constitutional institutions." I observe in passing that the learned judge considers the establishment of a church to be a departure from the broad equitable principles prevailing in modern British and other civilized institutions. "A constitution assumes a certain number of general principles," &c. [Reading down to line 34.] "Clearly intended to give legal sanction to the privilege enjoyed by practice." That puts in very clear language what is my contention. "To the contention that the new school law does not interfere with the privilege of any class of persons to have still denominational schools as private schools, the Roman catholics can justly say"——

Lord SHAND:—The learned judge all through uses such language——"the right or privilege to have them maintained." He means to say to have them maintained. coupled with an exemption. He does not always use the words but it is rather obvious he brings it up to this, that it is equivalent to a privilege of exemption. The question is whether it comes to that. I mean exemption from taxation.

Sir HORACE DAVEY:—"The Roman catholics can justly say: If the new act does not take from us the right of having our schools, it deprives us of the privilege of subscribing exclusively for our own schools." I do not follow that. "Prior to the union, the Roman catholics had the positive right of having their own denominational schools. They had besides the negative right, that is the privilege of never being compelled to support other schools." Their right, as I have repeated more than once, was the not being compelled to support other schools. They had that right and privilege as a matter of fact, and the words 'or practice' were inserted to prevent their being interfered with under the new constitution." That argument seems to me to be a great deal too far and altogether to paralyze the power to raise any rate for school purposes. "Besides considering the historical facts and circumstances," &c. [Reading down to line 27, page 67.] "That is one aspect of the question." I agree entirely. "The other aspect appears when we look at the other sub-sections," &c. [Reading down to line 40.] "Who might happen to be in the minority." My lords, that is not the construction which has been put upon this section in Mr. Logan's case, where it has been said that you cannot limit the words "any class of persons" in the 1st sub-section by reference to the mention of the catholic or protestant minority in the 2nd sub-section.

Lord MORRIS:—They might have decided differently in Logan's case.

Sir HORACE DAVEY:—Of course they might. "It is also said that the only privilege," &c. [Reading down to line 6, page 68.] "That was to be apprehended, because it was not in issue."

No doubt that may be so, but that is only given as an illustration of a way in which the rights or privileges, according to our construction, may be prejudicially affected. "On the argument it was contended by the attorney-general that, if the catholics have by the first sub-section in the Manitoba Act, the privilege of being exempt from contributing to the support of any other but their own denominational schools, the provincial legislature would be deprived of the power to pass any effective school law," &c. [Reading to the words on page 68, line 39.] "Reverting to the interpretation of statutes susceptible of more than one construction; it is an elementary rule that the construction which appears more just and reasonable will be adopted." Then he refers to a case in the queen's bench and to some words used by Lord Blackburn in the house of lords in Rothes *vs.* Kircaldy Waterworks Commissioners, and to Baron Parke, and a case in the house of lords. "In this case, however, we have not to resort to any such modification of the language of the enactment, nor to any addition thereto," &c. [Reading to the words on page 69, line 35.] "If the narrower construction of the provision in question is adopted, they will have to tax themselves to support their own schools," the learned judge uses "tax" in an inaccurate sense: of course they may have to ask for voluntary contributions—"the only schools which, in conscience, they can send their children to, and they will have besides to be taxed, and to pay for the support of other schools, schools from which the non-catholics will derive all benefit, and the catholics themselves no benefit whatever." My lords, that sentence contains two fallacies. In the first place it uses "tax" in different senses in the two limbs of it, and secondly, when they say that the catholics can derive no benefit whatever—that is their own choice. The schools are open to them if they choose to come. "Moreover the legislative grant, which is the people's money contributed by catholics as well as by other citizens will be exclusively devoted to assist the other schools, while the catholics will not get their proportionate share to maintain their own shcools. Would not that be most unreasonable and a great injustice to the Roman catholics, while the other portion of the community would get more than naturally they would be reasonably and justly entitled to? Now, if the broader and more equitable construction prevail, the Roman catholics, in being allowed to have their schools maintained and recognized by law would get nothing more than strict and fair justice, and the non-catholics would suffer no injustice." I may remark that the catholics had no such right before the union, to have their schools maintained out of public moneys. "Protestants and catholics have different views and different principles as to the education which children should receive in elementary schools." I do not think I need read the next two sentences. It is controversial matter.

Lord MORRIS:—I do not think it is controversial matter.

Sir HORACE DAVEY:—I will read it with pleasure.

Lord MORRIS:—No, I do not want you to read it, but it is not controversial matter that they have different views. That is not controversial matter.

Sir HORACE DAVEY:—I think many protestants would say that they hold the same quite fairly, but I will read it with pleasure.

Lord MORRIS:—No, but I do not admit it is controversial.

Sir HORACE DAVEY:—Very well, my lord. It comes to this, that catholics have conscientious objections to sending their children to non-sectarian schools, which, of course, may be admitted. "The state may hold that ignorance is an evil to be remedied by public instruction, and may see that certain secular subjects, which are known to form the basis of a proper education, be taught in schools assisted by public money," &c. [Reading to the words] "The desirability of having religious instruction combined with secular teaching in schools is, as stated by my brother Killam, considered as of the utmost importance by very many protestants as well as by Roman catholics." My lords, I venture to think we have nothing to do with these considerations, which are considerations for a different body, but I might add that it is rather odd to speak of the right of having your denominational schools maintained out of public money as flowing from the fundamental principle of liberty of conscience.

Lord MORRIS:—I think it only means this, that as Roman catholics they can obtain no benefits, as a matter of fact, from these non-sectarian schools.

Lord SHAND: That is their opinion, but, of course, they get the benefit of the general community being educated, in secular matters, in all ordinary branches—they get the benefit of intelligence being cultivated and general education spread.

Lord MORRIS:—That may be a very useful disquisition of Sir Horace Davey's, but as a matter of fact, it is sworn that the catholics in this district of Manitoba cannot, unless they change their religion, derive any benefit from schools that will be protestant schools.

Sir HORACE DAVEY:—They may not if they have a conscientious objection to do so. I do not propose to read these extracts from the report of the commission on education—I will with pleasure, if desired, but the learned judge finishes his judgment at line 30 page 72. That is on the respective value of religious and secular education. "On the grounds hereinbefore mentioned and on the authorities cited I believe that the re-enactment in the Manitoba Act, of the main provisions of the 93rd section of the British North America Act was for the purpose of ensuring, under the constitution of the new province to any class of persons who might desire it, the maintenance of the denominational schools existing at the time of the union, that the words 'or practice' added to the first sub-section of the 22nd section of the Manitoba Act can have no other meaning, and should receive no other construction than that they were clearly intended by the legislature to give a legal status to the said denominational schools, which as a matter of fact were known to exist at the time though not recognized by any law"—I am not sure that I understand what is meant by a "legal status" there—"that the said interpretation should be adopted on the ground, amongst others, that if the Roman catholics are allowed to have their denominational schools maintained under the law"—Here you see a different word introduced—"maintained under the law" "no injustice or detriment whatever will result to the other classes of the population, whilst otherwise, by being obliged to establish and support schools to which they could conscientiously send their children and paying at the same time for schools from which they cannot and will not derive any benefit, the Roman catholics will suffer a very great injustice, and the legislature, by inserting the words 'or practice,' intended to provide and in fact did provide against such injustice being done to the catholic minority in this province.

I am therefore led to the conclusion that the Public Schools Act of last session, by which the denominational schools heretofore existing are legislated out of legal existence"—Now I cannot understand that—"are legislated out of legal existence" I cannot understand how their legal existence is altered one single jot—"prejudicially affects the privilege which the Roman catholics had by practice at the time of the union with respect to denominational schools; that in consequence the said Public Schools Act is *ultra vires* of the provincial legislature, and that the two by-laws in question passed in compliance with the provisions of the said act are illegal and should be quashed."

Your lordships will no doubt have observed in the course of my reading this judgment, which is a very able document, that the learned judge does not condescend to particulars as to what is the right or privilege which he supposes is prejudicially affected. He plays between the schools having a legal status, and their being maintained by the state, and he appears to think that the effect of the act was to give them what he pleases to call a legal status—that is, a right to maintenance out of the fund provided by law by the act; but of course the preservation of existing rights could not confer any new rights such as that which the learned judge contemplates; and I entirely demur to his conclusion that the effect of the Public Schools Act is in any way to legislate them out of legal existence, or in any way to affect, in the slightest degree or particular, whatever legal existence they had before the union and still have. No doubt it alters their status under the legislation of 1871. That is undoubted, but that is not what is preserved. What is preserved is the *status quo* before the union.

Lord MORRIS:—What the judge I think was alluding to was, that they are legislated out of the legal existence that they had acquired under the act of 1871 and the subsequent acts.

Lord SHAND:—I do not think be refers to the subsequent acts at all. From beginning to end of his opinion he never refers to the subsequent acts.

Lord MORRIS:—I am not speaking of from the beginning to the end of the opinion, but of the particular passage on page 73 of three lines long.

Sir HORACE DAVEY:—I think he cannot refer to that.

Lord MORRIS:—I suggest that he referred to that, but I may be wrong. He says "I am therefore led to the conclusion that the Public Schools Act of last session"—that is the one we are dealing with—"by which the denominational schools heretofore existing, were legislated out of legal existence." Were not they in legal existence under the act of 1871 and the subsequent acts?

Sir HORACE DAVEY:—And they are still in existence.

Lord MORRIS:—Were they in legal existence as regards receiving any assistance? The Public Schools Act did not repeal the act of 1871.

Lord SHAND:—I think he is referring to the same thing on the previous page 72, line 33—"To any class of persons who might desire it, the maintenance"—that is the keeping up—"of the denominational schools existing at the time of the union." So be goes back to the union, but I am bound to say, I think, Sir Horace Davey, that the real point of this opinion from beginning to end is this: While he talks of it as maintenance, he thinks you strike a blow at maintenance if you take away what he assumes existed—it is a question whether it did exist, namely, what he calls a privilege of a negative character—the privilege of not being bound to contribute to the expense of the other schools; because he says so at the bottom of page 72—"By being obliged to establish and support schools to which they could conscientiously send their children, and paying at the same time for schools from which they cannot and will not derive any benefit." That is what he brings it round to. I think his opinion is that in effect these words "or practice" imply that there was a privilege of a negative character, namely that they should not be bound to contribute to state schools, and no doubt he always uses that word maintenance.

Sir HORACE DAVEY:—If that is so, it reduces the power of legislating as regards education to almost a nonentity because there could be no schools supported then out of public moneys. You cannot support, as I said yesterday, the denominational schools, because the right or privilege, if any, is of not being taxed at all for the support of schools: you cannot support non-sectarian schools because it is said that the Roman catholics object to it, and therefore it not only cripples but paralyses the power of the provincial legislature to make any arrangement for public schools in the province, either sectarian or non-sectarian, out of public moneys at all. That is the effect of it.

Well my lord, Mr. Justice Bain's judgment is a very powerful judgment in my favour; but if your lordships will excuse me, as you have heard so much of me, I will leave my friend Mr. McCarthy to deal with that judgment, which is a very powerful judgment in our favour.

Lord WATSON:—Unless there is something new in the judgments, it is not usual and I think it is not necessary to read them all.

Sir HORACE DAVEY:—That is what occurred to me, but no doubt your lordships would like to hear my friend Mr. McCarthy, and I do not wish, by passing it over, to prevent his referring to any portion of it he may desire.

Lord WATSON:—The more powerful it is, the less it requires repetition.

Sir HORACE DAVEY:—I propose to read two judgments of the supreme court, and I have selected those which appear to me—I may be wrong and of course that will not prevent my friend from referring to any other passages in his favour—the most powerful judgments; and those are the judgments of Mr. Justice Patterson and Mr. Justice Taschereau. The supreme court were unanimously against us.

Lord WATSON:—How many were there?

Sir HORACE DAVEY:—Five; the Chief Justice, Mr. Justice Strong, Mr. Justice Patterson, Mr. Justice Fournier, and Mr. Justice Taschereau. Mr. Justice Strong did not deliver a separate judgment. I will read Mr. Justice Patterson's, which I think my friends will agree is the most powerful judgment.

My lords, after referring to general subjects, on page 92, between lines 10 and 20, he says "What is meant by 'having by practice?' To have by law here means to have under some statutory provision, the preposition 'by' pointing to the law or statute as the means or instrument by which the right or privilege was acquired. Are we obliged to understand the term 'by practice' as intended to signify acquired by practice or user, involving some idea of prescription? It is arguable, and has in effect been argued, that that is the proper understanding of the term, that the word 'by' must have the same force when understood in the one place as when expressed in the other, leading to the conclusion that, inasmuch as no rights or privileges in respect of denominational schools had been acquired in the territory in that manner, the clause in question is wholly inoperative." Of course I do not know the argument addressed to the court, but I should not myself put the argument in that way. "The construction thus contended for may be capable of being supported by strict reasoning from rules of grammar or rhetoric, but it is not, in my judgment, appropriate to this clause," &c., &c. (Reading to the words at line 43, page 92.) "The right to establish and maintain such schools was not derived from statutory law. It was incident to the freedom of British subjects and was independent of and anterior to legislation." But I may remark, it might be modified and altered by legislation. "The Manitoba Act did not assume to preserve that right merely as an abstract and theoretical right, but it did so in favour of such classes of persons as at the union were practically exercising it. If this construction seems to do any violence to the language of the clause, it is only by treating the word 'by' where it is understood before the word practice, as not having precisely the same force as when expressed before the word 'law.' But, as once remarked by one of the most eminent of English judges, Lord Stowell, when Sir W. Scott: 'Courts are not bound to a strictness at once harsh and pedantic in the application of statutes.'" Then the learned judge refers to a case before this board of Salmon *vs.* Duncombe where a construction was put on an ordinance.

Lord WATSON:—Did not the board blame the draftsman in that case?

Sir HORACE DAVEY:—I think the board did, but it was an ordinance evidently drawn by a layman who did not know what the law was.

Lord WATSON:—I think the board found out that it was the draftsman in that case who was to blame.

Sir HORACE DAVEY:—They had to find out what the meaning of the words was. And the learned judge refers to what Lord Selbourne says in the well known case of the Caledonian Railway Co. *vs.* The North British Ry.

Lord WATSON:—It is generally not the draftsman who is to blame in these cases.

Sir HORACE DAVEY:—In Salmon *vs.* Duncombe it was undoubtedly the draftsman. It was a governor's ordinance in Natal, and it had been drawn in happy ignorance of what the existing state of the law was and it was very difficult to construe it. However your lordships construed it. "In my opinion the Roman catholics are a class of persons who had, within the meaning of the statute, rights and privileges with respect to denominational schools" &c, &c. (Reading to the words) "And the schools of the protestants were maintained by protestants, neither body contributing or being liable to contribute to maintain the schools of the other"—or their own schools in fact. "The fact is not without importance from a point of view which I shall presently notice, but I am not prepared to hold that the immunity enjoyed from liability to support schools of another denomination, at a time when taxation for school purposes was unknown in the territory, was a privilege in respect of denominational schools." My lords, I call your attention to this, because this learned judge who is delivering a judgment against me is in my favour to this extent, that he is not prepared to hold that the immunity enjoyed from liability to support schools of another denomination at a time when taxation for school purposes was unknown to the territory was a privilege in respect of denominational schools. "The provincial statute of 1890, which is attacked as *ultra vires*, renders every taxpayer liable to assessment for the support of the public schools," &c., &c. (Reading to the words on page 94 line 5.) "Which, as I construe section 22, they had as a class at the union." So that, so far, this learned judge takes the same construction as I do. "It is thus in effect asserted on the part of the appellant that the right or privilege has not been destroyed by the Public Schools Act of 1890," &c., &c. (Reading to the words at line 45.) "The contest is over the right or privilege, not of the individual but of the class of persons."

Lord SHAND:—This is not put on the conscientious objection. It is put on affecting the pocket.

Sir HORACE DAVEY:—Yes, my lord. "We are familiar with the expression 'injuriously affected' as used in the compensation clauses of the railway acts, and in the English Lands Clauses Act." Observe, my lords, that the argument comes to, any school rate for any purposes whatever. "It would be labour lost to cite cases turning upon the application of the provisions for compensating persons whose lands are injuriously affected by works done under sanction of law. They are very numerous, and the English cases will be found in Cripps on Compensation, cap. 9, and several other treatises. The claim to compensation failed in many of the cases in which lands were injuriously affected for reasons arising on the statutes under which the claim was made, as, *e.g.*, because the injury was caused by an act that would not have given a right of action at common law, or because it was caused by the operation only and not by the construction of the work; but all the cases agree in recognizing as something that injuriously affects a man's property whatever interferes with his convenience in the enjoyment of it, or of any right in respect of it, or prevents him from enjoying it to the best advantage, and whether the injury happens to be permanent or only temporary." My lords, I think that that is not a very happy illustration, because under the Lands Clauses Act nothing is injuriously affecting land within the meaning of the act, unless, apart from the act, it would give a right of action. "The same principle makes it imperative to hold that the right of a class of persons with respect to denominational schools is injuriously affected if the effect of a law passed on the subject of education is to render it more difficult or less convenient to exercise the right to the best advantage," etc., etc. (Reading to the words, page 95, line 40.) "There is therefore room for legislative regulation on many subjects, as for example, compulsory attendance of scholars, the sanitary condition of school houses, the imposition and collection of rates for the support of denominational schools." With great respect, the collection of rates for the support of denominational schools, would be equally an infringement of a right existing before the union.

Lord SHAND:—How do you understand these words, "compulsory attendance of scholars?"

Sir HORACE DAVEY:—I suppose the learned judge would mean that they must attend some school or other.

Lord MORRIS:—That is the law in England at present, he means.

Sir HORACE DAVEY:—Yes.

Lord MORRIS:—That is all he means.

Sir HORACE DAVEY:—That they must attend some school recognized by the elementary education department.

Lord MORRIS:—Yes.

Sir HORACE DAVEY:—"And sundry other matters which may be dealt with without interfering with the denominational characteristics of the school." To be quite accurate, I think that is not a general law, but it depends on the school board. I think so. I am not quite sure, but it does not matter—"And which, I suppose, were dealt with in the statutes of the province that were repealed in 1890, to make way for the system now complained of. I am of opinion that the appeal should be allowed and the by-laws of the city of Winnipeg, nos. 480 and 483, quashed, the appellant having his costs of the appeal and also of all proceedings in the courts below."

Now, my lords, this judgment is to a certain extent in my favour, because it recognizes that the only right or privilege was the right and privilege to maintain by voluntary contribution denominational schools for members of their own denominations. The learned judge agrees that that right is not taken away, but he says it is injuriously affected; and injuriously affected, how? Because (it seems to me very refined reasoning) the means of the taxpayers to contribute towards their voluntary schools will be diminished by having to pay the school rate; but they would be also equally diminished by any school rate at all; so that the argument, if it is worth anything, goes to the imposition of any taxation for the purposes of education at all.

Lord SHAND:—I suspect this learned judge stands alone in that passage on page 93, where he says: "I am not prepared to hold that the immunity enjoyed from liability to support schools of another denomination, at a time when taxation for school purposes was unknown in the territory, was a privilege." I suspect that most of the other judges make that really the ground of their opinions.

Sir HORACE DAVEY:—They do, my lord. That is one reason why I selected Mr. Justice Patterson, to show the difference.

Now, my lords, I propose to read from Mr. Justice Taschereau's judgment on page 108, and if your lordships will allow me I will read it in English instead of French, translating it as I go on. "The appellant in the present case attacks the constitutionality of the school act passed by the legislature of the province of Manitoba in 1890," &c., &c. [Reading to the words on page 108, line 43.] "Section 22 of the organic act of Manitoba of 1870 is in the French version, which it must not be forgotten is law as well as the English version." Then he reads it in French. The words in French are "ou par la coutume." It is textually section 93 of the British North America Act, with the simple addition of the words 'or by practice,'" &c., &c. [Reading to the words.] "His grace the archbishop of St. Boniface, in an affidavit which was produced, described it in the following words." I do not think we need read the archbishop's affidavit. I will go on at page 111, line 20, after the statement of the affidavit which I will not read again. He says: "The clear result of this affidavit, which constitutes the only evidence in the proceedings is" &c., &c. [Reading to the words at line 30.] "Catholic minority of the province." So that this learned judge goes on the negative privilege of not contributing to other schools than their own—of not being obliged to contribute. I have already commented on that—that that goes much further. The privilege, if it was a privilege, was of not contributing to the maintenance of schools at all. "The law of 1890, says the respondent, obliges, it is true, catholics to contribute to the free schools," &c., &c. [Reading to the words at line 40.] "What then does it all come to? To make it said by the non-catholic majority to the catholic minority: You have the privilege of having your schools; we leave you that, provided that you aid us to maintain ours." I beg his lordship's pardon. That is not the schools of the majority. That is just the fallacy. It is not the schools of the majority but the schools of the country. He puts it into the mouth of the non-catholic majority to say to the catholic minority: You have the privilege of having your schools; we leave you that, provided you aid to maintain ours. Of course that is not so. The schools are not the schools of the majority, but they are the schools of the country, to which every child in the country has a right of access.

Lord WATSON:—It is not quite as applicable to the period before the union. It is not quite easy to understand all these expressions, that is to say, the use of the word "privilege" as a privilege of the few over the many. It is nothing of that sort. They say it was the privilege of A over B, but it was a right existing in every man in the district to send his children to school.

Sir HORACE DAVEY:—Yes.

Lord WATSON:—The word "privilege" cannot be read as meaning what the few possess against the many. The question still remains as before. What is a privilege?"

Lord SHAND:—On the other hand, it may be further suggested that it was intended to save anything that could be called a privilege. It may be that there is nothing exactly to fit that word.

Lord WATSON:—There is no question between majority and minority or anything of that kind.

Sir HORACE DAVEY:—It was the right of every body of religionists to maintain schools at their own cost.

Lord WATSON:—The natural meaning of the word "privilege" means some exceptional favour shown to an individual or a class—an exceptional right belonging to an individual or a class, but there is no privilege of that kind in educational matters so far as regards the denominational schools existing at and before the union.

Sir HORACE DAVEY:—Privilege, strictly speaking, it was not, but it was in this sense, that it was the right of every body of religionists to maintain a school of their own denomination for the education of their own scholars.

Lord WATSON:—It was an equal right and equal privilege of every person.

Sir HORACE DAVEY:—Observe how this learned judge goes on in this imaginary conversation between the non-catholic majority and the catholic minority. I will read it again "You have the privilege of having your schools, we leave you that provided you aid us to maintain ours." Well I have commented on that. "You cannot send your children to our schools, but we do not oblige you to do so: all that we ask is that you pay for instructing ours." Well really, if it were not used by the learned judge, I should say that is a parody of the argument. No such argument was addressed to this board and the majority do not say anything of the kind. We say: We provide schools for the whole body which you can send your children to if you think fit to do so; if you have conscientious scruples about it we cannot help it, but we must legislate for the greatest happiness of the greatest number, and we provide public schools to which all have access; if any have conscientious scruples about using them we cannot help it.

Lord MORRIS:—What objection do you take to that statement of the learned judge?

Sir HORACE DAVEY:—He says "Vous ne pouvez envoyer vos enfants à nos écoles."—"You cannot send your children to our schools." I say you can send them to our schools if you like; they are open to all.

Lord MORRIS:—He does not mean that physically you cannot.

Sir HORACE DAVEY:—If he does not mean that, then the argument loses its force.

Lord MORRIS:—I do not think so.

Sir HORACE DAVEY:—The argument loses all its force if you do not mean that.

Lord MORRIS:—Nobody suggests that they could not be physically sent there.

Sir HORACE DAVEY:—Then it is a parody of the argument to say: "You cannot send your children to our schools, but we do not compel you to do that, all that we ask is that you pay to instruct our children." We do not ask you to instruct our children but we ask you to pay to instruct the whole of the children of the province.

Lord MORRIS :—So far from being a parody it strikes me as being literally the truth.

Sir HORACE DAVEY :—I am afraid I cannot repeat what I have said.

Lord MORRIS : - I did not like to allow it to pass by without saying that.

Sir HORACE DAVEY :—It is using language in two senses. If it was used in the sense in which it may be said to be true, then it is irrelevant, and it is only relevant if used in the sense in which it is not true. "I seek in vain in the proceedings the evidence that that was the custom before the union, &c., &c. (Reading to the words on page , line 32.) "And that the whole was then regulated by practice and by practice alone."

Lord WATSON :—You are not maintaining that by "practice" there is meant practice constituting law ?

Sir HORACE DAVEY :—No.

Lord WATSON :—Because I think there is a good deal of light thrown on the meaning of the word "practice" by its being used in distinct contradistinction to law.

Sir HORACE DAVEY :—I submit, as one of the learned judges says, it is rights and privileges secured by positive law; that is to say, by some ordinance or statute, or, although not secured by law, yet *de facto* existing at the time.

Lord WATSON :—When a man has a right or privilege by law, you generally find that he can defend that right or privilege; but whether he can when he has a right or privilege which has not the force of law, I think is more than doubtful.

Lord SHAND :—I do not think any judge of the whole of the judges who have dealt with the case, puts it any higher than you said, that it means the state of things existing at the time as a matter of fact.

Sir HORACE DAVEY :—The *status quo.*

Lord WATSON :—A right or privilege derived from a custom or practice that has the force of law is as capable of being defended, if it is invaded, as a right entirely arising from law itself; but when it depends on practice not having the force of law, I think it follows that it is not necessarily a practice which is capable of being defended.

Sir HORACE DAVEY :—I have conceded that the case goes beyond anything like prescription, and that it includes the *status quo ;* and the whole of my argument is addressed to what was the *status quo.*

Lord WATSON :—It may be that the practice did not exist, although it is defensible if invaded.

Sir HORACE DAVEY :—It was the preservation of the *status quo*, or rather, I ought to put it in the other way. What was conferred upon the province, according to my argument, was the right to establish a system of public education in the public schools in the province, and to tax the inhabitants of the province for the maintenance of such schools consistently with preserving the *status quo* of the denominational schools. "The defendant corporation and the attorney-general while they recognize in the minority, the abstract right to have these schools would prejudice the free exercise of it," &c. [Reading to the words] "And moreover, not only the private property of each catholic taxpayer, but each school house, even of catholic schools, and all property dedicated to the ends of the education of their children by catholics are taxable for the maintenance of free schools." Now he goes as far as confiscation. "The statute by section 179 goes as far as confiscating for the profit of the free schools in certain cases, the scholastic property of the Roman catholic minority." This is the most extraordinary argument ever used in a court of justice. Remember that by the legislation of 1871, all schools were public schools, some catholic and some protestant, but they were all public schools. In sections 178 and 179 of the Schools Act of 1890, it provides that the public property should remain the public property of the new school board, and it says this: "In cases where, before the coming into force of this act, catholic school districts have been established, covering the same territory as any protestant school district, and such protestant school district has incurred indebtedness, the department of education shall cause an inquiry to be made as to the amount of the indebtedness of such protestant school district and the amount of its assets. Such of the assets as consist of property shall be valued on the basis of their actual value at the time of the coming into force of this act. In case the amount of the indebtedness exceeds the amount of the assets, then all the property assessed in the year 1889 to supporters of such catholic school districts shall be exempt from any taxation for the purpose of paying the principal and interest of an amount of the indebtedness of such school district equal to the difference between its indebtedness and assets. Such exemption shall continue only so long as such property is owned by the person to whom the same was assessed as owner in the year 1889." That is to say, that if in a protestant school district there is a debt beyond the amount of the assets of the school district, the catholics are exempted from any taxes for payment of that indebtedness. That is for the benefit of the catholics. Then section 179 provides:—"In cases where, before the coming into force of this act, catholic school districts have been established, as in the next preceding section mentioned, such catholic school district shall, upon the coming into force of this act, cease to exist, and all the assets of such catholic school districts, shall belong to, and all the liabilities thereof be paid by the public school district. In case the liabilities of any such catholic school district exceed its assets then the difference shall be deducted from the amount to be allowed as an exemption, as provided in the next preceding section. In case the assets of any such catholic school district exceed its liabilities, the difference shall be added to the amount to be allowed as an exemption, as provided in the next preceding section." That is to say, when the act comes into force the public property, which up to that time has been appropriated to a catholic district, shall cease to be so appropriated. That is, of course, the scheme of the act, and that is what this learned judge calls the confiscation of the school property of the catholic minority. It never belonged to the catholic minority.

Lord WATSON:—They seem to have been the public schools of that denominational system.

Sir HORACE DAVEY:— Certainly, but the property is public property.

Lord SHAND:—Apparently the protestant schools were treated exactly on the same principle.

Sir HORACE DAVEY:—Exactly. "I am of opinion that this legislation is prejudicial to the rights and privileges which this minority enjoyed before the union, and consequently is *ultra vires*. It is possible, says the respondent, that this legislation may prejudicially affect the rights of the minority," &c., &c. (Reading to the words at the end of the judgment), "I am of opinion that the appeal should be allowed."

Now, my lords, in the course of the argument I think I have said what I have to say in answer to this learned judge and it would be inexcusable to trouble you at greater length. My submission may be summed up in one word, that the scheme of the act is to give the legislature of Manitoba full power to make such provisions as it thinks fit for public education throughout the province, whether sectarian or non-sectarian, supported by public money, and to make taxes for that purpose, provided that it leaves untouched the right of each community to support its own schools and to maintain its own schools for the education of its own scholars; and if I repeated myself for another hour I could not carry my argument further than that proposition.

Now, my lords, a few words as to the other appeal which is also before your lordships. My lords, I have told you that this appeal arises out of a proceeding by a gentleman named Logan, and Mr. Logan supported his appeal by an affidavit of the bishop of Rupert's Land, and his own affidavit; and I will ask your lordships' attention to the affidavit of the bishop of Rupert's Land, on page 4 of the record in this appeal. This most reverend person says that in 1865 he was appointed by the crown bishop of Rupert's Land. "The diocese of Rupert's Land in 1865 covered the whole of the North-west Territories of Canada, the district of Keewatin, the present province of Manitoba and that portion of the westerly part of the province of Ontario lying westerly of the height of land and running between Rat Portage and Port Arthur. Subsequently the diocese was sub-divided into eight bishoprics, one of which, still known as Rupert's Land, consists of the province of Manitoba and that portion of the province of Ontario referred to above;" and he says he is the bishop of that smaller diocese and metropolitan of the whole province. "Upon my arrival in the diocese in 1865, I found there existed a great want of schools for the education of the youth" &c., &c. (Reading to the words at page 6 line 40.) "Of these over 6,000 were Roman catholic, and nearly 5,000 were members of the church of England; the rest were chiefly presbyterians with a few of other denominations." I believe that those numbers are not acquiesced in. "The Christians residing in this province, as above set forth, resided in what was known as the Red River Settlement, and would practically be included in an area not exceeding 60 miles from the city of Winnipeg. In the year 1871, when the first Public Schools Act of Manitoba was passed, I joined heartily with the provincial executive in endeavouring to carry into effect the school law then enacted, believing that under that act public schools could be carried on giving such religious instruction as would be satisfactory to the members of the church of England and to myself."

Lord SHAND:—The act there referred to would be clearly for denominational schools. "I joined heartily with the provincial executive in endeavouring to carry into effect the school law then enacted, believing that under that act"——

Sir HORACE DAVEY:—Yes, but only as between protestants and catholics, only two classes of schools.

Lord SHAND:—I know that.

Sir HORACE DAVEY:—But it imposed taxation on presbyterians for the support of church of England schools, presbyterian or Jewish schools.

Lord HANNEN:—Was there any provision for Jewish schools?

Sir HORACE DAVEY:—I do not know that there was any in fact.

Lord HANNEN:—They do not seem to regard that, "But many of the members of the protestant section of the board of education did not hold the same views as myself," &c., &c. [Reading down to......] "Then I claim that the church of England is peculiarly entitled to such separate schools."

Lord SHAND:—What does that act mean; does that mean that there is to be an endowment?

Sir HORACE DAVEY:—No, it means separate schools, that is to say, Roman catholic or church of England schools are each entitled to exemption from the support of the public schools. Of course, if the Roman catholics and the church of England and the presbyterians, and if there be any other set of protestant Christians in Manitoba—all claim exemption, what becomes of the public school system? "As far as I have had any influence, I have always endeavoured to influence public opinion and the legislature," &c. [Reads down to......] "The children of parents of the church of England have been prejudicially affected." What presses one is that if this gentleman is right and the Roman catholic archbishop is right, between them they have such an enormous majority in Manitoba.

Lord SHAND:—As to that paragraph you have just read, it rather confirms what I have read.

Lord MORRIS:—That was in 1870. I should have thought the majority has shifted.

Sir HORACE DAVEY:—Between them the members of the church of England and the Roman catholics have a majority, one would think.

Lord SHAND:—What I was observing in this paragraph is, it is not a claim for exemption from the general taxation, but for a claim that he shall have re-establishment of denominational influence.

Sir HORACE DAVEY:—As I said in the other case, the privilege, if any, would be immunity from the taxation for the support of public schools. "Before the act of 1890 was passed I expressed my views on the schools question." I do not know that I need read this: "One of the schools conducted by the church of England as hereinbefore mentioned was situate in the parish of St. John's," &c. [Reads down to......] "In no way supported or aided by funds raised by general rates or taxation." Then Mr. Logan says in paragraph 13 of his affidavit, that he has three children of school age, and that he claims the right to have "My children taught religious exercises in school according to the tenets of the church of England, and I claim that such right was secured to me and other members of the church of England at the time of the said union by the provisions of the Manitoba Act"—undoubtedly, at his own expense—"I do not approve of the manner in which religious exercises are taught in schools where they are so taught under the provisions of the Public Schools Act, and I claim that the tax for the support of schools, imposed upon me by said by-law and pursuant to said Public Schools Act, or by any other act of the legislature, by which I am compelled to contribute for the support of schools not under the control of the church of England, prejudicially affects my rights as a member of the church of England, and if compelled to pay such tax I and other members of the church of England are less able to support schools in which religious exercises and teachings in accordance with our form of worship could be conducted." Then, a gentleman of the name of Hayward makes an affidavit to the same effect, and there are on page 13 regulations of the advisory board regarding religious exercises in public schools. I think I drew your lordships' attention to that in the course of the argument.

Lord SHAND:—It says there: "The following selections from the authorized English version of the Bible or the Douay version of the Bible." That is for the direction of the teacher, I suppose.

Sir HORACE DAVEY:—Yes. Then Professor Bryce makes an affidavit.

Lord WATSON:—It is all about what has happened since 1870.

Sir HORACE DAVEY:—Yes. I do not propose to read it. This case came before the chief justice, and it was decided before the chief justice, Mr. Justice Dubuc, and Mr. Justice Bain, and it was decided upon the authority of the previous case. The only point, which apparently was argued, was whether the members of the church of England were the class of persons within sub-section 1 of section 22, that is to say, whether you interpret the class of persons by reference to sub-section 2 and was the only class contemplated—catholics on the one side and protestants on the other; in other words, making only two categories or classes of persons. What they held there was this: The argument on page 23 is, that the Roman catholics had, at the time of the union, denominational schools in this province. That is in Barrett's case.

Lord WATSON:—They decided in that case, the cases were on the same question, and one was *res judicata* in the other.

Sir HORACE DAVEY:—The words are "any class of persons," and if Roman catholics are a class of persons I cannot see any valid argument that I could address to your lordships for the purpose of showing that the members of the church of England are not.

Lord SHAND:—I see Chief Justice Dubuc concurred in this case.

Sir HORACE DAVEY:—Because the decision was the way he would have liked to decide the others.

Lord SHAND:—I see it is the supreme court who decided.

Sir HORACE DAVEY:—That is why.

Lord MORRIS:—They were obliged to follow the decision of the superior court.

Sir HORACE DAVEY:—It was according to his own view. The chief justice and Mr. Justice Bain were constrained by the authorities of the superior court to decide contrary to their own opinion.

Lord SHAND:—Does that come from the queen's bench?

Sir HORACE DAVEY:—Yes, your lordship knows we require special leave to appeal from the supreme court in Canada, and it was a case in which leave was properly granted. But in truth we could have appealed Logan's case alone, and then impliedly appealed Barrett's case, but it was thought better that Barrett's case should come before your lordships. Now, my lords, just conceive; I cannot, I confess, draw any valid distinction between Logan's case and Barrett's case, because I think it is inadmissible to say that because sub-section 2 speaks of only two categories, therefore you must interpret the words "any class of persons" in sub-section 1, and confine that to the same category. It does not appear to me that that is reasonable from the language of the section, and I for one should not be prepared to support that at your lordships' bar.

Lord MORRIS:—What was the practice at the passing of that act in 1870?

Sir HORACE DAVEY:—The bishop of Rupert's Land says that the practice was that there were denominational church of England schools. That is what he says, and that seems to have been accepted.

Lord SHAND :—That is expressly sworn to, that they were all English church schools, and that they were so conducted.

Sir HORACE DAVEY :—So I understood the bishop's affidavit.

Lord SHAND :—It is very distinct in that affidavit.

Sir HORACE DAVEY :—I understand the bishop's affidavit to be to the effect that there were denominational church of England schools maintained by members of the church of England, and under the general supervision of the clergy and himself as bishop, and in which children were taught the English church catechism, and brought up according to the tenets of the church of England. If that is so, my lords, I am unable to see why the members of the church of England are not a class of persons whose rights and privileges, as they existed by practice at the time of the union were preserved just as much as the Roman catholics; and it seems to me inadmissible to say that there are only two categories in sub-section 1, because sub-section 2, which my learned friend contends has a larger sweep, refers only to two categories. Well, if that be so, just consider where the legislature of Manitoba, if those judgments are correct, is landed. They may not raise any general school rate for the maintenance of schools to which all have by law the right of going, because it is said that is contrary to the rights of the denomination. It is taxing members of the church of England for the maintenance of schools which are not denominational schools of the church of England, and it is taxing Roman catholics for the maintenance of schools to which they object to send their children, although they have by law the right to send them there. And it appears it is equally objectionable to tax the members of the protestant community, as was done under the act of 1871, for the maintenance of protestant schools, because the bishop has the right to say, as he does in his affidavit, that although he hopes for a better time, he is disappointed; and the members of the church of England have a right to say "We have a right to have schools under the control of the church of England, and therefore we object to pay taxes for the maintenance of schools under the control of presbyterian, or for teaching presbyterian tenets, and not the tenets of the church of England." And I do not see, as I have already said, how, if you carry the rights and privileges existing before the union to that extent, you can tax, that is, compel any class of persons to pay for education at all, because their right and privilege was to maintain their own schools with their own funds, and there was no power of imposing a compulsory tax, or constraining the members of any religious body—I use it in its proper sense—constraining them to contribute ratably towards the maintenance of their own schools, any more than there was to other schools. The right and privilege, if it did exist at all, was a right and privilege to be exempt from all taxation for school purposes. Now you have only before you members of the church of England and members of the Roman catholic church.

Lord MORRIS :—Is not there this difference between them: Does not the archbishop in the case of the Roman catholic church swear that by reason of the tenets of the church of England they cannot go to these schools?

Sir HORACE DAVEY :—Yes.

Lord MORRIS:—Very well, and the church of England does the same sort of thing.

Sir HORACE DAVEY :—What difference can that make?

Lord MORRIS :—I should think a good deal, because one is a matter of individual opinion.

Sir HORACE DAVEY :—So is the other. If they are members of the Roman catholic church they must agree with the tenets of the church of Rome. The archbishop of the church of England does not say it is a tenet of the church of England that a member of the church of England should not attend a Roman catholic church. It only means that is an opinion entertained by the Roman catholic church.

Lord MORRIS :—I beg your pardon. I do not find it.

Sir HORACE DAVEY :—When you say it is a tenet of the Roman catholic church, all you mean is that that is the opinion entertained, and conscientiously entertained, and the conviction entertained by members of that church. That is what you mean. It is only matter of opinion.

Lord MORRIS:—All the members of the church of England entertain the same opinion as the archbishop does.

Sir HORACE DAVEY:—I do not think he says so. I venture humbly to remark that it does not seem to me to make any difference.

Lord WATSON:—It has been in my mind to ask you for some time whether in any view the case is not narrowed a little by another element being introduced. I am merely assuming so. In the case of Logan, he says that at the time of the union there were denominational schools. He does not say he has any child attending school now.

Sir HORACE DAVEY:—Yes, in paragraph 13.

Lord WATSON:—Oh, he does?

Sir HORACE DAVEY:—"I have at the present time three children of school age, namely: one of the age of 14 years, one of the age of 11 years, and one of the age of 5 years."

Lord WATSON:—That is what I meant. What does it state in the other case? I do not think Mr. Barrett says anything about it?

Sir HORACE DAVEY:—No, he objects to being taxed. He says it is his right not to be taxed.

Lord WATSON:—What is the meaning of the "class of persons?" What is the meaning of the statute?

Sir HORACE DAVEY:—The class of persons is a body of individuals having one and the same characteristic.

Lord WATSON:—A person who is maintaining children of a denominational school desires to send his children to an independent school, his own denomination. He does not get any support for it, and, therefore, he has got to pay double. But is the member of a denominational sect, who neither sends his child to school, and who has no children in the denominational school, to support them?

Mr. MCCARTHY:—He has children.

Sir HORACE DAVEY:—Mr. Barrett, as a matter of fact, has children at the school.

Lord MORRIS:—You may be sure they took good pains to select a person who had.

Sir HORACE DAVEY:—No doubt the Dominion took care to select a good plaintiff. I suppose my learned friend says that the class are the Roman catholics, members of the church of England, members of the presbyterian church, and any other church, if there are any other bodies.

Lord WATSON:—Take a colony of single people—bachelors. What is their position?

Sir HORACE DAVEY:—That is what I venture to put before your lordships—that when you look at it, and analyse it, and see what the right and privilege, if any by law and practice really was, it was the privilege of immunity from any taxation at all for school purposes—that is their being compelled to pay anything for school purposes.

Lord MORRIS:—The act is not of general application. It only applies to that time.

Sir HORACE DAVEY:—The class of persons is any aggregation of individuals. The rights of the class are only the rights of individuals who compose the class. It is not a corporation. The class is only an aggregation of individuals, and you must look at the rights of the individuals in order to ascertain the rights of the class, and the rights, if any, of immunity from taxation for school purposes. I venture to think that Logan's appeal is unanswerable on the principle of Barrett's case. Your lordships may have before you a presbyterian who objects—who has a conscientious objection to support church of England schools which are tainted with the sin of prelacy; and you may have before you a wesleyan—I do not think there are any, but there may be. It may be shocking to a presbyterian to maintain schools in which children are taught the pernicious doctrine connected with prelacy and proatarial doctrines, and I see no end to it. If so, what becomes of the power which undoubtedly exists in the legislature of taxing for school purposes?

Lord MORRIS:—I suppose if the majority had been the other way, and if the schools had all been turned into Roman catholic schools, I suppose the presbyterian element would have had the same cause of complaint. I should say so, certainly. The presbyterians are then in the minority.

Sir HORACE DAVEY:—And therefore the state wisely—I will not say in my opinion, but in my submission—wisely holds an oven hand, and says: "We will maintain schools; we will outroot the curse of ignorance; we will do our duty as a government by maintaing schools without fear, favour or affection to any individual sect and to aid all your children if you like. But if you do not choose to come, then we will leave you as free as you were before the union, to provide your own education in your own way."

That is the theory which I submit is the effect of these acts, and is one which I venture to say will do justice between all parties.

Mr. MCCARTHY:—If I venture to add anything to my learned leader's very full argument on this question, it is on account of its great importance to the province that in point of fact I represent with Sir Horace Davey in this case, for it is a contest between the province on the one part and, as Sir Horace Davey states, also between the Dominion authorities (although they do not appear of course on the record) on the other part; and a contest in which it is not too much to say that the peace and welfare and good government of the province is very largely concerned.

Lord WATSON:—I was following the question I put to Sir Horace Davey. The Manitoba Act appears to confine the right or privilege which is pleaded here to the class of persons who are claiming that right or privilege "with respect to denominational schools." Now, do you conceive it must have been very much accepted as a matter of course in the opinions of some of the judges in the court below that the schools with which they are connected are really denominational schools within the sense of that clause?

Mr. MCCARTHY:—Your lordship means the earlier schools—the schools before 1871?

Lord WATSON:—No, I mean the two schools with which Mr. Barrett and Mr. Logan are respectively connected.

Mr. MCCARTHY:—We entirely repudiate that the schools established by the act of 1890 are denominational schools.

Lord WATSON:—I do not know that that will be disputed, that the right or privilege must be a right or privilege with respect to a denominational school within the meaning of section 22 of the act. What they have to show is that they have a privilege with respect to denominational schools which is affected.

Lord SHAND:—Prior to 1870.

Lord WATSON:—That is a denominational school within the meaning of this act. Do you think the schools with which they are connected are schools denominational in this sense only, that whilst they are established, partly supported by the state and partly by the province, and partly supported by the grant from the government, they are in a certain sense denominational as regards the Dominion? If they are not as regards religious denomination, then they are not denominational.

Mr. MCCARTHY:—All we can say to that is that certainly if the advisory board have attempted to introduce any denominational teaching, it is in direct violation of the object of the statute.

Lord SHAND:—I should expect that the act of 1890 does not introduce anything denominational.

Mr. MCCARTHY:—Non-denominational and non-sectarian.

Lord SHAND:—And several judges have said that these schools are not denominational.

Mr. MCCARTHY:—I do not think any judge holds that these schools are denominational.

Lord WATSON:—The schools of 1871 were in a different position. They were superseded. Then I do not find a word here that any person has set up a denominational school and is complaining of injury to that school.

Mr. MCCARTHY:—No, my lord, there is nothing of the kind, and that is just what I point out.

Lord WATSON:—That to my mind is rather a serious question in this case, and one of the questions we must consider, but of course they may say that that is a present system which prevents their setting up denominational schools.

Mr. McCARTHY:—That appears to me to be perhaps one error, if I may venture to say so, that runs through the judgments—a common error that we are opposing here.

Lord WATSON:—According to my view, the case would be rested very plainly upon the act, if a small community set up a school of their own and paid for it—the only denominational school, such as might have existed before 1870, and then if they could show that this act in any way interfered with that—if they said "Our interest in that school has been injuriously affected."

Lord SHAND:—I think it practically comes to this, that the intermediate legislature has nothing to do with this question.

Mr. McCARTHY:—Except as illustrating different views.

Lord SHAND:—That is an illustration. It really comes to this: Suppose there had been no denominational school between 1870 and now, people might still come forward and say we now insist on our privilege because we had schools before 1870, and we desire to re-establish them, and your legislation enforces that.

Mr. McCARTHY:—I do not think that would interfere with that—150,000 would be tied down by what the people in the first instance said, when there were only 15,000 to 20,000 as the bishop states.

Lord MORRIS:—They are bound by the same fetters by which the 100,000 people got the advantage of becoming a part of the general community. Therefore there is no question of 150,000 or 15,000.

Mr. McCARTHY:—All I meant was that they would not be tied down by what happened in the meantime.

Lord MORRIS:—It would show the action that was taken. I think it most material.

Mr. McCARTHY:—I was just going to mention the difference which your lordships will find in the British North America Act itself, which it is very important, as it seems to me, to get clearly before the board in the discussion. There was in the province of Upper Canada and that part of Canada which is Upper Canada, a system of schools known as separate schools,—a system which had been established after a very long and bitter contest between the Roman catholic section of the population, and a portion, not all, of the protestants, because others belong to the church of England as the bishop's affidavit shows. Their view always was, as in the other provinces of Canada, just as he holds still, that the church of England ought to have separate schools in which its own denominational doctrines would be taught. Then in the province of Quebec, where the Roman catholics were in a large majority, there were what were known as dissentient schools. The difference between the two was this, Ontario, as it is now, after 1863, any number of catholics living in a particular district, in a particular school section, the whole country being divided into school sections, that is, the townships being subdivided into school sections,—any particular number of Roman catholics, I think the minimum was 5, could make application for the establishment of a separate school which would be a Roman catholic school and from the establishment of that separate school all those who annually chose to serve a notice on the official officer, the municipal officer, became exempt from the support of public schools and became liable to the support of the separate school. Therefore there were two school corporations existing wherever those who were entitled to establish separate schools asserted that right. In Lower Canada, on the other hand, the great majority of the schools were Roman catholic and the protestant minority might object.

Lord WATSON:—Were they divided into school districts?

Mr. McCARTHY:—Yes, divided into school districts in the same way.

Lord WATSON:—In fact the whole province was divided.

Mr. McCARTHY:—Yes, but the school law was different. The school law which applied to Upper Canada, did not apply to Lower Canada except in this, that those who dissented, as Mr. Justice Killam shows, claimed the right to withdraw the contribution to the school which was, in point of fact, a denominational school, a school which was a Roman catholic school, whereas in Upper Canada the schools were schools in which nothing more was taught than in the Public Schools Act which is now in force in the province of Manitoba.

Lord SHAND:—Am I right in considering Justice Killam as giving a full account of what you are saying?

Mr. MCCARTHY:—Yes, an accurate account. The right of legislating in respect of schools which was contemplated in the scheme of the British North America Act was conferred on the provinces, but we do not find it in section 91 because owing to this contest about the right of separate schools it had to be limited and was limited by the language which your lordships will find in section 93 of the British North America Act. Now the first section to that preserves the right to denominational schools. I want to draw the distinction between denominational schools and the separate schools. It preserved the right to the denominational school. The second section adopts the law of Upper Canada as to separate schools and applies it to the province of Quebec which was then formed to form a province of Lower Canada. That is, the right of the Roman catholic minority in the province of Upper Canada being greater and more formally established than the right of the protestant minority in Quebec.

Lord WATSON:—Does that give the protestants in Canada the right when their number was a certain amount to demand a separate school which they supported?

Mr. MCCARTHY:—Yes, putting the two provinces of Lower and Upper Canada upon the same basis. Section 2 deals with Upper and Lower Canada. Quebec and Ontario. Section 1, however, dealt with the whole four provinces: New Brunswick, Nova Scotia, as well as Canada, and if rights were in existence in the province of New Brunswick and Nova Scotia, they were preserved by sub-section 1. Then sub-section 3 clearly points out the distinction between the system of separate and dissentient schools and the right or privilege of having denominational schools. "Where in any province a system of separate or dissentient schools exists by law at the union or is thereafter established by the legislature of the province the appeal shall lie," and so on, so that here at the time of confederation we find the four provinces dealt with upon that basis. Upper and Lower Canada were specially provided for. The other provinces had the general enactment of sub-section 1 and sub-section 3 followed by sub-section 4. As a fact, however, neither in Nova Scotia nor in New Brunswick had they any denominational schools; and therefore, so far as these provinces were concerned the limitation upon power as to education did not apply.

Lord SHAND:—Do you mean that those words "any right or privilege with respect to denominational schools" did not cover any right or privilege in New Brunswick or Nova Scotia?

Mr. MCCARTHY:—Because they did not exist.

Lord SHAND:—So that these words "affecting any right or privilege" had no meaning with respect to the two provinces although used with regard to them in the statute?

Lord HANNEN:—And that before Manitoba was introduced under the act?

Mr. MCCARTHY:—By this section, 146, the Dominion was to take in the province of Newfoundland, Prince Edward Island and British Columbia, and also it was assumed Rupert's Land, and the North-west Territories would be acquired and would be ultimately divided into provinces, just as the north-western states have been divided into states. And provision was made for taking in these various provinces, and accordingly they were taken, British Columbia first, if my memory serves me right, in 1871, and Prince Edward Island. There the general words applied no limitation at all. This clause 92 or 93 was made applicable to British Cloumbia, and in 1873 Prince Edward Island was taken in. This clause was also made applicable to British Columbia or Prince Edward Island but in neither of these provinces were there any denominational rights, nor has it been so pretended in respect of schools to be protected or reserved, but the scheme was to apply to the provinces, as they came in, the general terms of the British North America Act, where there were not special circumstances which rendered some other language or some other legislation necessary. Now applying that to the province of Manitoba your lordships have observed that there is the difference by the words "by practice" upon which all this controversy turns. There is another thing to be noted in it, and that is that parliament, it is quite clear, did not propose or intend to say that the province of Manitoba should have separate schools. If they had proposed that, nothing was easier than to say it. It was perfectly well known. The controversy was only 7 years old—the settlement of it rather—it was in 1863. Then in 1871 this act was passed. They have the British North America Act before them. They copy the words from the British North America Act into this particular section—almost the very words of it, but they carefully omit the imposition which we find provided for by sub-section 2 in the constitution which is conferred upon the province of Manitoba. I will point out by and bye that unless, as it seems to me with deference, this board came to the conclusion that separate schools have been established which is, in point of fact, the view taken by two at least of the judges of the supreme court—unless a system of separate schools has been established, that this appeal should succeed. Then another thing is to be noted showing that at this time when the controversy—when the embers of it still existed, at all events—they did not give the province of Manitoba or to the possible minority of that province, whatever it might be, the right which is conferred by sub-section 3, "Where in any province a system of separate or dissentient schools exists by law at the union or is thereafter established by the legislature of the province." Clearly, in Nova Scotia, New Brunswick and these other provinces, if at any time the legislature established a system of separate schools it thereby becomes a vested right which cannot be taken away, but, for some reason or another, the parliament of Canada did not confer that right upon the possible minority whatever the minority was ultimately to be.

Lord WATSON:—I think there is some considerable question. I do not think that is a clear point at all, that section 3 does not apply.

Mr. McCARTHY:—I was treating it for the moment as clear, because all the judges below have taken that view. The assumption, of course, in support of it not applying is that the rest of 92 has been applied in its own language, not of course, my lords, in express terms.

Lord SHAND:—It is very difficult to run the two sections into each other in regard to Manitoba.

LORD WATSON:—If they were to do what they have not done, there might be a question for establishing separate schools.

Mr. McCARTHY:—With great deference, it has always been thought that section 2 was to be in substitution for sub-section 3; and it is contended on the other side that the appeal is more on section 2 than it is on section 3.

Lord SHAND:—I understand in the case where separate schools were introduced the person subscribing to those schools got rid of the Public School Act.

Mr. McCARTHY:—Just so, and then became liable to a separate school rate. He could not, however, free himself from contribution to the educational fund, but he subscribed to one fund instead of another.

Lord WATSON:—Section 3 is really included in section 3 of the Manitoba Act.

Mr. McCARTHY:—Sections 3 and 4 are the identical sections. Your lordships will find that on page 4 of the Record in parallel columns.

Lord WATSON:—Assuming that they had done what they had power to do—the constitution of Manitoba I mean—if they were establishing separate and dissentient schools—a system of separate or dissentient schools, then their acts with regard to these schools might come under section 3.

Mr. McCARTHY:—That is what I was venturing to contend could not be done, because your lordships will see section 3 of the first act, the British North America Act, is re-enacted, or is partially re-enacted in section 2. So I think it is strong evidence that parliament intended to substitute so much of section 2, or to put section 2, which applied differently, in place of section 3.

Lord SHAND:—Am I right in thinking that what you are saying now is directed for the purpose of showing that Manitoba was treated in a separate way on its own basis?

Mr. McCARTHY:—My contention is that you have got to look at the whole scheme of legislation in connection with the constitutional system. You will look to see what was the intention with regard to education of the first four provinces.

We find that carried out with regard to the other two provinces. We find it carried out with variations, which must have full effect given to them in the province of Manitoba. We find that these words have no application. That will be my first argument. That it is not necessary to show there was any privilege. There was not any.

Lord SHAND:—You read the clause in this way: "Nothing in any such law shall prejudicially affect," and so on, but "if in any such case," and I see a number of the judges so put it.

[Adjourned for a short time.]

Mr. McCARTHY:—If I might be permitted perhaps to use the early legislation of Manitoba as illustrating the difference between the separate schools and the denominational schools properly so called, I think the first act of Manitoba, that of 1871, at page 39, might fairly enough be said to be a statute constituting denominational schools, but not separate schools. There the school board is divided into two sections, protestant and catholic. Each section has control over the books, and so on, to be used except in connection with religion and morals, but as to religion and morals they are left to the clergymen of the different denominations.

Lord WATSON:—They seem rather to be state schools, but each school to be a denominational school, leaving that to the determination of the local authorities.

Mr. McCARTHY:—No, pardon me, the act specially defines the sections which are to be catholic and protestant. Then there is not to be a separate school without the consent of the section. It is a denominational school under the act. It says it may "select books, maps and globes to be used in the common schools, due regard being had in such selections to the choice of English books."

Lord WATSON:—It is a state school in this sense, that the legislature provides that it shall be erected and means provided for it.

Sir RICHARD COUCH:—The schools are to be supported by an assessment on the property?

Mr. McCARTHY:—That is only if they pleased. That was not compulsory in the original act of 1871.

Sir RICHARD COUCH:—They may decide whether they shall do it by assessment or not.

Mr. McCARTHY:—Yes.

Lord WATSON:—It receives state aid?

Mr. McCARTHY:—Yes, and that was the main support. Whether they should have any additional support or not depended on the trustees of the different sections.

Lord WATSON:—It was really a denominational state school?

Mr. McCARTHY:—Yes, "But the authority hereby given is not to extend to the selection of books having reference to religion or morals, the selection of such books being regulated by a subsequent clause of this act." The subsequent clause of the act which regulates that says this—section 12:—"It shall not prescribe such of the books to be used in the schools of the section as have reference to religion or morals"—it is evidently a misprint of "shall." Then we come to the act of 1884. There we get for the first time Manitoba separate schools. It is at page 72. There there is provision made for separate schools. There was the earlier system of 1881, which is state denominational. Then there is the act of 1884 which for the first time introduces the principle of a system of separate schools, and then we have the act of 1890 and 1891 which is now in question.

Lord WATSON:—By a system of separate schools you mean permitting persons of a particular religious denomination within a school district to set up a school?

Mr. McCARTHY:—Yes.

Lord WATSON:—Does it go as far as the other? Were they relieve l of any expense of the burden of supporting?

Mr. McCARTHY:—Yes, adopting the Ontario system.

Lord SHAND:—I do not think Sir Horace referred to the act of 1884.

Lord MORRIS:—What do you say the act of 1884 did? Did it advance on the act of 1881?

Lord WATSON:—It introduced into Manitoba the separate schools of a parish.

Mr. McCarthy:—Perhaps I should say the act of 1881, not of 1884. It is the act of 1881, page 42. The act of 1884 is an amendment of the act of 1881.

Lord Morris:—That provides for a board of two sections, protestant and Roman catholic.

Mr. McCarthy:—That was so from the first. The difference made by the act of 1881 was that it permitted separate schools in the district.

Lord Shand:—Which is the clause which you say introduced what you call separate schools?

Mr. McCarthy:—Your lordships will see the different clauses on that point are 12, at page 44.

Lord Morris:—What do you deduce from this? In none of these acts, up to the act of 1890, do they interfere in any way with the denominational system.

Mr. McCarthy:—That, of course, depends on the construction put upon those words. According to our view, all these acts are *ultra vires*.

Lord Morris:—Did any of them conflict injuriously with what is called the denominational system as contrasted with the non-sectarian system?

Mr. McCarthy:—If Sir Horace Davey's argument is right that the exemption was against all taxation, then of course they did.

Lord Morris:—As contrasting denominational schools with non-sectarian schools, did they in any way cut in upon the denominational schools to their disadvantage?

Mr. McCarthy:—No, I think not. I was only pointing out the difference. It was merely to show the distinction between the denominational schools and the separate schools.

Lord Morris:—The denominational schools could not complain that they were in any way injuriously affected.

Lord Shand:—It seems to me that these acts were really compromises. Parties on both sides arranged them, both protestants and catholics. They look as if it were so. It may not be so. The effect is compromise.

The Attorney-General:—It must not be taken that we assent to that.

Lord Morris:—As I understand, the denominational system existed *de facto* in the year 1870, it is not cut in upon or interfered with until the year 1890. Nothing follows from that except the fact.

Mr. McCarthy:—The first point I desire to make, as I have already stated, is this: Bearing in mind the distinction between denominational schools, a system of separate schools, and the omission in the Manitoba Act to provide for a system of separate schools, I think the conclusion can fairly be drawn that the parliament of Canada did not intend to impose separate schools upon the new province, but left it for the new province to determine for itself as to its system of schools, preserving whatever vested rights there may have been at the time of the union, just as vested rights were preserved in all the other provinces, if any existed.

Lord Morris:—What were the vested rights in practice that were reserved?

Mr. McCarthy:—I am coming to that as my next statement of fact. Now, it is a very reasonable question to ask, as the judges below did ask, what was intended by the word "practice." Why was the change made with regard to the province of Manitoba by the introduction of the word "practice"? We answer in the first place, whatever was intended by the introduction of these words, it was not intended to impose separate schools. We answer, in the second place, that it is not necessary to find any existing condition of affairs to which the words apply. All that was intended, as we submit, was that if there were any existing privileges in this new territory which is to be taken in and constitutes the province of Manitoba, either by law or practice, they should be preserved. Now, the condition of things in the province of Manitoba was this: Part of what was constituted the new province had been formed into a district called the district of Assiniboia, after the re-purchase by the Hudson's Bay Company from Lord Selkirk's heir of the property which had been sold to Lord Selkirk in the early part of the century. In that particular district, I believe, forming 50 miles round the confluence of the rivers—the Red river and the Assiniboia—round what is now the city of Winnipeg, a radius of 50 miles around it—there was a council established, which council from 1834 onwards was in the habit of passing what might be called by-laws—I think they generally term them ordinances—meeting in council, generally annually, I think, once a year for that purpose, and as Sir Horace Davey mentioned, this council was not an elective body, but a body constituted by the Hudson's Bay Company, and had absolute powers of governing the territory conferred on them by the charter. Now it must be remembered that when the imperial act was passed handing over Rupert's Land to Canada, it was specially enacted that all the laws in force should continue to be in force recognizing to some extent those by-laws or ordinances which had been passed. Another portion of what is now the province of Manitoba was beyond the limits of this district of Assiniboia. It had a settlement in it. It is not a very large settlement, but a settlement just beyond the limits of Assiniboia and governed by the general laws which the Hudson's Bay Company enacted from time to time for the regulation of the affairs of Rupert's Land. Now there were laws recognized to some extent by the imperial statute, recognized by the Dominion statutes and recognized afterwards by the Manitoba statute—these laws of the district of Assiniboia. It is quite true there were no laws with regard to schools, but there were laws. Applying therefore this new constitution to the province of Manitoba, as Mr. Justice Bain says—and I adopt his reasoning upon that point—what could be more natural or proper than, in order that Manitoba should stand exactly in the same position as the other provinces with respect to any vested rights there might be as to education, that the word "practice" should be introduced? So that whatever rights or privileges in the other provinces they had by law, being organized provinces where they had for years and years exercised and had a system of laws, should not Manitoba, part of it, having had in some respects an organization also, some of it not being organized except on the Hudson's Bay—what could be more natural or reasonable I say——

Lord WATSON:—The words "or practice" were not introduced with special reference to education, but with reference to the fact that they had a very meagre system.

Mr. MCCARTHY:—They might have had laws with regard to education. They might have had practices in Assiniboia or practices beyond Assiniboia with regard to their system of education which it would be very unfair to deprive them of, more especially as the people there were half-breeds.

Lord MORRIS:—As I understand your opponents, not alone that they might have had, but that they had.

Mr. MCCARTHY:—I utterly deny that they had what you may call a system, while I do not dispute the fact that they had private schools here and there, some of which were in connection with the established church, some church of England, and some of the presbyterian church. There was nothing that can be called a system or in the nature of separate or dissentient schools.

Lord SHAND:—Have you a note of the passage of Mr. Justice Bain?

Mr. MCCARTHY:—Page 75, "The general power of the legislature to make laws in relation to education is subject then to the restriction that nothing in any such law shall prejudicially affect any right or privilege in respect to denominational schools, which any class of persons have by law or practice at the union." This sub-section differs from the 1st sub-section of section 93, in the British North America Act, only by the addition of the words "or practice," and as prior to the union, there were no laws in force in the territory which now forms the province, on the subject of education or schools, denominational or otherwise, the reason of the insertion of the words "or practice" is obvious.

Lord SHAND:—Does he go on to explain what he thinks was thereby introduced?

Mr. MCCARTHY:—Yes, I will refer to Mr. Justice Bain's judgment afterwards. I want in the first place to make the point about the distinction between the denominational and separate schools clear. There were schools and colleges. There was a college in connection with the Roman catholic church at St. Boniface. There was also St. John's college, as we know now from the bishop's affidavit in the parish of St. John's, and there were, I think, four Roman catholic schools altogether at different places. Those were not separate schools but isolated schools, so to speak, the only schools in the particular places, the Roman catholic settlement being in one place and the protestant settlement being in another place, each having Roman catholic schools in connection with the Roman catholic religious faith. So that not to repeat what has been so often said, and so much better said than I can hope to say it, by Sir Horace Davey, there was not a system of schools preserved. There was no system of schools to preserve. The right whatever that right was in connection with these denominational schools was preserved and it may be a right of some value and some use may be made of it, but that is far different from saying, as the judges in the court below and particularly in the supreme court say, that a system of separate schools existed which system of separate schools has been interfered with, as it undoubtedly has been interfered with if it did exist, by the passage of the act of 1890.

Now, perhaps it might be convenient as reference has been made to Mr. Justice Bain's judgment, if I read it, though it does not differ very materially from the judgments which your lordships have already heard. The earlier part of the judgment merely gives the history of the legislation, which I need not take up your lordships' time by reading, and I commence at page 75, line 22:—"The contention of the applicant is," etc. [Reading to the words at page 77 line 10.] "The advisory board is given power to prescribe forms of religious exercises to be used in the schools." I do not think I need trouble you with that. I do not think it will be contended here that these are denominational schools.

The ATTORNEY-GENERAL:—You must not assume that.

Lord SHAND:—I think it is at the basis of the argument of the other side.

Mr. McCARTHY:—Then I will read it. "The advisory board is given power to prescribe," &c. [Reading down to page 77 line 45.] "Controlled by the Roman catholic church and others by various protestant denominations." Then he quotes from a text writer on jurisprudence as to the meaning of the legal right, and he quotes the case which Sir Horace Davey referred to of Fearon *vs.* Mitchell as to the definition given of the right by the chief justice in that case and at line 29 [page 78] he continues:—"Had the words 'right or privilege' stood alone," &c. [Reading to the words at page 80, line 37.] "And expressly provided that the Bible when read in the parish schools by Roman catholic children, should, if required by parents, be the Douay version without note or comment." Perhaps I may just state here with regard to *exparte* Renaud that the facts in relation to it were these: There was a system of public schools called parish schools. They were intended to be and were in fact non-sectarian so far as the law went. But in settlements or districts where the Roman catholic population was in the majority they had been permitted to treat them as denominational schools, not by virtue of any law, but apparently in contravention of the existing law but acquiesced in by the minority in those several districts. The question there was whether the rights which they in that sense exercised were preserved to them not as separate schools, because I think the attorney-general is wrong when he insists that *exparte* Renaud raised the question of separate schools—the question was whether the right was preserved to them as denominational schools under the 1st sub-section of the British North America Act.

The ATTORNEY-GENERAL:—No; I said it might have been argued in that case.

Mr. McCARTHY:—"But the Common Schools Act, 1871, which repealed the Parish Schools Act, omitted this provision, and declared that all schools conducted under its provision should be non-sectarian," &c. (Reading to the words at page 82, line 10.) "The right to have separate schools and the immunity from supporting any but their own schools, the right would have been given in explicit terms." I may just state here that I think that view is strengthened by this consideration, that with regard to the North-west Territories, that is the remaining portion of the Dominion not incorporated into the province, parliament has expressly given to them separate schools—in express terms.

Lord SHAND:—Do you mean by another act?

Mr. McCARTHY:—Another act that has not been referred to, the North-west Act.

Lord SHAND:—Is that since 1871?

Mr. McCARTHY:—Yes, since the Manitoba Act. I forget at the moment the date, but it has given it in express terms.

The Attorney-General:—It is in 1875.

Mr. McCarthy:—"It was well known what agitation and bitter *ill-feeling* the question had caused in Upper Canada," &c. (Reading from page 82, line 10, down to end of Mr. Justice Bain's judgment.)

Lord Watson:—In reading over Mr. Barrett's statement, the statement comes to this, and nothing else: There were schools established under the act of 1871. There was a school board; there was a body of trustees under that act—statutory trustees—one of whom was catholic, the other protestant. That continued. I sent my children to a school where they were taught practical denominational matters, and he says since the act of 1890 came into operation I still send my children to that state school as before. I make no complaint of the teaching, but then he says: "Inasmuch as I am called upon to pay the same rate with all, and that rate is indiscriminately applied to the maintenance within the district in which I live of schools in which denominational teaching to some extent is allowed, I am not getting fair-play, because if you were to take the sum from the catholics within the area of which I am one, you would find it is more than sufficient to pay for all the catholic scholars, and, therefore, part of the sum raised from the catholics goes to subsidize protestant children." I can very well see this. The privilege must be a privilege according to the first sub-section in respect of a denominational school. It is a curious circumstance that under the act of 1890, the very school which he is using, and in respect of which he pleads a privilege as a denominational school, is not a denominational school. It is declared by this act to be a secular school, and he is availing himself of it. I can understand he would be in a different position altogether if he said: "I have an adventure school of my own—a denominational school such as existed before the act, not a state school, not a state regulated school."

Mr McCarthy:—In fairness I think I ought to say what I think Mr. Barrett means, is this: My children were attending the separate school, the Roman catholic school, under the act of 1881. The act of 1890 has been passed, but we take no notice of it. The school goes on just as it did before.

The Attorney-General:—And the same religious instruction? It is so stated in the affidavit.

Mr. McCarthy:—He is going to the old school which existed under the act of 1881.

Lord Watson:—The old denominational school; and we had a privilege there, and you simply take away that privilege.

Lord Shand:—It all comes back to this: I have to pay a share of the general rate. He has got his school, and his child is there just as before, but he says: It is infringing a privilege of mine.

Mr. McCarthy:—The difference is this, that prior to this act a portion of the public grant went to the support of that school.

Lord Watson:—Was the school of 1881 in any sense a denominational school also?

Mr. McCarthy:—It was a separate school—not only denominational but separate.

Lord Morris:—That is *a fortiori*.

Mr. McCarthy:—Yes, I say so.

Lord Morris:—It was controlled by a Roman catholic body, and the atmosphere and surroundings of the education were Roman catholic.

Mr. McCarthy:—Yes, it was a Roman catholic separate school.

Lord Morris:—You could not make it stronger than that.

Mr. McCarthy:—No, I have looked with some curiosity to see on what ground and in what way the appellants or the respondent here supports his contention. The respondent's own contention will be found at page 6 of his case, and he gives the reasons why this appeal should not succeed:—"Because the provisions of the Public School Act, 1890, prejudicially affect the rights and privileges of catholics in the province as they existed by law or practice at the date of the union." That does not advance the argument very much. "Because catholics cannot conscientiously permit their children to attend the public schools as constituted and carried on under the said act." Nor, do I venture to say, does that:—"Because by reason of the compulsory rate levied upon catholic ratepayers in support of the public schools, material impediments are cast in the way both of subscribing and of obtaining subscriptions in support of catholic denominational schools, and of setting up and maintaining the same, and the rights and privileges of catholics in reference thereto are thereby prejudicially affected. Because by the operation of the said act catholics are deprived of the system of catholic denominational schools as they existed at the date of the union, or are prejudicially affected in reference to such system. Because the public schools, as constituted by the said act, are or may be protestant denominational schools, and catholic ratepayers are by the said act compelled to contribute thereto." I pass over the fifth ground until I hear what the learned attorney-general has to say in support of it. So far none of the judges who considered the matter below take that view. The only ground here that is put forward as an argument is the third ground :—"Because by reason of the compulsory rate levied upon catholic ratepayers in support of public schools, material impediments are cast in the way both of subscribing and of obtaining subscriptions in support of catholic denominational schools."

Lord WATSON:—All of these propositions obviously imply that at the date of the union all catholics and other denominations who taught their own children efficiently in a school provided by themselves were exempted from liability to contribute to the education of any other children.

Mr. McCARTHY:—Undoubtedly that is what it comes to.

Lord SHAND:—That is the root of the whole thing.

Mr. McCARTHY:—When you come to analyse the reasoning the way they put it is this: Because we are compelled to contribute towards the support of other schools, therefore we are put in a worse position in supporting our own schools.

Lord WATSON:—That proposition is not expressed in terms, but it makes the foundation of all the reasons.

Lord MORRIS:—If a man had to pay for his dinner whether he ate it or not you would think he was injuriously affected with regard to what he had to pay for his dinner.

Lord HANNEN:—Or if he were called upon to pay for his bed—something totally different.

Lord MORRIS:—That is just as like as possible.

Mr. McCARTHY:—At page 8 of the Record your lordships will see the appellants put it in another way. At line 12 they say :—"At the union Roman catholics had by practice the right to support their own denominational schools," &c. (Reading down to the words) "Used by, and satisfactory to the various denominations of protestants." There is the same argument with regard to the payment of this money put in a different way, and if there was no privilege to be exempt, why it is hard to see how that privilege has been interfered with.

Then Mr. Justice Killam gives the reasoning, as he understands it, at page 34; and he understood the argument presented before him in this way; that the prejudice was first "by establishing in competition with the denominational schools a system of free schools supported by the public funds, and thereby placing the denominational schools at a great disadvantage; and, secondly, by withdrawing from the hands of those who would be desirous of supporting denominational schools, funds which they would otherwise devote to that purpose." The chief justice of Manitoba states the reasoning as he understood it at page 44: "The argument was pressed that, by section 22 of the Manitoba Act, parliament, in view of the controversy over separate schools in Ontario, could only have intended to secure for the Roman catholics of Manitoba the same rights and privileges as to separate schools which were by the British North America Act secured for Ontario and Quebec. I cannot, however, see that parliament intended more than is expressed by the language used." Mr. Justice Bain puts it at page 75, which I read to your lordships a moment ago. He puts the three grounds: "First, the right to separate from the rest of the community; secondly, the right to compete on equal terms with other schools; and, thirdly, immunity from contributing to the support of any other schools than their own." Mr. Justice Dubuc, at page 57, gives the grounds as he understands it. Now, that learned judge's reasoning is this: "If the words 'or practice,' inserted in the Manitoba act were as clear and unambiguous as to admit of but one construction"—and your lordships will find in a moment that the chief justice of the supreme court thinks they are clear and unambiguous and admit of only one construction—"the above rule would have to be applied, and there would be no use for prosecuting the enquiry any further. But such is not the case. They are said to mean that the Roman catholics, while compelled to contribute to the support of public schools, are by said words, allowed to have and maintain their denominational schools as private schools: this is the narrower construction. They are also alleged to secure to catholics the privilege of being exempt from compulsory attendance at public schools; another and more liberal construction is that the denominational schools, existing as a matter of fact at the time of the union were given by these words a legal status, so that they could not afterwards be interfered with by the provincial legislature."

Lord WATSON:—It would be very rash to assert in the face of the divided opinions of the judges of this court that the words were not capable of two constructions. You hardly would venture on that proposition now? There are six judges and five disagreed and there were four other judges on the other side.

The ATTORNEY GENERAL:—Three.

Lord WATSON:—And the question is still quite open which of those ought to be preferred.

Mr. MCCARTHY:—Although this judge seems to think they are open to two constructions, the chief justice think they are perfectly plain and admit of but one construction.

Lord WATSON:—It is always a hazardous thing to say that a clause is incapable of two constructions when a number of learned judges are of opinion that it is not only capable of two but capable of receiving a different construction from the first.

Mr. MCCARTHY:—Then at page 65, this same learned judge, whose judgment is a very long one, puts it in this way: "If the new act does not take from us the right of having our schools, it deprives us of the privilege of subscribing exclusively for our own schools." The learned judge there appears to be speaking on behalf of the minority. At page 69, the same learned judge speaks of the grant: "If the narrower construction of the provision in question is adopted, they will have to tax themselves to support their own schools, the only schools which in conscience they can send their children to, and they will have, besides, to be taxed and to pay for the support of the other schools, schools from which the non-catholics will derive all benefit, and the catholics themselves no benefit whatever. Moreover, the legislative grant, which is the people's money, contributed by catholics as well as by other citizens, will be exclusively devoted to assist the other schools, while the catholics will not get their proportionate share to maintain their own schools. Would not that be most unreasonable?" and so on. Then we have Mr. Justice Patterson's view that the right has been prejudicially affected by the compulsion upon all of contributing to the support of the public schools; and we have Mr. Justice Taschereau and Mr. Justice Fournier for the first time, and I think, logically, holding that there were separate schools before the union, and that this system interferes with the separate schools. None of the judges in the province took that view; nor does the chief justice, but Mr. Justice Taschereau and Mr. Justice Fournier distinctly say that as a fact there were separate schools before, and the separate schools have been interfered with by the passage of this act which is now in question.

Lord MORRIS:—Do they say "separate" or "denominational" schools?

Mr. MCCARTHY:—Separate schools.

Lord MORRIS:—Does anything turn on the use of the word "separate" as distinguished from "denominational"?

Mr. MCCARTHY:—I think, my lord, a very great deal turns on it. I think the greatest distinction is to be drawn with regard to separate and denominational schools.

Lord SHAND:—The separate schools are explained in a sentence, and I understand that is a school that a body was entitled to open as a separate school and then relieve themselves of rates by so doing.

Mr. McCarthy:—Yes. It implies that there was another school from which it was separated; that there was some system from which the minority became separated.

Lord Shand:—With the attendant privilege that they got rid of the rates.

Mr. McCarthy:—With the attendant privilege that they got rid of the rates.

Lord Morris:—If there was a country, province, or place where all the schools were denominational, which was the primary thing from which the other was separated? Which was separated from the other?

Mr. McCarthy:—They were all denominational. There was none separated at all. They were all private schools—there was a school in each locality just as here.

Lord Morris:—They were separate schools in one sense—in the sense that they were separated into different sects.

Lord Watson:—I cannot help thinking that supposing the state or country establishes schools after the act of 1870, and says this: So far as practicable we will divide these into schools of different denominations so as to suit the different denominations, so that each parent shall, so far as is reasonably practicable, have his child taught at a school in the religion which he professes; and the legislature at the same time levy an equal tax, or what is generally considered an equal tax, namely, a tax according to means, on all persons in the state, some of them bachelors, and some of them otherwise—some married and some unmarried and some married and childless; and then these funds are distributed equally by giving a capitation grant to each scholar to help the schools, and the schools are maintained—it would be very difficult to say in that case that the government pecuniarily were dealing unequally with any persons because there they are getting the advantage. There may be a great many persons who are not bound to provide schools; who do not want schools, such as wealthy bachelors, and who, but for the interference of the state, might never contribute to schools, and would not be compelled to do so; and if each denomination had to find its own school, how follows it that it would be better? They are getting, through the intervention of the state, a great deal of money from persons who have no children to teach, and it is an uncommonly difficult thing to say who may be prejudiced. It would be very difficult to say in point of fact whose the pecuniary privilege was. It would come to be very much more strong if it were said:" I cannot stand the schools established, but I will build a school, and, having built the school and taught my own children in it, I am not to be called upon to pay for other schools." I do not see the inequality of the system. I am not at all clear it is made out that there is any inequality. Where you have this system, you have no separate schools of that kind—no independent schools, I mean to say—but simply an attempt—an honest attempt, made by the legislature to give effect as near as possible to the ratio which fluctuates every day.

Mr. McCarthy:—I do not know that I quite follow your lordship's argument.

Lord Watson:—You might have a district in which the catholics were poor and where the protestants were wealthy.

Mr. McCarthy:—That frequently happens.

Lord Watson:—And just the other way you might have a district where the protestants are poor and the catholics wealthy, but all this system assumes that everywhere you require to have a careful calculation, which would fluctuate from year to year, of the number of catholic children taught within the school district and the comparative wealth and assessable means of the protestants on the one hand and the catholics on the other, and to take the ratios existing.

Mr. McCarthy:—In order to carry out the system of denominational schools.

Lord Watson:—Yes.

Lord Shand:—And the argument of the other side is practically that you must do that.

Lord Watson:—It would become practically, to my mind, almost impossible to tell to what extent it ought to be carried.

Mr. McCarthy:—It would be impracticable in the sense that in a new country like Manitoba it would virtually destroy the school system. As an historical fact which I am at liberty to mention, I think, even in the province of Ontario many catholics allow their children to go to public schools in towns, and in country districts they do not.

Lord WATSON:—I do not say that it is the right view, but it is quite possible the court may take the view that in providing a system of that sort the government were providing a system which really did not work perfect justice.

Mr. McCARTHY:—Then to push the argument to its legitimate conclusion, as I think I have a right to do—in point of fact they did do it—normal schools, that is, schools for the education of teachers were established.

Lord MORRIS:—Where?

Mr. McCARTHY:—In Manitoba, and they were also made denominational at first. There are schools now for the deaf and dumb; the same claim would be made that they must be denominational.

Lord MORRIS:—Certainly. I do not think anything follows from that. Of course that would follow.

Mr. McCARTHY:—It reduces it to an absurdity.

Lord MORRIS:—No, because that is "by practice."

Lord SHAND:—What about the schools for reading, writing and arithmetic; must they be taught by catholics?

Mr. McCARTHY:—Yes.

Lord SHAND:—It is the same principle?

Mr. McCARTHY:—It is the same principle.

Lord HANNEN:—Or medical schools, or schools of art.

Mr. McCARTHY:—Yes, or industrial schools.

Lord SHAND:—Take the three R's.

The ATTORNEY-GENERAL:—We say four R's: reading, writing, arithmetic and religion.

Lord SHAND:—Yes, you want a fourth R in addition to reading, writing and arithmetic.

Lord MORRIS:—It may be a very foolish thing for particular religionists to believe in these things, but we must accept them as we find them because a good many observations lead to the inference that it is a very foolish thing but, however, people do believe in foolish things; for instance I think it very foolish of those people of India who will not eat with anybody else, but still you must accept it as a fact generally and not look at what a particular individual may regard it to be.

Mr. McCARTHY:—There is no doubt very great difference of opinion on that subject, and in no place more than in the country from which I come.

Lord MORRIS:—The fact that certain persons in Ontario take exception to it cannot affect the question.

Mr. McCARTHY:—No, I was only saying that of course we have to find out the meaning of the words, and where there was this difference of public opinion—a very strong body of public opinion on the one side opposed to separate schools—denominational schools—and a strong body of public opinion on the other side in favour of them.——

Lord MORRIS:—I am not intolerant: I may not agree with these extreme opinions but still there they are and you must deal with them.

Mr. McCARTHY:—There is one thing which has not been mentioned, and perhaps it is not entitled to very much weight. I mention it with some diffidence and some reluctance.

Lord WATSON:—I cannot make out altogether what Mr. Logan wants.

Mr. McCARTHY:—He wants church of England schools.

Lord WATSON:—He says this: "I have at the present time" (he does not say where they are instructed) "three children of school age, namely, one of the age of 14 years, one of the age of 11 years, and one of the age of 5 years and I claim the right to have my children taught religious exercises in school." Has that been refused? It rather suggests that the children are apparently at one of the schools under the act of 1890. "I claim the right to have my children taught religious exercises in school according to the tenets of the church of England, and I claim that such right was secured to me." Now was it secured to him in that school?

Mr. McCARTHY:—Not in that school, of course.

The ATTORNEY-GENERAL:—I think my friend has stated Mr. Logan's position.

Mr. McCARTHY:—I am just endeavouring to do so in answer to a question.

Lord WATSON:—"I do not approve of the manner in which religious exercises are taught in schools where they are so taught under the provisions of the Public Schools Act, and I claim that the tax for the support of schools, imposed on me by said by-law"—I can find nothing in the act of 1870 to prevent the state establishing such schools in which religion would not be taught.

Mr. McCARTHY:—That is what is contended.

Lord HANNEN:—You repudiate his assistance?

The ATTORNEY-GENERAL:—Yes.

Lord SHAND:—He is sent to give point to your argument as it were.

The ATTORNEY-GENERAL:—Yes.

Mr. McCARTHY:—I do not know why my friend should say so. Here is the bishop's affidavit.

Lord SHAND:—The bishop seems very sincere and determined about it.

Lord WATSON:—He says, "I have a right to keep my children at the school and I have a right for them to be taught in the religious fashion which I approve of." That seems his first complaint. That seems to me to be a very strong thing.

Mr. McCARTHY:—Of course the point he desires to make here is that he has got the same right that Mr. Barrett claims—to have a separate school, and if Mr. Barrett has got a right to his denominational school because it was existing in practice at the time of the union, then why has not Mr. Logan got his right because the church of England schools not only existed, but they were much more numerous at the time of the union, and if so, why have not the presbyterians got it, and why have not the wesleyans got it? In *exparte* Renaud your lordships remember that that point came up, and this board approved. I do not know whether of all, but they approved of the judgment in Renaud's case, in which it was established that this first sub-section was to protect the right of all denominations. I was going to mention this fact. Your lordships will remember that the Hudson's Bay Territory was governed by the laws of England at the time that the charter was granted in 1670. The charter was conferred upon the Hudson's Bay Company in these words —I am reading from a copy of the charter here,—"And the said governor and company shall have full liberty, power and authority to appoint and establish governors and all other officers to govern, &c., &c. [Reading the charter to the words] "According to the laws of this kingdom and to execute justice accordingly." And the laws that prevailed in the Hudson's Bay Territory up to the time of the handing over to Canada were held to be the laws of England at the year 1670. That was distinctly held in the Manitoba courts. Now amongst those laws some of the laws that were in force—I mean technically speaking in force, though perhaps not effectively in force—were the penal laws against catholics, and it may well have been that the legislature desired to protect the people who had been enjoying religious liberty notwithstanding those laws, and to prevent any question being raised in the new province of Manitoba, that they were deprived of their rights by virtue of the statutes against catholics. Some of those statutes did extend to all the Dominion.

Lord MORRIS:—But this section only applies to schools.

Lord SHAND:—To education only.

Lord MORRIS:—To education. All the penal laws were in existence.

Mr. McCARTHY:—Well some of the penal laws were certainly very strong even so far as education went. One prevented children being sent out of this kingdom for the purpose of being educated at Roman catholic convents or schools.

Lord MORRIS:—That is sending them abroad.

Mr. McCARTHY:—Yes.

Lord MORRIS:—But what was there penal about Roman catholic education?

Mr. McCARTHY:—Well I think there were laws that might be said if they had not fallen into disuse—

Lord MORRIS:—I am not saying there were not, but I do not remember them. There were in Ireland.

Lord WATSON:—I think it is quite obvious from the statements of the judges on either side, who took different views of the case, that there was no privilege or right acquired prior to 1870 into or concerning any state system of teaching—nothing whatever. There was a privilege of setting up a school and teaching your own child;

and really the only question seems to me to be this, whether in respect that there was not levied at that time, and no power under which there could be levied, a public rate for public schools or a compulsory rate for private schools—the real question is whether the mere absence of that power, and the mere non-existence of any legal warrant for raising such a tax, constituted an exemption of the privilege which those persons got under the act of 1870. That they got the privilege of educating their own children is not disputed by any one.

Mr. McCarthy:—Of course not.

Lord Watson:—The question is whether that right or privilege carried with it the right or privilege of being exempt from taxation for educational purposes when they had fulfilled their duty in that way. But really and truly there is no question of any right to be taught in any one way or other in a government school. If government accompanied that with such restrictions that they could not lawfully set up a school of their own and teach their own children that would be a different matter.

Mr. McCarthy:—Or if they attached any disadvantage to the fact that they were not taught in the public schools.

Lord Shand:—Or any disability such as Sir Horace Davey put: "You shall not enter a government office unless you have attended some state school."

Mr. McCarthy:—In the state of Massachusetts you have this law, that no child can work in a factory that cannot bring a certificate that he has attended a public school. That is an adjoining state. So that you can give full effect to the words of this statute if it is necessary to do so, which I do not at all concede or admit, by saying that the law would not permit of Roman catholics or any other denomination to contribute and support its own school or set it up and maintain it—you can give full effect to it by holding that the Roman catholics, or any of the children of the different denominations could not be compelled to attend the public school, and, in the way which Lord Shand has just mentioned, that no disability should attach to their non-attendance. Now, that is what we admit. That is what we say gives full effect to the language of the statute.

Now, what is the contention of the other side? What must it go to? They must contend that any school law that interferes with the schools of Roman catholics, episcopalians, presbyterians or methodists, all of them having schools at the time, would be beyond the power of the legislature, and that any attempt to expend the public money——

Lord Watson:—In clause 22 the exemption there is: "Nothing in such clause shall prejudicially affect any right or privilege"—not with respect to denominational education, but "with respect to denominational schools which any class of persons have by law or practice" and so on. Now, what within the meaning of that exception is a "denominational school?"

Mr. McCarthy:—That is a view which I must confess had not occurred to me. We have been treating it all along as if it was "denominational education" and not "denominational schools." It is "denominational schools."

Lord Watson:—In other words, can a school which is by law declared to be a secular school and the assessment for which is made on the footing that it is a secular school, but in which also denominational teaching is allowed after hours, be a denominational school? Can they come into that school, share its advantages, and say it is a denominational school within the meaning of section 22?

Lord Shand:—Upon that section allow me to say that in the claim here made—in the application for this remedy the claimant says: "By the law impeached the Roman catholics are compelled to bear a ratable share of the charge for the schools thereunder established, schools which are not denominational." Therefore he himself says in his complaint that the schools of 1890 are not denominational. He has expressly so said in article 11.

Lord Watson:—Mr. Barrett does not say that he has built or intends to set up a denominational school in his own right, but he says they are not entitled to charge me for the teaching which my children get there. Then he requires to split it up.

Lord Shand:—It is at page 8 of the Record.

The Attorney-General:—I am obliged to your lordship. It is the factum on appeal.

Sir RICHARD COUCH :—That is the factum on appeal; it is not the application for the remedy.

Lord SHAND :—I thought it was the application.

The ATTORNEY-GENERAL :—It is put forward on his behalf.

Lord WATSON :—What it rather points to, to my mind, is this, that when you are taking that view of the act it really comes to this, as long as you choose to come in and educate your children at these state schools you must pay as the state provides, but you may go outside the state schools and set up any school you like and, if it turns out in doing so you are availing yourself of a privilege given, that privilege is still open to you, and nobody disputes it. You must then try whether part of your privilege consists in ceasing to be liable to payment when you have set up your own schools. You are coming into the state schools upon those terms.

Mr. MCCARTHY :—I do not think I can usefully occupy any more of your lordships' time. I think our case has been fully presented. My learned friend who is with me suggests I should say a word on the question which was discussed very fully yesterday, and that is as to the right of appeal to a court of law.

Lord WATSON :—We do not require to hear you on that point. We are quite satisfied.

The ATTORNEY-GENERAL :—Mr. McCarthy contends there is no liability.

Lord WATSON :—You are going to contend that there is none?

Mr. MCCARTHY :—Yes, my lord.

Lord SHAND :—After the intimation you have heard it will not be a very hopeful argument, to say the least of it.

Lord WATSON :—You cannot be denied if you come before us in that way.

Mr. MCCARTHY :—I would only say this on the point. Your lordship will see the power to legislate with respect to education is exclusively given to the province subject and according to the following provisions. That is, the exclusive right of dealing with education is subject only to these provisions: the first provision is the limitation that we have been dealing with in the first clause; and the second provision is an appeal to the governor; and the third provision is as to the manner of working out that appeal. Now the ordinary rule is that when a special matter of this kind—a particular remedy is pointed out in the statute which confers the right, of course that special remedy must be followed. Now when you look at the curious words of the statute, that the exclusive right to legislate as to education is given to the province, with the right in the only case that I know of, to the parliament of Canada to interfere with the provincial power—this is the only case in the British North America Act——

Lord WATSON :—Then, on the other hand, we have this very plausible suggestion—it made a very great impression on my mind at the time—that that means an appeal in ordinary course. It does not contemplate an excess of jurisdiction either in the appeal court or in the other court.

Mr. MCCARTHY :—I will not waste your lordships' time by repeating what Sir Horace Davey said on the subject.

Lord WATSON :—That is an appeal on the merits.

Lord SHAND :—Besides Sir Horace Davey said you were most anxious to get a decision of this board.

Mr. MCCARTHY :—Yes we are anxious to get a decision on the merits.

The ATTORNEY-GENERAL :—My lords, the discussion that this case has undergone in the most fair arguments of my friends Sir Horace Davey and Mr. McCarthy will shorten my labours in the matter. I have also, as I indicated to your lordships yesterday, the great advantage of the assistance of my learned friend Mr. Blake, and therefore, I shall to a certain extent, ask him to inform your lordships more fully, if it be necessary, upon any matters which touch upon the historical aspect of the case, or any question involving local knowledge with respect to facts in Canada. But, my lords, I should like to state at once, in the shape of perhaps a somewhat formal propositition, that for which we contend. In the first place, my lords, a distinction has been attempted to be drawn by my friend Mr. McCarthy between separate schools and denominational schools. We shall humbly submit to your lordships that there is no such distinction to be drawn, that a Roman catholic school was a separate school and that a protestant school was a separate school; and that when you come to look at what was the existing practice; when you come to consider the facts in the light of the knowledge of the learned judges, they have recognized that speaking of the year 1870 there was one dividing line and that was between the Roman catholics of the province and the protestants of the province. Whether there were, as it is quite probable there were, some minor denominations which would enter into one or the other division, and which might be more correctly enumerated by some separate distinguishing name, for the purposes of this legislation, that was the distinction which was intended to be drawn. Then, my lords, we shall submit to you that the right and privilege which at that time existed, was the right and privilege of each section to maintain by its own contributions its own schools and not to be taxed directly—I will deal with the question of the indirect grant later on—to contribute to schools which it was not to their interest to support, to which they could not conscientiously send their children, and which were from their constitution opposed to everything which to Roman catholics, on the one side, was regarded as most sacred, and had the question been raised as to contribution by protestants to Roman catholic schools in those times, there would have been an equally strong feeling on the part of the protestants that they ought not to be called upon to contribute to Roman catholic schools. Further, my lords, we shall humbly submit that, speaking simply as a proposition of law, the intermediate statutes between 1870 and 1890, as far as the question of construction is concerned, may be disregarded. I should not argue before your lordships that, assuming that you were satisfied that the act of 1890 is *intra vires*, I could possibly contend that a different construction was to be put upon the language of the act of 1870, because there had been intermediate legislation with respect to separate or denominational schools; but, my lords, we shall venture to submit that the importance of what has occured during the twenty years is this, that it enables your lordships to see that the allegations of fact as to what was the existing state of things at the time of the passing of the Manitoba Union Act are true and are not exaggerated. We shall submit that the legislation from 1871 down to 1890 carried into effect, what were the existing rights and privileges at that time, namely, putting it broadly, that the protestants maintained protestant schools, that the Roman catholics contributed to and maintained the Roman catholic schools. The system of contribution was different I admit, it was by rating or assessment or it was by some other kind of contribution recognized by the statute,—that was merely a question of machinery—but under all circumstances during that time the right of the Roman catholics to contribute to Roman catholic schools and the rights of the protestants to contribute to protestant schools—the obligation of the Roman catholics to contribute only to Roman catholic schools, and the obligation of the protestants to contribute only to protestant schools was recognized and maintained.

Lord WATSON:—I think that you may assume, as I think all the judges below have assumed, that prior to 1870 it was the inseparable and universal practice in the district which is now called Manitoba, that each denomination provided and supported its own schools without any obligation to contribute anything towards the support of any other denominational schools.

Lord SHAND:—And not only is that so in the judges' opinions but I think it is universally accepted. Both parties are now agreed about it, as I understand. I do not think there is any difference about it.

The ATTORNEY-GENERAL:—I should not question, if I could quote it from recollection accurately, the brief summary of the rights and privileges made by one of your lordships, Lord Hannen, this morning as to what he, for the moment, indicated may be the rights and privileges which the several parties had, but following out what I have said with regard to these 19 or 20 years, I will ask your lordships kindly to remember this, that I say during all that time, notwithstanding it may be that the population had increased as my friend Mr. McCarthy said, who I am sure will assist me on all questions of fact—he always does most loyally and fairly—notwithstanding that the population has increased from 15,000 to 150,000, and notwithstanding that denominations may have been growing and swelling in importance within the protestant section, and for aught I know within the Roman catholic sec tion, yet, during the whole of that time, the line of clevage or division has been the same. It has been Roman catholic on one side, and protestant on the other.

Now, the next point that I shall humbly submit to your lordships, when I come to examine the act of 1890 is that in effect the act of 1890 does establish separate schools to which the Roman catholics are compelled to contribute, and in which schools there is either religious teaching or the absence of religious teaching—I care not which you call it, either religious teaching or the absence of religious teaching —which was wholly inconsistent with the schools which were being supported by the Roman catholics prior to the year 1890.

Lord HANNEN:—Where no religion is taught, to what denomination is it attached?

The ATTORNEY-GENERAL:—I knew what was in your lordship's mind. If your lordship will forgive me, I can promise you not to overlook that matter; because, my lord, I humbly submit that too much has been made of what I may call the technical meaning of the word "denominational," and that it has been forgotten to look at the history of these schools in the year 1870. I shall humbly submit to your lordships that most unquestionably for this purpose "denomination" does mean Roman catholic on the one side and protestant on the other, and I shall contend before your lordships that the distinction attempted to be drawn by my friend Mr. McCarthy between denominational and separate is ill founded, and that it is essential to the success of the argument of the appellant.

Lord WATSON:—Does "denomination" refer at all to a race or rank or nationality? I thought it referred to the common religion.

The ATTORNEY-GENERAL:—I should like to answer Lord Hannen, as he would know, perfectly fully. I would suggest, my lord, that we have got to consider what were the schools which, from a religious point of view, the protestants were satisfied with, and what were the schools, which, from a religious point of view, the Roman catholics were satisfied with. I say it is absolutely and entirely foreign to this question to consider whether within the protestants there were wesleyans, baptists, congregationalists and other sects of importance.

Lord WATSON:—Laying aside race altogether, if one set of schools were such that the protestants would send their children to them, and the Roman catholics would not, and the other such that the Roman catholics would send their children and the protestants would not, I should say those were denominational schools.

The ATTORNEY-GENERAL:—It is only my argument now, that, as I shall submit, when you look either at the history or at the legislation, that is what is meant by denominational in the British North America Act of 1867 and in the Manitoba Act of 1870; and I know Lord Hannen will follow what I have in my mind. What I am endeavouring to submit respectfully to your lordships is this, that if you come and endeavour to argue this case by construing the word "denominational" as though you were dividing the protestant sects up into a number of grades, you will lose sight entirely of what was the reason and object of the act.

Lord WATSON:—Experience may be different in America or in Canada, but I know of no school which can be called purely sectarian which any denominationalist would approve of. Denominationalists would not be satisfied, as far as my experience goes, with schools in which there was no religious teaching.

The ATTORNEY-GENERAL:—I am anxious to confine my mind at present to the particular points which I had hoped to enumerate before your lordships to-day. I am not suggesting that there is not difficulty in my way, and I am not suggesting that we may not have to consider whether denominational has not got the meaning that Lord Hannen indicated it might have in certain places.

Lord HANNEN:—Does your argument amount to this, that no non-sectarian school is denominational?

The ATTORNEY-GENERAL:—I should suggest that these sectarian schools constituted under the act are clearly denominational as compared with the Roman catholic schools. My lord, a Roman catholic school is denominational in one sense.

Lord HANNEN:—Of course it is.

The ATTORNEY-GENERAL:—Therefore, your lordship will forgive me for a moment. I merely wanted to say that I was not overlooking the point.

Lord HANNEN:—But everything that is not Roman catholic is not necessarily denominational.

The ATTORNEY-GENERAL:—Certainly not. I perfectly agree. I would like to put a case which, it seems to me—I do not know that I may not get into difficulties —would be clear: for instance, take a school of cookery. I do not know, I am sure, whether there are any rules of the Roman catholic church that a school of cookery would have to be preceded by any grace or religious ceremony before the lesson was commenced, but I will accept any form of education in which it would be admitted by all persons religious principles would not be supposed of necessity to be introduced.

Lord SHAND:—The archbishop's affidavit goes the length of saying that whatever the branch of education is, it must be taught by a Roman catholic, and a Roman catholic thoroughly imbued with Roman catholic principles.

The ATTORNEY-GENERAL:—Let me explain that when I come to it; but I only desire your lordships to follow my argument when I suggest that I am not here to say for a moment that it is to be pressed to the length that everything must be imbued with Roman catholicism. But I do say this, that the strength of our argument depends upon an examination of what this statute of 1890 is; and I say that upon the facts, whether you regard the statute itself, or whether you regard the affidavits which speak of the schools referred to in the statutes, they are denominational—and I accept the word at once—in the sense that they are of that class which was intended to be separated from the Roman catholics in the year 1870.

My lords, will your lordships allow me to make one or two very brief references upon this question of separate schools and denominational? I think, but I speak with great deference in the presence of my learned friends from Canada, that there is a mistake with reference to the use of the word. I will ask your lordships to be kind enough to refer to page 109, where Mr. Justice Taschereau cites the French statute Your lordships will remember that the law is equally law in both French and in English. I believe the original document is written in French.

Mr. McCARTHY:—No.

The ATTORNEY-GENERAL:—The, law, at all events, is written in French as well as in English. Mr. Justice Taschereau at any rate says so, and I will take it from him.

LORD WATSON:—Although it does not apply strictly, I think you may apply the rule which is formulated by the Quebec code; you must take that construction which appears to be most in conformity with the spirit of the legislation.

The ATTORNEY-GENERAL:—That is the principle of my argument. It is because I humbly submit the distinction, which my friend Mr. McCarthy told your lordships was of great importance, between denominational and separate, is inconsistent with the general scope of the legislation, that I have called your lordships' attention to this.

LORD SHAND:—I may have misunderstood him, but I thought he used that more historically than anything else—the moment you have a separate school undoubtedly it then is a class school, the moment you have a separate school it is a denominational school.

The ATTORNEY GENERAL:—I am not comparing separate with class, but separate with denominational.

Lord SHAND:—The moment you get what he called a separate school, it is undoubtedly denominational.

The ATTORNEY-GENERAL:—Nobody knows better than your lordship that I do not desire to press anything Mr. McCarthy said, unduly against him. I meant to say that we considered that undue stress has been laid on the word "denomination."

Lord MORRIS:—Mr. McCarthy suggested that Mr. Justice Taschereau rather fell into a mistake by using "separate" as a synonymous term with "denominational."

The ATTORNEY-GENERAL:—Yes. Of course we all understand, standing here, we are only endeavouring to answer one another, but when the question was put by one of your lordships to my friend, Mr. McCarthy, whether he considered it important, I think he said it was of very great importance. Will your lordships look at page 109, where the French language is given: "Rien dans ces lois ne pourra préjudicier à aucun droit ou privilége conferé, lors de l'union, par la loi ou par la coutume." It is a little curious to notice that that is translated "practice." I am not sure that "custom" would not be rather stronger, but it makes no difference—"à aucune classe particulière de personnes dans la province, relativement aux écoles séparées,"—then the parenthetical translation put, I have no doubt, by Mr. Justice Taschereau is "denominational schools."

Lord WATSON:—It is quite possible that the word "séparées" may have had a special meaning, or technical meaning, in Ontario and Quebec. That is quite possible, because even in the act of 1867, the words separate or dissentient are used there as indicating, in the provinces to which the act then applied, at all events, two varieties of denominational schools.

The ATTORNEY-GENERAL:—"Separate" in one province and "dissentient" in the other.

Lord WATSON:—But they both refer back to the word "denomination." They are special provisions with regard to special classes or denominations.

The ATTORNEY-GENERAL:—I hope not to fall, if it be an error, into the same error, as I humbly submit it is, by attaching undue importance to the word "séparée" or separate, but I do say that when you start with the history and look at the legislation of 1870 and look at the subsequent legislation, it is not correct to allege that denominational means sectarian in the sense of breaking up the protestants into a number of different sects. On the other hand, it is correct to say that the people intended to be protected were the protestant religionists on the one side and the Roman catholic religionists on the other.

Now, my lords, I think a little error was made, quite unintentionally, by one of your lordships with regard to Mr. Barrett's affidavit, and I should like to call your lordships' attention to what Mr. Barrett complains of, because I now desire to submit to your lordships what is the strength of our position from the Roman catholic point of view. We say that the schools under the act of 1890—call them non-sectarian or sectarian, or call them denominational or undenominational—call them what you like—public schools—are schools to which, according to their consciences, Roman catholics cannot send their children, and we submit that to force Roman catholics, in the event of necessity, namely, there being no other school, either to leave their children in ignorance, or to send them to these schools, and at the same time to force them to contribute to these schools in places where they are minded to establish the Roman catholic schools does prejudicially affect rights and privileges as they existed. I must not be drawn to-day into arguing before your lordships what "right or privilege" means, or what "prejudicially affected" means. I am going to protest against the doctrine that it is to be construed by some technical meaning like *privilegium*. I shall submit presently that the reference to the word "practice" indicates clearly that that is not the way in which the word "privilege" has been used, but in a far wider sense. But, my lords, I am about to point out, when I come to argue on the statute of 1890, that the schools which are therein by law established are schools to which no conscientious Roman catholic, whose rights and privileges are to be respected, can send his children, or to which he would willingly be called upon to subscribe, and it is, my lords, because I think that it was a little too readily assumed on the statement by my learned friend that you must regard these schools as absolutely unsectarian—as absolutely undenominational, because they are called so in the statute—that an error has crept in upon which, at any rate, we are entitled to address some argument. I shall point out that on the admitted facts the schools are acceptable to the protestants. I entirely deny that Mr. Logan is a *bona fide* objector—entirely. He is here to assist and sent here by the provincial government to assist them.

Lord HANNEN:—You do not suggest that the bishop is not sincere.

The ATTORNEY-GENERAL:—I say the bishop's affidavit is very much in my favour. I know I am entitled to refer to it, and I shall refer to it.

Lord MORRIS:—By his affidavit he does not allege that there was any doctrine objectionable to the church of England: he only says that a great many bishops and persons do not like it.

The ATTORNEY-GENERAL:—He says more. He says that the protestants are satisfied with these schools. Would your lordships kindly turn to page 12 and just see what Mr. Barrett really says. I think Lord Shand or Lord Watson referred to it. "I am a ratepayer and resident of the city of Winnipeg, and have resided in the said city continuously for the past five years, and am a member of the Roman catholic church. On and prior to the 30th April last, a school district (having some years before been established) existed in the city of Winnipeg, and such school district was under the direction and management of the corporation, known as the school trustees for the catholic school district for Winnipeg no. 1 in the province of Manitoba. The said corporation has established and in operation a number of schools in Winnipeg under the provisions of the various provincial statutes relating to schools, to one of which, namely, St. Mary's school, situate in Hargrave street, I have for three years past sent my children for instruction, which children are aged respectively ten, eight and five years. That the said St. Mary's school is still in existence, and the same teaching and religious exercises are continued as before the passing of the said act, and my children still attend said school."

Lord WATSON:—In point of fact, St. Mary's school had become a school under the provisions of the act of 1871, the act of 1870 having come to an end.

The ATTORNEY-GENERAL:—Your lordships will see how that is when I look at the statute. It is very important, because my friend, not unnaturally, called your lordships' attention to the fact that he was continuing to send his children to schools where there was no religious instruction at all. That is not so.

Lord WATSON:—He said the very reverse. I referred to that.

Lord SHAND:—I suppose there is no doubt that that is a denominational school in every sense of the word.

The ATTORNEY-GENERAL:—I have said so.

Lord MORRIS:—Is not that his complaint, that the school which was paid for up to the year 1890, being a denominational one, he still continues sending his children there, but it is now struck off? That is the point.

The ATTORNEY-GENERAL:—May I point out, though I am going into another matter now, that that school would have been paid for and contributed to out of catholic contributions, and yet it will become a public school and non-sectarian under the act of 1890. I will call your lordships' attention to the actual language of the statute which deals with that point; but it is very important that I should point out that he distinctly confirms the affidavit of the archbishop so far as he is concerned as a parent of the child. He says he has read it, and so far as the same lies within his personal knowledge, it is true, and as to the rest he believes it to be. Then in paragraph 13, he says that "the effect of the by-laws is that one rate is levied upon all protestant and Roman catholic ratepayers in order to raise the amount mentioned in the said exhibits "C" and "D," and the result to individual ratepayers is, that each protestant will have to pay less than if he were assessed for protestant schools alone, and each Roman catholic will have to pay more than if he were assessed for Roman catholic schools alone." I am not on the question of *quantum*: I do not propose to argue this case on that, but I am about to point out, when I come to deal with the act of 1890, that the position is this, that to a school which we are entitled to say is not Roman catholic, as it existed at the date of the passing of the act of 1890, the Roman catholics are called upon to contribute and that those are schools at which conscientiously they cannot allow their children to attend.

[Adjourned to to-morrow at 10.30.]

IN THE JUDICIAL COMMITTEE OF THE PRIVY COUNCIL.

COUNCIL CHAMBERS, WHITEHALL, Thursday, 14th July, 1892.

Present:

The Rt. Hon. Lord Watson,	The Rt. Hon. Lord Hannen,
The Rt. Hon. Lord Macnaghten,	The Rt. Hon. Lord Shand,
The Rt. Hon. Lord Morris,	The Rt. Hon. Sir Richard Couch.

THE CITY OF WINNIPEG

vs.

BARRETT,

and

THE CITY OF WINNIPEG

vs.

LOGAN.

[Transcript of the shorthand notes of Messrs. Marten & Meredith, 13 New Inn, Strand, W.C.]

Counsel for the appellants:—Sir Horace Davey, Q.C., Mr. McCarthy, Q.C., and the Hon. Mr. Martin.

Counsel for the respondent Barrett:—The Attorney-General (Sir Richard Webster, Q.C., M.P.), Mr. Blake, Q.C., Mr. J. S. Ewart, Q.C., and Mr. Gore.

Counsel for the respondent Logan:—Mr. A. J. Ram.

Third Day.

The ATTORNEY-GENERAL:—When your lordships adjourned yesterday I had discussed what was the condition of matters at the time of the union of Manitoba with Canada. In our submission to your lordships, had this act of 1890 been passed in the year 1871 it would have been extremely difficult for anyone to contend that it did not interfere with rights or privileges with respect to denominational schools which some class of persons had by law or practice in the province at the union. It is because that is our main contention before your lordships that I postpone altogether for the present any consideration of what had happened between the year 1870 and the year 1890. It is well that I should very briefly recall your lordships' attention to the affidavit of the archbishop with regard to this matter at page 14 because I cannot quite accept the view presented by my learned friends as to what was the fair effect of the affidavit and of the other evidence as to the state of the facts. If your lordships will look at the top of page 14 of the record he says: prior to the passing of the act—that is the act of 1870—"there existed in the territory now constituting the province of Manitoba a number of effective schools for children," &c. [Reading to the words at line 14]. "The members of the Roman catholic church supported the schools of their own church for the benefit of Roman catholic children, and were not under obligation to, and did not contribute to the support of any other schools." My lords, I do not know that my learned friend will dispute it, but I am going to contend that the exemption from subscription to the schools of protestant denominations was a privilege of the class of persons called Roman catholics. "In the matter of education, therefore, during the period referred to, Roman catholics were as a matter of custom and practice separate from the rest of the community, and their schools were all conducted according to the distinctive views and beliefs of Roman catholics as herein set forth." I venture to read this again and to press it upon your lordships' attention once more. I know of course that it was very fairly read two days ago by my learned friend, but at the same time I venture to press it again because it has rather been suggested that there was practically no educational system at all in Manitoba prior to this time, and it has been rather put by my learned friends as though it was a school here and a school there. I submit that upon the facts which must have been in the minds of those who framed the act of 1870, it is clear that the Roman catholics were arranging their own educational establishments—their own schools, and the protestant denominations were doing the same. Then I ask your lordships to consider what must be a matter of very great importance, and that is the allegation in paragraph 7:—"Roman catholic schools have always formed an integral part of the work of the Roman catholic church," &c. [Reading to the words at line 30.] "In education the Roman catholic church attaches very great importance to the spiritual culture of the child, and regards all education unaccompanied by instruction in its religious aspects as positively"—I think it must be "possibly"—"detrimental and not beneficial to the children."

Lord SHAND:—It is "possibly" in the affidavit in the other case.

Lord MORRIS:—One must judge of what he was likely to swear. He would not swear that it was "positively."

The ATTORNEY-GENERAL:—"With this regard the church requires that all teachers shall not only be members of the church, but shall be thoroughly imbued with its principles and faith; shall recognize its spiritual authority, and conform to its directions. It also requires that such books be used in school, with regard to certain subjects as shall combine religious instruction with those subjects, and this applies peculiarly to all history and philosophy."

Lord MACNAGHTEN:—I suppose that is true of all denominations, is it not?

The ATTORNEY-GENERAL:—At any rate, it is sufficient for my purpose to say that it is true of the Roman Catholics for this purpose, because we are considering what was the constitution of the denominational schools which the Roman catholics were entitled, as we submit, to have protected at the time that the act introducing Manitoba into the union was passed.

Lord SHAND:—I think the last two paragraphs of section 7 are peculiar to the Roman catholics.

The ATTORNEY-GENERAL:—Probably; I ought, perhaps, to read paragraph 8: "The church regards the schools," &c. [Reads paragraph 8.] My learned friend Sir Horace Davey has used that passage in the affidavit as an admission that there was no interference with any right or privilege. I shall have to argue on the meaning of the words "prejudicially affected" in a very few moments. I humbly submit it is not right to assume that, because his grace the archbishop has said that they will revert to the system, that therefore there is no prejudicial affection in regard to their rights and privileges.

Lord MACNAGHTEN:—I do not see what authority he has to speak on behalf of protestants. Of course, everything he says is worthy attention.

The ATTORNEY-GENERAL:—I am going to point out that the protestants say it for themselves.

Lord MACNAGHTEN:—It has not the same effect.

The ATTORNEY-GENERAL:—But, on the other hand, when the statement is made and not contradicted, and this is an affidavit in the proceedings, I submit I am entitled to call attention to it.

Lord MACNAGHTEN:—He speaks with a different weight of authority when he is speaking of his own church.

The ATTORNEY-GENERAL:—I accept what your lordship says as a criticism on it.

Lord MACNAGHTEN:—It does not seem to be accurate with regard to protestants.

The ATTORNEY-GENERAL:—I propose to point out that the protestant bishop does not object to the schools in so far as they go. He would like something more. The point I am desirous of making here is that the statement that the archbishop makes—of course your lordships may say it is not to be regarded——

Lord MACNAGHTEN:—I do not say it is not to be regarded, but I say it has not the same weight.

The ATTORNEY-GENERAL:—In that view I think I ought to submit to your lordship that this allegation is not going one bit too far.

Lord MORRIS:—There was an affidavit made by Mr. Bryce.

The ATTORNEY-GENERAL:—I am going to call attention to it in a moment. "Such schools are in fact similar in all respects to the schools maintained by the protestants under the legislation in force immediately prior to the passing of the said act." We have a form of prayers used here both before and after the passing of the act of 1890, and it is the fact that the prayers which are in use in the schools under the act of 1890 are identical with those which were in use in the protestant schools prior to the act of 1890.

Lord HANNEN:—The question is what were in use in 1870? What was done between 1870 and 1890 is not important.

The ATTORNEY-GENERAL:—I was not applying my mind to that for the moment. I was meeting the observation of Lord Macnaghten's that the statement that the protestants were willing that their children should attend these schools might not be entitled to weight. That is the whole point of my observation. It has no reference to a comparison between the period of 1870 and the period of 1890. I was dealing with the allegation made that the affidavit was not in this respect entitled to so much respect as in other parts.

Lord SHAND:—The prayer was adopted on the 21st May, 1890, by the advisory board. This affidavit is made in October, 1890, and there is no objection taken to the prayer in any way.

The ATTORNEY-GENERAL:—I have the forms here. I have not made my meaning clear. I am not saying that he raised any objection to the prayer. I am simply on the point that the protestant members are satisfied with the schools as they stand at present.

Lord SHAND:—I think it would be very difficult to make that out if you take the other affidavit out of Bishop Machray.

The ATTORNEY-GENERAL:—I have a great difficulty in dealing with more than one thing at a time. I was for the moment dealing with this allegation.

Lord SHAND:—My observation bears upon that very matter.

The ATTORNEY-GENERAL:—Certainly.

Lord WATSON:—Is the act of 1890 except in that one matter of imposing an equal assessment and thereby, it is said, creating a distinction doing away with the privileges possessed before 1890—is the act not capable of being worked so as not to injure any person?

The ATTORNEY-GENERAL:—No, with great deference, I submit not.

Lord WATSON:—The complainant in this case, the objector Mr. Barrett, states a much smaller case against the act.

The ATTORNEY-GENERAL:—He distinctly refers to this affidavit of the archbishop and confirms it. I mentioned that yesterday. I propose to call your lordships' attention to the act of 1890. Your lordships will remember he is sending his children, at the time this application is made, to a school which is conducted as a catholic school had been conducted, and not as a protestant school, but at present I only desire before passing on to point out to your lordships the allegation is that the schools are in fact similar in all respects to the schools maintained by the protestants under the legislation in force immediately prior to the passing of the act.

Lord WATSON:—Am I to assume that he was dissatisfied with the teaching before the act?

The ATTORNEY-GENERAL:—No, certainly not. I shall have to show your lordship that that school, if continued, will not be entitled to have its share of the grant; that under the act of 1890 it would cease to be a public school, and to have its share of taxation; and in fact will not be a public free school within the terms of the act of 1890.

Lord MORRIS:—By the act of 1890 it has been.

The ATTORNEY-GENERAL:—He is speaking of a time at which the act has not come into force. I will not overlook that, because I have noted the sections of the act of 1890 to which your lordships' attention has not yet been called, which, we venture to think, interfere, and prejudicially affect the rights and privileges to a much greater extent than the mere question only of being bound to contribute, though that in itself is extremely important. I would ask your lordships' permission to call attention to the passage I was reading at the top of page 15:—"Such schools are in fact similar in all respects to the schools maintained by the protestants under the legislation in force immediately prior to the passing of the said act. The main and fundamental difference between protestants and catholics with reference to education is that while many protestants would like education to be of a more distinctly religious character than that provided for by the said act, yet they are content with that which is so provided, and have no conscientious scruples against such a system."

Lord SHAND:—Do you submit that to be the fact?

The ATTORNEY-GENERAL:—I do.

Lord SHAND:—That protestants are quite content with this system?

The ATTORNEY-GENERAL:—No, I did not say "quite content."

Lord SHAND:—"Content." The distinction between "quite content" and "content" is small.

The ATTORNEY-GENERAL:—My reason for only asking your lordships to let me put it in my own way is this: that I do understand the affidavits to indicate that many protestants are quite content that their children should go to this school intending to provide them with a religious education elsewhere, whereas the Roman catholics say that a school so conducted is not a school to which they can conscientiously send their children.

Lord WATSON:—One would suppose that that must be the case to some extent, or else the act of 1890 would not have been passed.

Lord MORRIS:—Why is it necessary for the archbishop to go into the question of what protestants think? It is enough for you what the catholics think.

The ATTORNEY-GENERAL:—It is quite enough for me that when the point has been put by some of your lordships that they are not asked to subscribe, or to make any contribution, to any school which is in any sense denominational. I think upon the affidavits the facts show that the public schools which have been established, and which are paid for by catholics, are schools which are in the main, I do not say entirely, but in the main, satisfactory to the protestant denominations; and therefore they do directly prejudice and interfere with the schools which are satisfactory to the Roman catholic denominations.

Lord MORRIS:—I do not follow how that takes the argument farther than the fact that the Roman catholics cannot go there. If they cannot attend these schools, these schools are as if they never existed, as far as they are concerned.

Lord SHAND:—What Bishop Machray says on this very subject is:—"With the great majority of the bishops and clergy of the church of England, I believe that the education of the young is incomplete, and may even be hurtful if religious instruction is excluded from it." That is identically what the archbishop says.

The ATTORNEY-GENERAL:—He does not say that the children will not be sent to those schools. The distinction I am endeavouring to draw is the distinction which is in the mind of Lord Morris.

Lord MORRIS:—It is very much in my mind, because I am very conversant of a country in which the whole thing comes up every day, and in which I am the senior member of the board of education which has to deal with the subject. Protestants, as a matter of fact in Ireland, will send their children to the model school, although some of them may prefer this, that, and the other; but they are under a ban so far as the Roman catholics are concerned.

The ATTORNEY-GENERAL:—I cannot neglect any point that is made against me. I think it is important to consider whether the public schools established under the act of 1890 ——

Lord SHAND:—I think the other element you desiderated is also given by bishop Machray: "I have no doubt that if religious training is excluded from the public schools, as is threatened, this will be the policy in future of the church of England, and of myself. The re-establishment of our parish schools is merely a question of means and time." That is identical with the archbishop.

Lord MORRIS:—I do not see that it is identical. The Roman catholic archbishop swears that it is substantially against the tenets of the Roman catholic church for Roman catholic children to attend these non-sectarian schools.

Lord SHAND:—There is that distinction.

The ATTORNEY-GENERAL :—That is the point I was upon.

Lord SHAND :—I thought the protestant view was that their children would still go to the public schools.

The ATTORNEY-GENERAL :—The distinction is not that they will not supplement the protestant education of other schools, but that they will be content.

Lord WATSON :—I do not know whether one can rely upon one's own experience. These kind of questions were more or less burning questions in Great Britain about the year 1865 or 1866, and during the whole of that period, as far as my knowledge and experience goes, there were large classes of protestants, and especially presbyterian protestants, who I am glad to see are recognized as Christians in Manitoba, who were in favour of secular education, and think that religious education ought to be imparted in the family, or by the church, and not in a secular school, where they are learning the rudiments of knowledge. On the other hand there are a great number of episcopalian protestants who take a different view: but I have never yet met a Roman catholic who took that view.

THE ATTORNEY-GENERAL :—What I would desire to be allowed to submit as part of my argument is this: that there are two questions, the one question whether the several respective denominations, protestant and catholic, will supplement the school by religious instruction, upon which I admit, and was going to have said if I had not been anticipated, I think the views of Bishop Machray accord with the views of the archbishop; the other question, whether the protestants will permit their children to go to these schools, whereas the Roman catholics honestly and conscientiously cannot.

Lord SHAND :—I do not take the view you have been suggesting on that second point.

The ATTORNEY-GENERAL :—I desire merely to be allowed to present my argument to your lordships on the point. Of course it is not for me to suggest that my argument is right; but I ask your lordships' consideration of it. Will your lordships turn to Mr. Bryce's affidavit, pages 20 and 21. I had no knowledge of the Logan papers until they were given me for the purposes of this case. He says: "That the presbyterian church is most solicitous for the religious education of all its children. It takes great care in the vows required of parents at the baptism of their children, and in urging its ministers to teach from the pulpit the duty of giving moral and religious training in the family. It is most energetic in maintaining efficient Sunday schools which have been called the 'children's church,' and in requiring the attendance of the children at the church services, which is made a great means of instruction. I think it is our firm belief that this system, joined with the public school system, has produced and will produce a moral, religious and intelligent people." So far I submit it confirms the view I have taken that they do not object on conscientious principles to the children going to a public school. They are satisfied by supplementing those schools by their own schools. He says in terms "That the presbyterians are thus able to unite with their fellow Christians of other churches in having taught in the public schools (which they desire to be taught by Christian teachers) the subjects of a secular education, and I cannot see that there should be any conscientious objection on the part of the Roman catholics to attend such schools, provided adequate means be provided of giving elsewhere such moral and religious training as may be desired; but on the other hand there should be many social and national advantages." Possibly Lord Macnaghten will not object to my saying— and I should like to make the observation——

Lord MACNAGHTEN :—I do not think Mr. Bryce has added anything to the weight of his argument or affidavit by stating his view of what Roman catholics do or ought to do.

The ATTORNEY-GENERAL :—My whole point is to show that there is this broad distinction with regard to the right and privilege that in the one case protestants are willing and can conscientiously avail themselves of the benefits of the public schools supplementing that by their religious instruction.

Lord SHAND :—He speaks for presbyterians only.

The ATTORNEY-GENERAL :—For presbyterians who are an important protestant body.

Lord MORRIS:—They are much the largest body.

The ATTORNEY-GENERAL:—Yes, much the largest body among the protestants.

Lord MORRIS:—And I believe the methodists come next. The church and catholics come down very low.

The ATTORNEY-GENERAL:—It is a completely different point to the one which I am humbly submitting to your lordships that in the case of a Roman catholic they cannot conscientiously avail themselves of the advantages of the public instruction because of their view with regard to what education should be.

Lord MORRIS:—Looking at this as a matter of fact anybody who takes the trouble of reading the report of the commission to inquire into the national system of education in Ireland will see that Cardinal Cullen claims what this archbishop claims also; namely, the exclusive right of the church to superintend education. That may be right or wrong; we are not going discuss theological questions; but that is asserted as a matter of fact.

Lord WATSON:—In Winnipeg, as far as one can judge from the sum expended on the respective schools belonging to the protestant and the catholics, the protestant element must be to the catholics as 30 to 1. There are 75,000 dollars required for the protestants, and 2,500 for the catholics.

Lord MORRIS:—I do not see the object of all this, except to ascertain the fact that the members of the Roman catholic church will not go to those schools.

Mr. MCCARTHY:—The actual population taken from the census in Winnipeg is 2,470 Roman catholics, 6,850 church of England, 4,310 methodists, 5,952 presbyterians, 1,000 baptists and 5,000 all others.

Lord MORRIS:—That is the town of Winnipeg, but what is the proportion in the province of Manitoba?

Mr. MCCARTHY:—There is a total population of 152,000; baptists 16,000, Roman catholics 20,000, church of England 30,000, methodists 28,000, presbyterians, 39,000 and all others 17,000.

Lord MORRIS:—That is the reason I said the presbyterians were by far the largest body.

The ATTORNEY-GENERAL:—I am merely anxious to direct your lordships' attention to one or two matters in this particular connection and to pass on. I do not want to occupy your lordships' time by unnecessary discussion, but it is important that I should make my meaning clear. I am only here to submit what I think is entitled to some weight. Now I turn to Professor Bryce's affidavit in the Logan case. I only use it because it has been referred to by my learned friends. I do not know that I am entitled to use it, but it does bear directly on the point which I mentioned, especially with reference to an observation of Lord Shand's as to what the attitude of the presbyterian body was. It is at page 19 of the Logan case, paragraph 5.

Lord SHAND:—I spoke of the protestants, not of a section of them, the presbyterians.

The ATTORNEY-GENERAL:—This bears directly at any rate upon my argument.

Lord SHAND:—I merely made my observation. I did not assert anything about the presbyterians.

The ATTORNEY-GENERAL:—At page 20:—"The presbyterian synod of Manitoba and the North-west Territories, which represents the largest religious body in Manitoba, passed in May, 1890, a resolution heartily approving of the Public School Act of this year, and I believe that it is approved of by the great majority of the presbyterians of Manitoba." Then he proceeds to deal with the question of supplementing public education of a secular character by a religious education.

Lord SHAND:—I think you have made out that presbyterians have little, if substantially any objection.

The ATTORNEY-GENERAL:—Then will your lordships kindly turn back to Bishop Machray's affidavit at pages 6 and 7. The important paragraph is the 21st:—"When the School Act was passed as above mentioned," &c. [Reading down to line 44, page 7 of the Logan case.] "The re-establishment of our parish schools is merely a question of means and time." I understand that gentleman to say not that they object to their children going to these public schools, but that they will supplement them by the establishment of parish schools in which religious instruction will be given.

Lord SHAND:—I do not take that view of it, particularly if you take with it the passage:—" With the great majority of bishops and clergy of the church of England, I believe that the education of the young is incomplete and may even be hurtful if religious instruction is excluded from it." He means to say he will be obliged to re-establish parish schools and thereby have double rates to pay—a public school rate and a parish rate.

The ATTORNEY-GENERAL:—If so, it is an argument in my favour from the church of England point of view.

Lord SHAND:—Quite so; I think it is. That is exactly what I have been indicating.

The ATTORNEY-GENERAL:—I did not conceive upon the general scope of the affidavit that there was the same objection, particularly as I know, from the official documents which we have, that the prayers which are being continued and the religious instruction which is being continued are the same as existed in the protestant schools before the passing of the act of 1890.

Now, my lords, in this state of things, may I for a few moments ask your lordships to consider what is the real construction of the act of 1870?

Lord MACNAGHTEN:—That is the only question. To my mind everything after 1870 may be put on one side.

The ATTORNEY-GENERAL:—I ventured to say so to your lordships yesterday. There are two matters which I must ask your lordships to consider beyond that, and one of them is what has been done by the act of 1890? Your lordships must not overlook that, and further I desire to enforce what I said yesterday, that the only denominations regarded by the legislature at any time, 1867, 1870, or later periods, are the denominations of protestants and Roman catholics.

Lord MACNAGHTEN:—That is a question of construction of the act.

The ATTORNEY-GENERAL:—It is; but I shall submit to your lordships that from a historical point of view—I am not saying for the purpose of construction—I endeavoured to disclaim that as strongly as I could yesterday, my learned friends cannot point to anything, to any other dividing line, except that between protestants and Roman catholics. That is my object in referring to it again. I should not have done so but for your lordship indicating what I was saying was not material.

Now, what was the position of things when the act of 1867, the British North America Act, was passed? In Upper and Lower Canada, in Ontario and Quebec, as it was subsequently called, there was legislation with reference to the existence of separate schools and contribution to them. I care not whether they are called separate, whether they are called denominational, or whether they are called dissentient. I think that that difference of language is simply adopted because different names had been used in different acts of the various provinces and under different circumstances, but they all point to the same things, namely, schools which were established in the interests of Roman catholics, and schools established in the interests of protestants.

Lord WATSON:—Unquestionably the dissentient schools are spoken of in the British North America Act as denominational schools.

The ATTORNEY-GENERAL:—I am reading from page 4 of the Record—sub-section 2, section 93 of the act of 1867. If you look at the words "denominational" in the first sub-section, and at "separate" and "dissentient," and remember what had existed in Upper Canada and in Quebec, that in the one part there had been a majority of Roman catholics, and in the other a majority of protestants, you will see that this distinction between these expressions is not of any importance and was not inserted by the legislature with any intention of conveying a different meaning. I desire to supplement a statement made by my learned friends, Sir Horace Davey and Mr. McCarthy, with which I in no way quarrel, by telling your lordships that most unquestionably in Upper Canada—that will be in Ontario—this exemption from contributing to the other schools existed by law, and was regarded as being a right existing by law. I have the statute before me. It is the act of 1863. It is called "an Act to restore to Roman catholics in Upper Canada certain rights in respect to separate schools." By the 14th section of that act "every person paying rates, whether as proprietor or tenant, who by himself or his agent on or before the 1st of March gives, or has given to the clerk of the municipality notice in writing that he is a Roman catholic and supporter of a catholic school, situated in the said municipality, or in a municipality contiguous thereto, shall be exempted from the payment of all rates imposed in support of common schools and common school libraries, or for the purpose of purchase of land or erection of buildings for common school purposes." The reference is to 26 Victoria, chapter 5, in the Statutes of Canada. So I point out that at the time this British North America Act was passed, in one of the provinces there existed by law a right that the Roman catholic should not be called upon to contribute to what they there call common schools.

Lord SHAND:—That was extended to Quebec—was it by section 2?

The ATTORNEY-GENERAL:—I rather think they had got legislation in Quebec under another statute, which, practically speaking, was to the same effect; but at any rate your lordships will find it in chapter 15 of the Consolidated Statutes of Lower Canada. I think they were published in 1861. "Whenever the arrangements made by the school commissioners for the conduct of any school are not agreeable to any number whatever of the inhabitants professing a religious faith different from that of the majority of the inhabitants of such municipality, the inhabitants so dissentient may collectively signify such dissent in writing to the chairman of the commissioners, and give him the names of three trustees chosen, such trustees shall bear the same powers and duties as the school commissioners." Unfortunately I have not had this act before. I do not remember whether there was the actual prohibition that the persons who dissented should not contribute, but I will ask my learned friend just to look and see whether that be so, and if necessary, Mr. Blake will call attention to that. But it is sufficient for my purpose to show that in some of the provinces there existed by law this exemption from having to subscribe to the schools of another denomination, meaning thereby, as I humbly submit, protestant as distinct from Roman catholics.

Lord MACNAGHTEN:—Sub-section 1 is general. Then we come to sub-section 2.

The ATTORNEY GENERAL:—That is only applying it to Lower Canada.

Lord SHAND:—The effect of section 2 is that whatever is going on in Upper Canada shall now go on in Quebec.

The ATTORNEY-GENERAL:—Yes, but for the purpose of the protection of Upper Canada, it must depend on sub-section 1, I think.

Lord SHAND:—You say there were such privileges in Upper Canada and even in Quebec, but I suppose you do not dispute, on the other hand, what was stated to us by the learned counsel who last addressed us that neither in New Brunswick nor in Nova Scotia was there any such privilege.

The ATTORNEY-GENERAL:—Yes, I do dispute it as regards New Brunswick. As to Nova Scotia I do not know. I think my learned friend may be right. I must be permitted to make my point with reference to that. I am going to point out when I come to consider the Manitoba Act of 1870, that they have framed a section bearing in mind what was the condition of things in Manitoba and also bearing in mind what questions had been raised with reference to New Brunswick. I understand that the protection given to Upper Canada or Ontario is by virtue of sub-section 1. Sub-section 2 is to extend to Lower Canada the same protection that exists in Upper Canada. That is my idea. Of course the question would arise whether Upper Canada got the protection which we are contending for. I shall submit that when the British North America Act was passed it was intended to reserve to Upper Canada and by virtue of sub-section 2 to give to Lower Canada the statutory exemption from having to subscribe to schools of another denomination,—meaning thereby catholics not to subscribe to protestant schools and *vice versa*, for all I know, but at any rate that—which existed in Upper Canada.

Lord SHAND:—I rather thought that was not disputed. I do not think it is. Whatever privilege they had was certainly retained to them.

The ATTORNEY-GENERAL:—Now, with regard to the questions which were put to me with regard to New Brunswick, it stood in this way: There was a statute relating to schools in New Brunswick and the only point that was decided in the Renaud case was not that there were no schools or that there were no privileges of a class in relation to denominational schools, but that that privilege had not been taken away or interfered with, that is to say, the privilege they claimed. They claimed that whatever was read in the Scriptures must be read from the Douay Bible, and that, inasmuch as there was a discretion given by the New Brunswick Act of 1871 to allow the teacher or allow the board to direct the teacher to read from another version of the Bible the privilege had been interfered with.

Lord SHAND :—Then is the head note wrong? It says: "At the union the law with respect to schools in the province of New Brunswick was governed by the Parish School Act, under which no class of persons had any legal right or privilege with respect to denominational schools, and a subsequent act, 34 Victoria, cap. 21, providing that the schools conducted thereunder should be non-sectarian."

The ATTORNEY-GENERAL :—I think the head note is wrong, but I will read the passage which I had in my mind which is at the bottom of page 466. "Those relied on are that the Common Schools Act has no enactment similar to section 8 of the Parish Schools Act, that the Parish School Act had no enactment similar to section 58, sub-section 12 of the Common Schools Act, and this section it is alleged, prohibits the granting provincial aid to any but schools under the Common Schools Act; and that by the 60th section of the Common Schools Act, all schools conducted under its provisions shall be non-sectarian—a provision not to be found in the Parish School Act, and it is contended, that the omission in the one case, and the express enactment in the other, prejudicially affect the rights and privileges which the Roman catholics, as a class of persons and a denomination, had in the schools established or which might have been established under the Parish School Act; in other words, that the rights and privileges which they had under the one, the omission and the enactments referred to prevented their claiming or obtaining under the other. With reference to the omission, the Parish School Act no doubt declares that the board of education shall secure to all children, whose parents do not object, the reading of the Bible, and that when read by Roman catholic children, if required by their parents, it shall be in the Douay version, without note or comment. Here we have expressly directed to be secured to all children, what many persons no doubt consider a great right and privilege; and Roman catholic parents have a great right secured to them, viz..—to have, if they require it, a particular version of the Bible read." That is under the old act which existed in New Brunswick before the passing of the Common Schools Act of 1871. "As to the reason why a similar provision, securing these important rights, in which protestants and catholics were both interested, was excluded from the Common Schools Act, it is not our business to inquire; what we have to determine is, does this omission make the law void, if in other respects unobjectionable? We think not. If this was a right or privilege which existed at the union, the legislature certainly has not protected it by any express enactment. But is the right taken away? May it not still exist, provided always it is a right which legitimately comes under sub-section 1, section 93? Because that section declares that nothing in any such law shall prejudicially affect any such right, and in such case, reading the Common School Law by the light of this section, would it not be the duty of the board of education under the Common Schools Act, instead of making regulation 21, declaring as follows :—that it shall be the privilege of every teacher to open and close the daily exercises of the school by reading a portion of Scripture (out of the common or Douay version as he may prefer), and by offering the Lord's Prayer—any other prayer may be used by permission of the board of trustees; but no teacher may compel any pupil to be present at those exercises against the wishes of his parents or guardian, expressed in writing, to the board of trustees, to secure by regulation, just what the board of education were bound to secure under the Parish School Act of 1858, that is, to make just such a regulation as the Parish School Act required to be made? We have seen they have precisely the same, and only the same powers to make regulations, as the board had under the Parish School Act. By this simple means, the rights of all the children and their parents in the province—as well protestants as Roman catholics—which existed at the union, would be preserved, and all just cause of complaint on this head removed. Why the board of education should have departed from the principle and policy of the Parish School Act, and taken from the parents of all the children of the country—protestant and Roman catholic alike—the great boon and privilege of insisting on the Bible being read in schools, as they have done, and should have conferred on the teacher, not only the privilege of reading the Bible or not as he likes, but out of the common or Douay version—not as the children or their parents may choose, but as the teacher may prefer, though he cannot compel the attendance of the pupils,—is not for us to explain, we simply point out the fact. But if the right secured by the Parish School Act is protected by the British North America Act 1867, we fail to see because the board of education may not have made such a regulation as they ought in such case to have made or have made a regulation they ought not to have made, that the action of the board or its non-action can render the action of the legislature inoperative."

Lord SHAND:—That was a privilege that had been secured by statute.

The ATTORNEY-GENERAL:—I was criticising the contention that there was no privilege by statute in New Brunswick prior to the passing of the British North America Act, and I was pointing out that when rightly understood, as the chief justice himself says in his judgment, they did not intend to decide in the Renaud case that there was no privilege by law; but what they did decide was that the privilege by law had not been infringed by the statute made, but had only been temporarily abrogated by a direction of the education department, which need not have been made under the statute, and, therefore, that the law was not objectionable, but that the declaration was.

Now, my lords, with regard to Nova Scotia, my learned friends informed me that they are not aware, and of course Mr. McCarthy would have told you if he was aware, that there was any act. Therefore, there was in that case, apparently, what I may call no protection existing by law at that time, as far as that province was concerned.

I think it must be taken that at the time that the British North America Act was passed they meant to protect whatever rights and privileges the persons had by law. It is important to observe when the Manitoba Act was passed. I will ask your lordships just to refer to page 61, where you will find a very convenient reference to dates in the judgment of Mr. Justice Dubuc. He points out that the New Brunswick case had been under discussion, and that there had been active discussion with reference to this matter shortly before the introduction of the Manitoba Bill. Now, my lords, it may not have the slightest effect on the language used any more than what happened afterwards, but it is important to see whether or not the difference in language used with reference to the Manitoba Act was not aptly chosen with reference to what was the known state of things at the time that Manitoba Act was passed. I remind your lordships once more that in some of the provinces—which is sufficient for my purpose—under the act of 1867, there was an exemption against having to subscribe to schools of a different denomination. Your lordships will forgive me for not always repeating: when I say different denomination, I am arguing from the point of view of protestants and catholics—I say that the exemption in some of the provinces from having to subscribe to schools of another denomination existed by law; it did not exist by law in Manitoba. Perhaps I may ask your lordships here to refer to Mr. Justice Fournier's judgment, which has not been read I have a translation, and it is on the first page. "It is important for the decision of this question to advert to the circumstances which led to the entry of this province into the Canadian confederation. It must be remembered that it was at the end of a rebellion which had thrown the population into a profound and violent agitation, raised religious and national passions, and caused great disorders, which had rendered necessary the intervention of the federal government. It was with the view of re-establishing public peace and of conciliating this population that the federal government accorded to them the constitution which they have enjoyed up to the present time. The principle of separate schools introduced in the British North America Act, section 93, was also introduced into the constitution of Manitoba and declared to apply to separate schools which existed *de facto* in that territory before its organization into a province. The population was then divided almost equally between catholics and protestants. While giving to the province the power to legislate concerning education, sub-section 1 of section 22 adds to the restriction of section 93 of the British North America Act, not to prejudicially affect any right or privilege conferred by law respecting separate schools, that in addition to not prejudicially affecting separate schools existing by the custom of the country (by practice)." If your lordships want the page in the book for the French, it is page 109.

Lord SHAND:—I have it before me. I was looking at the act.

The ATTORNEY-GENERAL:—It is upon this extension of the prohibition contained in the 93rd section, which protected separate schools existing by custom, that the legislature of Manitoba acted in introducing the principle of separate schools. I will not refer to that, because that is an argument which I do not think I desire to press, although I am going to refer to it in another connection. Now that is not the only difference in the 22nd section between the two statutes. I will ask your lordships' kind attention to the opening words of sub-section 3 of the British North America Act, and the corresponding words in sub-section 2 of the Manitoba Act. Sub-section 3 of section 93 of the British North America Act begins in this way: "Where in any province a system of separate or dissentient schools exists by law at the union, or is thereafter established by the legislature of the province, an appeal shall lie," and so on. Therefore, at the time that the Manitoba Act was passed, rights had been intended to be given to the protestant and catholic minorities under the British North America Act in the event, either of their being "separate or dissentient," which I submit is exactly the same as denominational, "schools existing by law at the union, or thereafter established by the legislature of the province." Those words are omitted from the commencement of sub-section 2 of section 22 of the Manitoba Act. If your lordships will look, kindly, at the parallel columns on page 4 of the Record, you will see exactly what I mean. Sub-section 2 begins: "An appeal shall lie to the governor-general," without any of the introductory words, "Where in any province." I am justified, and entitled to submit, that the reason of the omission of these words is because both parties—I have no right to say both parties—but both contending parties in the state, who would have to influence the legislature, knew that the schools did exist. There is no necessity for a condition precedent in this respect. Your lordships must remember that they are modifying it in connection with practice, as distinguished from law alone, and, therefore, having widened sub-section 1 by the inclusion of the words "or practice," when they come to frame the corresponding section to sub-section 3, they leave out the narrowing words there, because I point out to your lordships that if an appeal had been brought under sub-section 2 of the Manitoba Act, it might have been contended, had those words been left in, separate and dissentient schools did not exist in Manitoba by law; they had not been established by the legislature subsequently, and, therefore, no question of the rights of the protestant and catholic minorities could be considered by the governor-general under the sub-section. I, therefore, point out that the whole framing of the section 22 of the Manitoba Act of 1870 indicates that the legislature knew and were informed of that which the learned judges of course say everybody did know at the time; that in fact there had been in Manitoba a separate system of education by protestants and Roman catholics, each separately supported, the one by the protestants and the other by the Roman catholics.

Lord SHAND:—There is this distinction, that in order to make a difference about the word system, in the one case you had a mere voluntary series of schools, and in the other case there were government schools.

The ATTORNEY-GENERAL:—I do not think they were government schools.

Lord SHAND:—They were state schools.

The ATTORNEY-GENERAL:—They were regulated by statute.

Lord SHAND:—They were state aided.

The ATTORNEY-GENERAL:—No, I do not think so.

Mr. MCCARTHY:—Yes.

The ATTORNEY-GENERAL:—There was state aid?

Mr. MCCARTHY:—Yes.

Lord SHAND:—They were all getting state aid.

The ATTORNEY-GENERAL:—That is why I ventured to explain what the word "state" meant.

Mr. MCCARTHY:—They get a portion of the government grant.

Lord WATSON:—The difference would be this: that, if you are right, there would be some distinction in Manitoba. The schools before the statute were private schools, erected, set up and managed privately, and any person who set up and managed a private school at that time was not liable to be called upon for any school assessment; but in Ontario it seems to have been somewhat different. In Ontario there were schools formed—separate schools for catholics, which were set up under the provisions of an act, under certain conditions as to teaching and so forth, and it was only when he supported one of these schools that he got any exemption. If he set up any school of his own, as was done in Manitoba before the passing of this act, there would have been no exemption from the law to contribute to the school rate.

The ATTORNEY-GENERAL:—I have not suggested, of course, that the circumstances are identical. I quite agree that your lordship has pointed out certain differences.

Lord WATSON:—One, if I may say so, is a much wider right.

The ATTORNEY-GENERAL:—I am, of course, submitting to your lordships that it is because there were these differences that you find that an expression has been used to which the widest meaning is intended to be given, and should be given. I want, my lords, to test it by two observations. First, my learned friends say: This may have been directed to some possible legislation or *quasi* legislation of the Hudson's Bay Company. Now, I say there is no trace of it in any one of the judgments in the court below, nor in any of the facts stated as to the existing facts in Manitoba. There is absolutely no suggestion made in the whole course of the previous proceedings which can be directed to that. Then, my learned friends say, and I think it was more Sir Horace Davey's argument—that "privilege" is a sort of technical word—*privilegium*. Well, it would be strange if it had been used in that sense in any such statute as this, but it is very difficult, if I understand the law, to understand what a *privilegium* by practice would mean. If *privilegium* is to be construed in the strict sense which my friend Sir Horace Davey indicated, I should have thought it was, I will not say a contradiction in terms, but almost a contradiction in terms, to speak of such a *privilegium* as existing by practice. My lords, I submit to your lordships that this is a kind of legislation which is intended to be construed by giving a liberal and wide meaning to the words, and that the meaning is to be gathered from what was to be protected. I say that the words "rights and privileges" are general words. I do not know that I should assist your lordships much by citing authorities, but of course I could cite to your lordships several authorities indicating that the word "rights" and the word "privileges" have been given wider meanings than the narrower meanings which are suggested by my learned friends. My lords, my learned friend Sir Horace Davey endeavoured to draw a distinction in which he said one of the privileges was, not being compelled to attend any school at all—that there was no obligation on a Roman catholic prior to the act of 1870 to send his children to any school.

Lord WATSON:—Is not it almost an inversion of the use of language to speak of *privilegium* as existing by practice.

The ATTORNEY-GENERAL:—I was not using this as an argument in my favour, but I was endeavouring to answer the argument used by my friend Sir Horace Davey against me. He said there still is preserved in the act of 1890, so to speak, by there being no section compelling attendance, that privilege of non-attendance; but, my lords, surely, the answer is obvious. There were no public schools at all before the act, and therefore it cannot be said that there was an exemption by practice from attending schools in the sense that Sir Horace Davey means. In fact, the same argument which he uses to answer our argument with reference to exemption from subscription to schools of other denominations.

Lord SHAND:—It is the same point taken against you. Sir Horace Davey says because there were no schools before, you were not enjoying any privilege such as you say now you are to have protected.

The ATTORNEY-GENERAL:—Then of course my reply would be, what do they say is to be preserved to us in the words "rights and privileges."

Lord SHAND:—I think there are two things said. He says in the first place it preserves your right to open such schools, and it would also protect you against any act creating disabilities against Roman catholics.

Lord WATSON:—His argument may be expressed in these words. He said, a privilege of this kind is of the nature of an exemption, but there cannot be an existing exemption when there is no rule from which to exempt it. That was the gist of his argument.

The ATTORNEY-GENERAL:—I was fully alive to those points which I had in my mind, and I was about to enumerate them. Let us take the exemption from civil disability by the legislation which would exclude catholics who had not gone to protestant schools.

Lord HANNEN:—Which would exclude catholics who had not gone to public schools.

The ATTORNEY-GENERAL:—Yes, my lord, who had not gone to public schools.

Lord SHAND:—There is such a law in one of the other provinces we are told.

The ATTORNEY-GENERAL:—Oh! no, my lord, my friend was referring to the United States—to the state of Maine, I think.

Mr. MCCARTHY:—Massachusetts.

The ATTORNEY-GENERAL:—That has nothing in the world to do with Canada, not the least in the world. That was given by my friend Mr. McCarthy as an illustration.

Lord SHAND:—I thought it applied to one of the provinces.

The ATTORNEY-GENERAL:—But, my lord, acts could be passed excluding catholics from civil employment. There is absolutely nothing to prevent the legislature doing it. Far wider powers have been used under such legislation.

Lord HANNEN:—But is that example applicable? We are supposing the legislature to point to their not having attended a particular public school.

The ATTORNEY-GENERAL:—My argument is because the legislature has been prevented in this respect from imposing restrictions upon catholics, that is the reason why the particular matter has been picked out. It is all very well for my friend to say that is one thing that is preserved, but I am entitled to say what we argue for is preserved also. I submit it is not because those who are arguing for the other contention can pick out a thing and say we admit that this particular thing is something which is preserved to them.

Lord SHAND:—I think the argument was only used to show that they could satisfy the language of this act.

The ATTORNEY-GENERAL:—But why are they entitled to satisfy it in that way? Supposing a law was passed excluding persons from employment who had not gone to the public schools, taking the more accurate expression which Lord Hannen was good enough to give me, why should not they say in reply, "It is all very well, but you had no privilege at the time of the union in that respect; it is perfectly true there was no law respecting it; there was no practice one way or the other with regard to the matter; the matter had not formed the subject of legislation. I submit that you are not entitled to pick out one particular burden that might be imposed by legislation and say that was prevented; that was barred, and at the same time exclude that which we humbly submit must have been present to the legislature at the time that they were dealing with the system of education.

Lord WATSON:—I can understand this view that you found on the language of the statute. "Law and practice" is an expression that one is familiar enough with, and in that case it generally signifies some practice having the force and effect of law; but when you have the expression "law or practice," which makes them alternative and contrasts "law" with "practice," I take it that "practice" there can hardly mean practice having the effect and force of law. Then that raises the question, What in that case does "practice" mean?—A right or privilege arising from practice, which has not the force of law. It may be that privilege in that sense simply means arising or depending on practice; and practice, using the word in that sense, simply means that they were in practical enjoyment of immunity—

that they did not do certain things at the time and they were not liable for them. Can you put the statute higher than that?

The ATTORNEY-GENERAL:—I do not know that I want to put it higher than that.

Lord WATSON:—That seems to me to be the most favourable aspect in which it can be put for you, that "practice" here cannot mean practice equivalent to law.

Lord HANNEN:—The effect of this is, I think, as though it had said that any practice with respect to denominational schools shall have the force of law.

The ATTORNEY-GENERAL:—May I endeavour to illustrate my argument by assuming that "churches" were there instead of "denominational schools." Supposing there had been a completely voluntary church system, as I dare say there was a church system, and supposing the section had read in this way:—"In and for the province the legislature may exclusively make laws in relation to religion, subject and according to the following provisions:—Nothing in any such law shall prejudicially affect any right or privilege with respect to churches which any class of persons have."

Lord WATSON:—But in conventional language—not strictly legal language—I take it "privilege" has a much wider meaning. Take a place where there is little taxation: there is nothing erroneous in saying that a resident in that country is in the enjoyment of privileges because he can do this, that, and the other because the force of law has not yet stepped in to prevent it.

Lord MORRIS:—Just as, in the case of Jersey, the residents have not the privilege of paying duty on their wines.

Lord WATSON:—If you go into a part of the world where there is no law against trespass, you may say the fact that there is no law enacted against trespass, gives you the privilege of going into another person's land.

The ATTORNEY-GENERAL:—May I say what I desired to say with respect to the illustration of churches?

Lord MACNAGHTEN:—I think that is rather adding to your difficulties.

The ATTORNEY-GENERAL:—Of course I did not intend to do so in putting it. I thought that it was not an unfair parallel to put "religion" corresponding to "education," and "churches" corresponding to "schools," and I assume that there are voluntary church rates for both.

Lord MORRIS:—Have you any objection to deal with what Lord Watson says—that they are not to do anything to prejudicially affect the condition of things which these two churches practically enjoyed at the time of the passing of the act?

The ATTORNEY-GENERAL:—Certainly not. I hope I was not understood as dissenting from what Lord Watson put to me. I was submitting an illustration and I was going simply to consider whether the illustration was not a good one, but if Lord Macnaghten says it is not, I am sure I must be wrong. It does help sometimes to consider what may be thought to be parallel cases.

Lord MORRIS:—I do not think you can put it higher than what he says was the highest point—that the condition of things as regards denominational education, which was then practically enjoyed, was not to be altered prejudicially.

Lord MACNAGHTEN:—You say that it means, with respect to denominational schools, no class of persons shall be put in a less favourable position than they occupied at the time of the union?

The ATTORNEY-GENERAL:—That is my submission, my lord.

Lord MACNAGHTEN:—You put it as high as that?

The ATTORNEY-GENERAL:—Yes. I submit it means "prejudicially affect the rights or privileges of a class of persons." They are very wide words.

Lord MACNAGHTEN:—Yes, they are very wide words.

The ATTORNEY-GENERAL:—To prejudicially affect does not mean to take away absolutely.

Lord MACNAGHTEN:—But would not that prevent them from legislating with regard to education at all?

The ATTORNEY-GENERAL:—No, I say most distinctly it would not.

Lord MACNAGHTEN:—You will come to that presently. I wanted to know exactly how high you put it. May I take it from you that you accept that?

The Attorney-General:—I do.

Lord Macnaghten:—May I take it that you say that the real effect of this section is that with respect to denominational schools no law shall be passed which would put any class of persons in a less favourable position than they occupied at the time of the union?

The Attorney-General:—With respect to their own denominational schools, and with respect to the denominational schools of the other party. I put that in for this reason: I think too much stress has been laid upon the view that there is only one side on this question. There are the denominational schools of the Roman catholics which they have to maintain, as to which they have rights and privileges; there are the denominational schools of the protestants, which the protestants have to maintain, and as to which they have rights and privileges. There are also rights and privileges *inter se.*

Lord Macnaghten:—No doubt—as we have seen the presbyterians, as a body, seem to take a different position from the church of England.

The Attorney-General:—I do not only mean that. I am afraid your lordship thought it was more in my favour than I meant to put it. I was putting this: I submit that the right to conduct, and the privilege of conducting, your own education without having anything to do with the schools of the other denomination is just as much a right and privilege of a class of persons with respect to your own denominational schools, as to say you may yourselves keep your own——

Lord Macnaghten:—Would not that exclude all government interference?

The Attorney-General:—No, I will come to that at once, because I have no difficulty in arguing the point.

Lord Macnaghten:—Before you go to that, I put down what I thought you said "right or privilege" was, and I want to see if I put it down correctly. It was the right or privilege to maintain by their own contributions their own schools, and not to be taxed directly for the maintenance of schools to which they conscientiously objected, and to which they could not send their own children.

The Attorney-General:—That is in substance what I meant to say. I wished to put the two limbs, the freedom of contribution and the exemption from contribution to other schools. I submit both those were by practice, rights or privileges of the Roman catholics and the protestants respectively.

Now I should like to grapple at once with the point, which is a point evidently pressing upon your lordship.

Lord Shand:—Of course in the second branch of that the idea of exemption occurs.

The Attorney-General:—Certainly.

Lord Shand:—And it all comes back really practically to the second.

The Attorney-General:—Yes.

Lord Macnaghten:—Then on the other side it was said that was not fair, because if they had a right or privilege at all not to be taxed directly for any education——

The Attorney-General:—No I did not say that, my lord.

Lord Macnaghten:—No, you did not say it, but the other side did.

The Attorney-General:—Yes. I am going to say that my friend, Sir Horace Davey, goes too far, and I should like to take the point now, because it really fits in with the argument and it has been mentioned by both your lordship and Sir Richard Couch. Will your lordships look at the section once more? "The legislature may exclusively make laws in relation to education." Therefore they are intended to legislate with respect to education, but they are to be subject to provision number one, which I need not read again. I say that provided they did not put the Roman catholic denomination in a worse position than the protestant denomination the legislature clearly was entitled to legislate, and I desire to point out that it is not sound to say that all this legislation has been *ultra vires.* That was put compendiously to my friend Sir Horace Davey by one of your lordships yesterday; provided that the law up to 1890 preserved equality as between the Roman catholics and the protestants, the legislation was perfectly *intra vires.* My learned friend put it that we say it was a compromise.

Lord WATSON:—I do not think it can be said for one moment that this reservation in favour of denominations was intended to stifle or deprive the legislature of a free hand in saying who should be educated, how they should be educated, and what standard of education there should be.

The ATTORNEY-GENERAL:—But Lord Macnaghten was putting to me while your lordship was absent for a moment that my argument paralyzed, or might be said to paralyze, the hands of the legislature, and that they could not legislate at all. I am endeavouring to answer that, by pointing out that there was a permission to the provincial legislature to legislate, with the condition that no such law shall have the prejudicial effect intended to be provided against.

Lord SHAND:—The difficulty I have about that is, that if you interpret the condition in the strict way you are doing, I cannot see very much what is left to the legislature to do, except to keep up denominational schools.

The ATTORNEY-GENERAL:—What I am endeavouring to answer is this: I would take every section of the act of 1870, and the act of 1881, and I think it could be honestly contended that not one of them infringed that first condition—not one of them. The whole point that is suggested is this: that because there being a customs taxation, and because the result of that customs taxation was handed over to the Dominion, and then the Dominion might make to the province a payment in the nature of a grant—that because when the state—that is the province—came to make the grant towards education, supplementing a rate, that would be or might be supposed to be, a product of the customs, paid by Roman catholics, and therefore that was an illegal application of moneys by the province.

Lord WATSON:—For instance, take the act of 1871—the education act. I certainly have been unable to see any enactment in the statute which would not infringe the right you claim.

The ATTORNEY-GENERAL:—We are not entitled to say our educational rights are not to be interfered with at all—that they are not to be governed or controlled, but as between the classes there is not to be a prejudicial affection of our rights.

Lord SHAND:—Is not it a just observation to say that both the act of 1871 and the act of 1881 are acts which establish or keep up denominational schools?

The ATTORNEY-GENERAL:—Yes, I think it is a right observation.

Lord SHAND:—Then this follows if that be so that what I have said and think about this, subject to what you can say, is that your argument comes to this, that from the day the Manitoba act was passed, the government could have established nothing but denominational schools, because both the statutes you have referred to establish denominational schools. Now is it the case that the government cannot establish schools of a non-sectarian character?

The ATTORNEY-GENERAL:—No, I do not say in the least that the government cannot establish schools of a non-sectarian character.

Lord SHAND:—But the moment they do, then the question arises.

The ATTORNEY-GENERAL:—I do not say that in the least.

Lord SHAND:—But they must relieve the protestants and the catholics from payment.

The ATTORNEY-GENERAL:—Your lordship is asking me to put it too much in the concrete, though I do not shirk the responsibility. I say that when I come to examine the act of 1890 what the legislature has done is to take away catholic schools and turn them into public schools, and insist on taxing the catholics for those schools. Those are the rights interfered with by the legislation of 1890. But I would willingly take hypothetically any part of the acts of 1871 and 1881—I have studied them carefully, and I am not aware of any provision down to the act of 1890, which interfered with the equality and freedom of Roman catholics and protestants.

Lord SHAND:—I take it so, but on the other hand, both those acts establish denominational schools. Now the question is whether the government having been told that they are to legislate on education can establish anything but denominational schools? It is no answer to say they were all allowed under these acts because they were denominational. Do you contend that they cannot establish non-sectarian schools? I do not think these acts help in the argument.

The ATTORNEY-GENERAL:—I do not say that they cannot establish non-sectarian schools but what they have established under the act of 1890 does in fact interfere prejudicially with our rights.

Lord SHAND:—What class of schools would not do that? Is there any class of schools that you can mention that would not by your argument infringe the act?

The ATTORNEY-GENERAL:—I am bound to answer the questions which your lordship puts, but I should say for instance a school of gymnastics—a most useful thing.

Lord SHAND:—That is a very limited class of school.

The ATTORNEY-GENERAL:—It is not very limited, I can assure your lordship. I speak with some knowledge of the educational system of the present day and I can assure your lordship that it forms a very substantial element of expense in the board schools.

Lord SHAND:—I was rather referring to schools for educating the mind than to schools for educating the body.

The ATTORNEY-GENERAL:—The Swedes tell us that both are equally important. In the Swedish system we are told the best products are obtained from those schools which educate both the mind and the body. I am rather disposed to suggest that there may be schools of that sort which would not infringe the act.

Lord MORRIS:—Is not this intended to be confined to what may be substantially called primary schools?

The ATTORNEY-GENERAL:—Certainly.

Lord MORRIS:—What light is thrown upon the subject by going into schools of that sort or schools of medicine or training?

Lord SHAND:—Well, take schools for teaching "the three R's." Could the goverment establish such schools? A Roman catholic, according to what the archbishop says, would not allow one of his children to go.

The ATTORNEY-GENERAL:—I think that in this province if a Roman catholic was made to contribute to a school that taught "the three R's" without any religious teaching at all, that would be an infringement of the act of 1870.

Lord SHAND:—Does not that show that you are paralyzing the government if you will not allow them to have schools for teaching "the three R's?"

The ATTORNEY-GENERAL:—I submit distinctly not.

Lord MORRIS:—In such a school in the teaching of writing any atheistic teacher would set a line. "There is no God." You get into an extraordinary line of controversy when you get into that.

Lord WATSON:—I can quite conceive that there might be a very great many branches of education taught in schools set up for both classes of religionists without any distinction of creed, such as cookery, science and a number of things—things that we are quite intimate with and not within the meaning of the word denominational.

The ATTORNEY-GENERAL:—I really put my proposition higher than that. I put it, and I meant to put it, including and not excluding these debateable subjects. I say that the act of 1881 is an instance to show that useful legislation could be passed by the legislature controlling protestants and controlling catholics and yet not prejudicially affecting their rights.

Lord WATSON:—My own impression is this: I do not think that a school of that kind set up for teaching these branches has ever been heard of as a denominational school. I never heard of such a thing.

Lord MORRIS:—These are very chimerical things.

The ATTORNEY-GENERAL:—As to the words used, "privilege with respect to denominational schools," they could not apply that with respect to a school which no human being would think of calling a denominational school.

Lord SHAND:—Take a science school, which Lord Watson mentioned: that would be the very first thing they would object to; they would say that the government could not open a science school.

The ATTORNEY-GENERAL:—I can assure your lordship I am not, on behalf of the Roman catholics of this province, here to ride off on a minor point, but I am here to submit that within the four corners of this 22nd section there may be, not only useful legislation and useful legislation, controlling and interfering with the rights of both parties, protestants and Roman catholics, but that it was intended to protect *inter se* the rights which these two classes had by practice with regard to each other's denominational schools and their own denominational schools.

Lord MACNAGHTEN:—Then, do you object to this, that according to your view—I do not know whether I am putting it right—the only legislation which could be effected under this section would be legislation with regard to education more or less on the denominational system and not on a national system?

The ATTORNEY-GENERAL:—I think, my lord, it must be more or less on the denominational system, if it is to apply to the whole community, I should be disposed to say that they might legislate for protestants in protestant schools and they might legislate for Roman catholics in Roman catholic schools.

Lord MACNAGHTEN:—But there could be no general system of national education according to your view?

The ATTORNEY-GENERAL:—Is not it a little involved in what is a national system of education?

Lord MACNAGHTEN:—It is one of the most difficult questions.

The ATTORNEY-GENERAL:—What your lordship puts is a general system of national education.

Lord MACNAGHTEN:—I do not want to put words into your mouth.

The ATTORNEY-GENERAL:—No; but does not it require a definition of what a general system of national education means?

Lord WATSON:—Even in Ireland, it would be news to me to be told, and I should be very much surprised if I was told that the teaching of the Dublin university in the arts schools and science schools is denominational.

The ATTORNEY-GENERAL:—I think Lord Macnaghten was pressing me a little too far in asking me to say that no general system of national education could be established. I can conceive it being a general system applicable to all, but still so erected within the general system that there was no infraction of the sub-section. I can imagine a general system contemplating schools established for Roman catholics and schools established for protestants.

Lord MACNAGHTEN:—That would be easy enough with regard to such a place as Winnipeg, but with regard to a large district of this size sparsely inhabited, would it be possible?

The ATTORNEY-GENERAL:—I am about to point out, when I come to the act of 1890, they have gone a great deal further than that. I say when you look at what the act is, this act has crushed out the Roman catholic schools. I know not whether it is in consequence of any violent agitation on behalf of Orangemen or others, but that is the fact.

Lord MACNAGHTEN:—I think you need not bring Orangemen into it.

The ATTORNEY-GENERAL:—I do not know, my lord. I am not sure that before this argument is over, your lordship may not hear from my friend, Mr. Blake, something which may render it necessary to introduce the word, but I will say "strong protestants or others."

Lord MACNAGHTEN:—I do not know what a "strong protestant" is.

The ATTORNEY-GENERAL:—I will say "protestants or others."

Lord MACNAGHTEN:—You may leave out all epithets.

The ATTORNEY-GENERAL:—I will leave out all epithets. I am very much obliged to your lordship for your assistance; but I do say this, that when you come and look at this act of 1890, our contention on behalf of the Roman catholics is that it has crushed and killed any possibility of schools in which there should be such education as the Roman catholics think they are entitled to have and to maintain freely. That is why we are here. It is absolutely unfounded to say that our argument stifles and crushes all legislation in Manitoba with regard to education. We appeal to the legislation of twenty years, which has been absolutely successful, and we say that to contend that there is a stifling of legislation by this contention is not sound. If you only look at the provisions of the act of 1890, we say it is a stifling of any school at the public expense to which Roman catholics can conscientiously send their children, and therefore we say that the legislature of the province has legislated with respect to education, as they are bound to do if they think it right, so as to most materially prejudice the rights of the Roman catholic class.

Lord MORRIS:—Is not the only system of education founded by this act of 1890 one which Roman catholics in Manitoba cannot conscientiously avail themselves of?

The ATTORNEY-GENERAL:—That is my contention.

Lord MORRIS:—It is not a bone of contention, but that is the fact.

The ATTORNEY-GENERAL:—Of course, I am only here as an advocate.

Lord MORRIS:—What is the use of discussing other matters. Nobody can deny that the Roman catholics cannot avail themselves of the system.

The ATTORNEY-GENERAL:—Surely your lordship will be of opinion that it is useful to discuss such questions as have been put to me, because it helps the ultimate decision on the argument.

Lord MORRIS:—But supposing those questions are put on the theory that that ought not to be the theory of the Roman catholics?

Lord SHAND:—I think it is put in this way, that these schools have been proved to be unacceptable to Roman catholics, but if you carry the principle far enough there could be no schools which would be acceptable, and therefore you could not have a national system.

The ATTORNEY-GENERAL:—I do not agree with that.

Lord SHAND:—That is the point.

The ATTORNEY-GENERAL:—That is the point, but I do not agree with it.

Lord MORRIS:—I understand there is a national system in England, but I am not so acquainted with that as I am with Ireland—I understand there are schools which are acceptable to the Roman catholics, and, therefore, why should not there be in Winnipeg?

The ATTORNEY-GENERAL:—Will Lord Morris pardon me. Why should I go to England? Why not take Manitoba?

Lord MORRIS:—So I say.

The ATTORNEY-GENERAL:—I have been trying to stick to Manitoba. I say for eighteen years there has been a perfectly legitimate, lawful and *intra vires* working out of this act.

Lord MORRIS:—Not by any undenominational schools.

The ATTORNEY-GENERAL:—I do not care whether or not. I do not quite agree that it was so. In one sense I will accept that it is denominational.

Lord SHAND:—All that it shows is that if you have a denominational system it is not objected to, but the moment you make it undenominational it is objected to.

The ATTORNEY-GENERAL:—I think that is too narrow, if you come to look at the act of 1881. I do not shrink from it because it may well be that section 22 did mean it may be necessary to maintain a denominational system. I do not shrink from it from that point of view, but I say that it is narrow, because I think it is an illiberal view of the acts of 1871 and 1890, simply to refer to them as being purely what I may call denominational schools. I admit the catholics manage the catholic schools, and the protestants manage the protestant schools, but in no other sense do I admit it was denominational. I admit it was baptist for baptist, or presbyterian for presbyterian, or churchman for churchman. It was denominational in that sense of the word, denominational under the 22nd section of the act. May I trouble your lordships to look at the act of 1890. It is really of very considerable importance. First your lordships must be possessed of what the advisory board were, and I can further briefly explain that. I will ask your lordships' attention to pages 107 and 108 of the statutes. The advisory board is established. Four members are nominated by the department of education; two are elected by the teachers, and one by the university by ballot. Then there are two important matters the advisory board have to deal with, and this is entirely new. They have first under 14 B "to examine and authorize text books and books of reference for the use of pupils and school libraries." May I point out at once a most important point as to which legislation could take place, and that is sub-section A:—"To make regulations for the dimensions, equipment, style, plan, furnishing, decoration and ventilation of school houses, and for the arrangement and requisites of school premises. That is a most important branch of legislation which would be perfectly independent of, and could not infringe the rights of catholics or protestants, because it could not be said that it could be a right of the Roman catholics to have the children educated in unhealthy schools.

Lord HANNEN:—That is only as to the school houses. It is not in relation to education.

Lord SHAND:—At all events, those are the words of the act.

The ATTORNEY-GENERAL:—The school houses would mean the buildings in which the children are. Then there is sub-section G.

Lord WATSON:—It is not made requisite that the advisory board should contain any catholic.

The ATTORNEY-GENERAL:—I was going to mention that. Sub-section G is to prescribe the forms of religious exercises to be used in schools. Now, on this advisory board there is no representation of any denomination, and no provision that any catholic element should be included, therefore, from the point of view of Roman catholics, it is a purely secular board. Then if your lordships will turn to the statute, knowing what the advisory board is, at page 111, there are certain sections which I think ought to be considered. The first is the 3rd. Remember that prior to this statute there were catholic and protestant districts, and the people were taxed. The grant was given to the schools by capitation, I think, or in some way or other of that character, and the catholics were taxed.

Lord WATSON:—They were either taxed or contributed.

The ATTORNEY-GENERAL:—They were either taxed or contributed. "All protestant and catholic school districts, together with all elections and appointments to office, all agreements, contracts, assessments and rate bills, heretofore duly made in relation to protestant or catholic schools, and existing when this act comes into force, shall be subject to the provisions of this act." Therefore that puts all the protestant and catholic districts under the provisions of the act. Then section 5 is:—"All public schools shall be free schools, and every person in rural municipalities between the age of five and sixteen years, and in cities, towns and villages between the age of six and sixteen, shall have the right to attend some school." Then section 6 is:—"Religious exercises in the public schools shall be conducted according to the regulations of the advisory board. The time for such religious exercises shall be just before the closing hour in the afternoon." Then the parent may notify that he wishes the pupil to be exempt. "Religious exercises shall be held in a public school entirely at the option of the school trustees for the district, and upon receiving written authority from the trustees it shall be the duty of the teachers to hold such religious exercises." Therefore the school may be one in which there is absolutely no religious exercise at all. "The public schools shall be entirely non-sectarian and no religious exercises shall be allowed therein except as above provided."

Lord SHAND:—I think that necessarily excludes doctrinal teaching.

Lord HANNEN:—Of course.

The ATTORNEY-GENERAL:—"No religious exercises shall be allowed therein except as above provided."

Lord WATSON:—I do not understand how a school purely non-sectarian can teach religion on the one side and can refuse to teach religion on the other.

Lord SHAND:—I agree in that.

Lord WATSON:—We call them non-sectarian in Scotland also, but I do not understand it.

Lord MORRIS:—Really the word should be "secular," but they do not like that word.

The ATTORNEY-GENERAL:—What I wish to point out is this, that really the use of the word "sectarian"——

Lord HANNEN:—It means not to teach the doctrines of any particular sect.

The ATTORNEY-GENERAL:—I should have said myself that "sectarian" there means to draw a distinction between the various sects of religion. It is not used in the sense that "denomination" is used in the act of 1870. It is not used with reference to the broad dividing line between Roman catholics and protestants. It is used in a more limited or a more definite sense, of the sects of religion.

Lord MORRIS :—In all the legislation as affecting Manitoba up to 1890, beginning with the act of 1871, is there any reference at all to anything except protestants on the one side and Roman catholics on the other?

The ATTORNEY-GENERAL :—Not the slightest, my lord. Not a word. The whole of the legislation proceeded on the lines of drawing that sole distinction and proceeded on an absolute equality between the two sections, protestant on the one hand and Roman catholic on the other.

Lord MORRIS :—I mean, the legislation never seemed to contemplate any provision for the different sects of protestants.

The ATTORNEY-GENERAL :—Never, my lord. I may ask your lordship's consideration of this. Neither before 1870 nor between 1870 and 1890 has there been any reference in any of the statutes relating to Manitoba, or in the practice, to any distinction between sects, properly so called. The sole distinction is between Roman catholics and protestants.

Lord MORRIS :—That is continually put forward.

The ATTORNEY-GENERAL : – Certainly.

Lord SHAND :—There is one matter I have never had information about. What became of the school buildings, were those just appropriated?

The ATTORNEY-GENERAL :—I am coming to that directly, my lord.

Lord SHAND :—Do not let me induce you to take it out of its order.

The ATTORNEY-GENERAL :—I mentioned it yesterday by anticipation. I might point out to your lordship that the school buildings which had been created by catholic money would become and be public schools under this act. I mentioned that with reference to an argument which my learned friend Mr. Blake may use to-day, that it amounts, to a great extent, to the confiscation of catholic property.

Lord SHAND :—It has occurred to me, for example, that after the act of 1870—I mean the Manitoba Act—if the government had appropriated the catholic schools, I think that would have been invading a right or privilege. I confess that is my impression if that had been done at that time. Whether it may make a difference that in the two years the schools had changed their character or not, is another matter.

The ATTORNEY-GENERAL :—I shall show your lordships, if I may be permitted to refer to it only for the purpose of illustration, what the system was under the act of 1881. Of course I have borne in mind that your lordships have told me, and I have myself submittted, that I am not entitled to refer to it for the purpose of construction, but only for the purposes of illustrating what was the real positi on of the parties at the time. Now, I will pass the reading of the grant sections, to which I have to refer later on, and I will ask your lordships kindly to pass at once to section 141, page 140 : "No teacher shall use or permit to be used as text books any books in a model or public school"—a model school, I am told, is for teaching teachers—"except such as are authorized by the advisory board, and no portion of the legislative grant shall be paid to any school in which unauthorized books are used." Now, from the point of view of catholics, that is an extremely important section. Your lordships will be good enough to remember that the books are to be selected by the advisory board, upon which the catholics are not given any representation, and as to which it is obvious that religious considerations may not enter into the mind of the board at all ; but further than that, that is the board that is to. control the religious exercises. I think your lordships would be of opinion that, at any rate, from the point of view of a conscientious Roman catholic, section 141, with regard to books that are to be used in the schools, has a very important bearing. Then of course there are sections as to penalties with regard to the use of books, which are only following out the same thing.

Lord MACNAGHTEN :—What is the meaning of the reference there at the end of that section, R. S. O.?

The ATTORNEY-GENERAL :—That is the Revised Statutes of Ontario, chapter 225. It is the Consolidation Act.

Lord MACNAGHTEN :—I suppose that was.

The ATTORNEY-GENERAL :—Now, will your lordships turn to sections 178 and 179, which is the point that Lord Shand asked me about. I will read section 179 first: —"In cases where, before the coming into force of this act, catholic school districts have been established, as in the next preceding section mentioned, such catholic school districts shall, upon the coming into force of this act, cease to exist, and all the assets of such catholic school districts shall belong to, and all the liabilities thereof be paid by the public school district. In case the liabilities of any such catholic school district exceeds its assets then the difference shall be deducted from the amount to be allowed as an exemption, as provided in the next preceding section. In case the assets of any such catholic school district exceeds its liabilities, the difference shall be added to the amount to be allowed as an exemption." Now, will your lordships go back to section 178?—"In cases where, before the coming into force of this act, catholic school districts have been established, covering the same territory as any protestant school district, and such protestant school district has incurred indebtedness, the department of education shall cause an inquiry to be made as to the amount of indebtedness of such protestant school district and the amount of its assets. Such of the assets as consist of property shall be valued on the basis of their actual value at the time of the coming into force of this act. It case the amount of the indebtedness exceeds the amount of the assets, then all property assessed in the year 1889 to supporters of such catholic school districts shall be exempt from any taxation for the purpose of paying the principal and interest of an amount of the indebtedness of such school district equal to the difference between its indebtedness and assets. Such exemption shall continue only so long as such property is owned by the person to whom the same was assessed as owner in the year 1889." So that your lordships observe that the property which has been created in catholic school districts has under section 179 to be handed over to the public schools board under this act, the only protection being that if the assets are more than the debts for the time being there shall be a partial temporary exemption from taxation in respect of that particular excess, but, assuming the debts and assets to be equal, the catholic school districts cease to exist and the schools go over to the public school trustees to be held under this act. If your lordships look back there is another section which is to the same effect as that I have mentioned.

Lord HANNEN:—Is there anything to show that any property that a Roman catholic school body possessed before 1870 has been transferred or could be transferred?

The ATTORNEY-GENERAL:—Only this, that if you look at the legislation of 1871 and 1881 you will find that the existing schools, practically speaking, come under the existing legislation.

Lord WATSON:—There were no school districts in 1870.

The ATTORNEY-GENERAL:—No. If your lordships think it right to look, as I shall ask your lordships to look, at the legislation of 1871 and 1881, your lordships will find that the schools in existence get certain benefits by certain contributions being made and come under the then existing legislation; but if your lordships ask me whether there was a building here or there ——

Lord HANNEN:—Or any funds or any assets.

The ATTORNEY-GENERAL:—I have no detailed information about that point, but I shall submit it clearly must have been so. Possibly one of my learned friends can help your lordships on that matter.

Sir RICHARD COUCH:—That would not affect anything existing at 1870.

The ATTORNEY-GENERAL:—No, I think not; but the outcome of what existed in 1870.

Sir RICHARD COUCH:—It affects them.

The ATTORNEY-GENERAL:—What I want your lordships to have in your minds is this: I said that the schools in existence in 1870 came under the acts from 1871 to 1881, grew up, were improved and increased in efficiency with the growth of population by the contributions of the catholic supporters in the one place and the protestants in the other. Now comes the act of 1890 and sweeps all that into the common schools trust.

Lord MORRIS:—The boy of 1870 became the man of 1881.

The ATTORNEY-GENERAL:—The infant before 1871.

Lord MORRIS:—And is now transferred, man and boy, bodily.

The ATTORNEY-GENERAL:—I must ask your lordships to look at the taxing section for a moment. Your lordships are aware that the council levy an equal rate on all property. Section 89 says that it shall be the duty of the council to levy and collect by assessment upon the taxable property an equal rate on all property, and by sections 92 and 93, it is charged on all school property. I only mention this as affording an illustration that a catholic school voluntarily maintained would have to pay to the school rate for the purpose of the schools under this act. If your lordships look at section 93: "The taxable property in a municipality for school purposes shall include all property liable to municipal taxation, and also all property which has heretofore been or may hereafter be exempted by municipal council from municipal taxation, but not from school taxation. No municipal council shall have the right to exempt any property whatsoever from school taxation." It is only an aggravation of the grievance, but it is worth a word of notice that owners of Roman catholic school property would have to contribute to this rate for school purposes.

Lord SHAND:—Even voluntary schools would be subject to assessment?

The ATTORNEY-GENERAL:—Even voluntary Roman catholic schools would be subject to assessment to this rate for other schools. Then the legislative grant depends on the school maintaining its character. That your lordships will find at section 108: "Any school not conducted according to all the provisions of this or any act in force for the time being, or the regulations of the department of education or the advisory board, shall not be deemed a public school within the meaning of the law, and such school shall not participate in the legislative grant." Therefore, of course, that makes it absolutely impossible for any school in which there has been any religious teaching other than that permitted by the advisory board to receive its grant.

Lord WATSON:—Do you say that excludes anything like an adventure school that complies with the terms of the advisory board and the education act?

The ATTORNEY-GENERAL:—From any benefits under the act. It excludes any school.

Lord WATSON:—It rather suggests a school which is not a public school.

The ATTORNEY-GENERAL:—I think it is in the nature of restriction.

Lord WATSON:—A school other than that maintained by the district board may be a public school and may participate in the grant.

Sir RICHARD COUCH:—If not conducted according to the regulations of the board.

Lord MORRIS:—No school could get any public grant in which there was any religion taught other than that which was prescribed by the advisory board, who are entitled to form a sect of their own. By calling it non-sectarian they become a sect, because they could prescribe what religion they liked.

The ATTORNEY-GENERAL:—Would it be convenient if I say to your lordships now what was the system under the act of 1881? It is quite sufficient for me if I state that the whole of that legislation preserved absolute equality between the two sections, and the state managed the schools of the catholic and protestant sections respectively.

Lord MORRIS:—It never contemplated anything but the broad and known distinction historically and theologically on this subject between protestants and catholics.

The ATTORNEY-GENERAL:—There is one section that does bring that out in clear relief, and that is at page 42, namely, that the board is only divided into two sections. That is the act of 1881. Originally, there was equal representation of catholics and protestants. Now, in the year 1881, it is 21, 12 being protestants and nine Roman catholics. The board is to resolve itself into two sections, the one consisting of the protestant and the other of the catholic members. It is clear, I should think, that the reason why there were more protestants than catholics was because there was a larger population, but they do not intermix. The sections are still simply the protestant section and the Roman catholic section.

Lord SHAND:—Each has the management of its own schools.

The ATTORNEY-GENERAL:—Yes.

Lord SHAND:—So that these schools are purely denominational schools.

The ATTORNEY-GENERAL:—Are purely under Roman catholic management and protestant management respectively.

Lord SHAND:—Therefore the system is one of purely denominational schools.

The ATTORNEY-GENERAL:—Your lordship will understand why I do not quite accept that.

Lord SHAND:—You do not admit that?

The ATTORNEY-GENERAL:—I do not dispute it at all, but only that denomination may be used in two senses. It was used yesterday in argument, by Sir Horace Davey, as meaning baptists and as meaning presbyterians. I want it to be understood in adopting the word denominational——

Lord SHAND:—You recognize only two denominations?

The ATTORNEY-GENERAL:—That is what I meant.

Lord SHAND:—I have understood that quite.

The ATTORNEY-GENERAL:—If your lordships observe, each of the two sections selects its own books. If you look at the top of page 43, sub-section C, the protestant members select the protestant books, and the Roman catholic select the Roman catholic books. "Provided, however, that in the case of books having reference to religion and morals, such selection by the catholic section of the board shall be subject to the approval of the competent religious authority." That is because over the Roman catholics there might be still, according to their conscience, a higher authority than their own judgment with regard to that matter. Then section 9, a protestant member of the board shall be the superintendent of the protestant schools, and a catholic member superintendent of the catholic schools. Then section 12:—"It shall be the duty of the council of the municipalities to establish and alter, when necessary, the school districts within their bounds, and if any of the said councils shall refuse or neglect so to do, then on the petition of at least five of the ratepayers of the school district, or proposed school district, of the section of the board of education to which the same belongs, the said section of the board shall establish or alter the same as may by them be deemed expedient. (a.) The establishment of a school district of one denomination shall not prevent the establishment of a school district of the other denomination in the same place, and a protestant and a catholic district may include the same territory in whole or in part."

Lord MORRIS:—That sub-section shows that what was meant by denominations was nothing but protestants and catholics.

The ATTORNEY-GENERAL:—That is why I ventured to call attention to it, particularly with reference to the question put to me. It is obvious there they are referring to denominations in the sense of protestants and Roman catholics.

Lord SHAND:—I have not a doubt about it that the scheme did refer generally to protestants and catholics, but it remains that the system the government established under that was denominational.

The ATTORNEY-GENERAL:—Was catholic, and the other.

Lord SHAND:—Those are two denominations, but purely denominational, I should think. I do not see how it could possibly be put otherwise.

The ATTORNEY-GENERAL:—I was meeting the point made by Sir Horace Davey and pressed with great force upon your lordships that if we were right this work was to be broken up into a number of various sections.

Lord SHAND:—That depends upon another matter altogether—the particular section of the act of 1890 which was the word "class."

The ATTORNEY GENERAL:—Oh! no, my lord.

Lord SHAND:—You will deal with that when you come to Logan's case.

The ATTORNEY-GENERAL:—I should rather deal with that now. I am not instructed in Logan's case, and have no right to deal with it. The only proviso is "with respect to denominational schools which any class of persons have by law or practice in the province at the union." One class of persons who had privileges and rights were Roman catholics on one side and protestants on the other.

Lord SHAND:—That is a question of fact.

Sir RICHARD COUCH:—They were the only recognized classes of persons at that time.

The ATTORNEY-GENERAL:—Certainly, so far as the evidence goes.

Sir RICHARD COUCH:—No subdivision of protestants seems to have been contemplated.

The ATTORNEY-GENERAL:—The affidavits state that the protestants combined for the purpose of the protestant schools.

Mr. MCCARTHY:—Not before 1871.

Lord MORRIS:—They did not dream of anything but the two denominations of protestants and catholics.

Lord SHAND:—There is nothing in section 22 about either catholic or protestant. It is "denominational schools which any class of persons have by law or practice."

The ATTORNEY-GENERAL:—Your lordship must look at the next section—"affecting any right or privilege of the protestant or Roman catholic minority of the queen's subjects."

Lord SHAND:—That is not the section that is founded on. Section 1 is founded on by Mr. Logan, who says I had denominational schools; they were a large and important class of schools, and I am affected in the same way as Barrett.

The ATTORNEY-GENERAL:—I am not counsel for Logan, and knowing the position in which Logan stands now——

Lord MORRIS:—As far as I am concerned, I am not capable of trying two cases at the same time. That is an objection I have to it—I could not.

The ATTORNEY-GENERAL:—I will judge it with reference to what your lordship said just now. I must be permitted to point out that I do not admit that "denomination" in sub-section 1 of the 22nd section means anything other than protestant and Roman catholic; and if you look the whole way through the British North America Act and everything in this case I humbly submit it points to identically the same consideration.

Lord HANNEN:—Do you say it would not apply even if it was proved in evidence, as I am not aware it was at all, that there were several presbyterian schools, and that the class of presbyterians had established schools of their own.

The ATTORNEY-GENERAL:—I think it would apply and I think it ought to be held to apply, but that was not my main argument as to what led to the words being inserted. I do not deny that it would apply and that they would get the benefit of it, because sufficiently strong language had been used; but denomination in Manitoba in 1870 meant the distinction between catholics and protestants.

Lord WATSON:—You might put it in this way: Supposing you had a presbyterian school teaching religion in a form of Calvinism which was very objectionable to episcopalians in the district, who would not send their children there. Would the persons maintaining that school be entitled to an exemption on a question of school rate for protestants?

The ATTORNEY-GENERAL:—I should have thought that if there was a class of persons representing Calvinism they would be entitled to say they were one of those included under the term denomination. We admit we were part of a larger group, but were included under the word denomination, and, therefore, come in, but not because they were Calvinists, but because they form part of that which the statute was regarding, the distinction between Roman catholics and protestants. Then if your lordships would be good enough to note that by section 25 there was power to assess in each school district, that is to say the catholic district and the protestant district, equally to supplement the grant, and it was to be laid equally—that is section 27.

Lord HANNEN:—I have not caught where the legislative grant is provided for?

The ATTORNEY-GENERAL:—In section 84, I think. It would be convenient to take it now, because I wanted it myself. The rate only supplements the grant in section 25. Section 84 says: "The sum appropriated by the legislature for common school purposes shall be divided between the protestant and Roman catholic section of the board of education in the manner hereinafter provided, in proportion to the number of children between the ages of five and fifteen, inclusive, residing in the various protestant and Roman catholic school districts in the province where schools are in operation as shown in the census returns." Then there are provisions for the apportionment, and provision for representation of the catholics and protestants respectively, and provision for the payments being made to the various sections. Then going back to section 25, the legislative grant is supplemented by an equal rate, which is to be levied equally upon the various sections, and if your lordships would kindly look at section 30: "The ratepayers of a school district, including religious, benevolent or educational corporations, shall pay their respective assessments to the schools of their respective denominations, and in no case shall a protestant ratepayer be obliged to pay for a catholic school, or a catholic ratepayer for a protestant school."

Lord SHAND:—I am not sure that I follow the object with which we are looking at this statute just now.

The ATTORNEY-GENERAL:—Perhaps your lordship would not mind looking at section 30 in connection with this. It is for two objects—to show that "denomination" meant, for the purposes of the act of 1870, catholics on the one side and protestants on the other; and to show that when the legislature of Manitoba worked out, as they did in 1871, as well as 1881—because I could show the same thing in 1871—the rights and privileges of each class of persons, they recognized that very same exemption which had existed in Ontario by law, was applied to Quebec by law, although it did not exist in Manitoba by law, but existed, as I submit, by practice. Section 30 is at page 48: "The ratepayers of a school district, including religious, benevolent or educational corporations, shall pay their respective assessments to the schools of their respective denominations, and in no case shall a protestant ratepayer be obliged to pay for a catholic school, or a catholic ratepayer for a protestant school." Then the next section, 31: "When property, owned by a protestant, is occupied by a Roman catholic, and *vice versa*, the tenant in such cases shall only be assessed for the amount of property he owns, whether real or personal, but the school taxes on said rented or leased property shall, in all cases, and whether or not the same has been or is stipulated in any deed contract or lease whatever, be paid to the trustees of the section to which belongs the owner of the property so leased or rented, and to no other, subject to the exemptions aforesaid."

Lord MORRIS:—If that was done in 1881, Logan would have no case.

The ATTORNEY-GENERAL:—Certainly not.

Lord MORRIS:—I have not heard his case yet. In the year 1881 no catholic would be obliged to pay for a protestant school, and no protestant would be obliged to pay for a catholic school. That is all.

The ATTORNEY-GENERAL:—Then section 34: "The school trustees in each school district shall be a corporation under the name of 'the school trustees for the protestant or catholic, as the case may be, school district'" of so and so. Then section 84 again, in reply to Lord Hannen's question, dealing with the grant, also divides it between catholic and protestant, and section 101 provided for regulations being made for compulsory attendance at the various schools. If your lordships would kindly take it from me—I will make good the statement—in substance, subject to slight alterations, the scheme of the act of 1871 was exactly the same exempting the protestants from rating or subscribing to the catholic schools or catholics to protestant schools.

My lords, there is one part of the case that has not been read, which I think is entitled to respect and to some words of comment, and that is the judgment of the chief justice, Sir William Ritchie, because I submit to your lordships that he puts one or two arguments in my favour which are entitled to some consideration. I am not going to read the whole of it, of course. Your lordships are aware that the judgment of the five judges of the supreme court was unanimous, and this judgment, I think, does contain some rather important arguments. I read at page 85, from the second paragraph: "It must be assumed that in legislating with reference to a constitution for Manitoba, the Dominion parliament was well acquainted with the conditions of the country to which it was about to give a constitution, and it must have known full well that at that time there were no schools established by law, religious or secular, public or sectarian. In such a state of affairs, and having reference to the condition of the population, and the deep interest felt and strong opinions entertained on the subject of separate schools, it cannot be supposed that the legislature had not its attention more particularly directed to the educational institutions of Manitoba, and more especially to the schools then in practical operation, their constitution, mode of support and peculiar character in matters of religious instruction. To have overlooked considerations of this kind is to impute to parliament a degree of short-sightedness and indifference which, in view of the discussions relating to separate schools which had taken place in the older provinces, or some of them, and to the extreme vigilance with which educational questions are scanned, and the importance attached to them, more particularly by the catholic church, as testified to by Monsigneur Taché, cannot, to my mind, be for a moment entertained. Read in the light of considerations such as these, must we not conclude that the legislature well weighed its language and intended that every word it used should have force and effect? The British North America Act confers on the local legislature the exclusive power to make laws in relation to education, provided that nothing in such laws shall prejudicially affect any right or privilege with respect to denominational schools which any class of persons had by law in the province at the union, but the Manitoba act goes much further and declares that nothing in such law shall prejudicially affect any right or privilege with respect to denominational schools, which any class of persons had by law or practice in the province at the union. We are now practically asked to reject the words 'or practice' and construe the statute as if they had not been used, and to read this restrictive clause out of the statute as being inapplicable to the existing state of things in Manitoba at the union, whereas on the contrary, I think, by the insertion of the words 'or practice' it was made practically applicable to the condition at that time of the educational institutions which were, unquestionably and solely, as the evidence shows, of a denominational character. It is clear that at the time of the passing of the Manitoba Act, no class of persons had by law any rights or privileges secured to them, so, if we reject the words 'or practice' as meaningless or inoperative, we shall be practically expunging the whole of the restrictive clause from the statute." Then his lordship referred to some authorities on the question of the construction of statutes, which I do not wish to trouble about, but it is important I should read the passage on page 87 with regard to Renaud, because he was the presiding judge who decided Renaud. Perhaps I ought to begin a little earlier than that, at the second paragraph of page 87: "It cannot be said that the words used do not harmonize with the subject of the enactment and the object which I think the legislature had in view. But if the legislature intended to recognize denominational schools, how could they have used more expressive words to indicate their intention, since the words used read in their ordinary grammatical sense admit of but one meaning and therefore one construction? and I do not think we should speculate on the intention of the legislature, more particularly as that intention is very clearly indicated by the language used, considering the condition of the country and the state of education in that country. And the object appearing from these circumstances that the legislature must have had in view in using them, which in my opinion was clearly to protect the rights and privileges with respect to denominational schools which any class of persons had by law or practice, that is to say had by usage at the time of the union."

Lord Shand:—I do not think there is very much difference between the judges as to the meaning of the words. It is rather in the application of the words that the difficulty arises. I do not think anything could be clearer than the way in which Mr. Justice Bain puts it. He puts it exactly as this judgment has done. I think they are really all practically agreed about the meaning, but it really comes to be a question of application.

The Attorney-General:—Yes. "The decision of the court in the case of *exparte* Renaud turned entirely on the fact that the Parish School Act of New Brunswick, 21 Vict., c. 9, conferred no legal rights on any class of persons with respect to denominational schools. It was then simply determined that there were no legal rights with respect to denominational schools, a very different case from that we are now called on to determine. It may very well be that in view of the wording of the British North America Act, and the peculiar state of educational matters in Manitoba, the Dominion parliament determined to enlarge the scope of the British North America Act, and protect not only denominational schools established by law, but those existing in practice, for, as I am reported to have said, and no doubt did say in *exparte* Renaud, that in that case, 'we must look to the law as it was at the time of the union, and by that and that alone be governed.' Now, on the other hand, in this case, we must look to the practice with reference to the denominational schools as it existed at the time of the passing of the Manitoba Act. That this was the view taken by the legislature of Manitoba would seem to be indicated by the legislation of that province up to the passing of the Public Schools Act, which very clearly recognized denominational schools and made provision for their maintenance and support, providing that support for protestant schools should be taxed on protestants, and for catholic schools should be taxed on catholics, and conferring the management and control of protestant schools on protestants, and the like management and control of catholic schools on catholics. This denominational system was most effectually wiped out by the Public Schools Act, and not a vestige of the denominational character left in the school system of Manitoba. Mr. Justice Dubuc gives an accurate synopsis of the legislation as follows." Then his lordship cites Mr. Justice Dubuc. Then the bottom of page 90 bears on the question of confiscation. He has gone through the whole of the sections to which I have called attention, and he says:—"It is easy to see from the above that the new act makes a complete change in the system. The denominational division of catholics and protestants is entirely done away with, and by section 179, where, as in this case, the catholic school district is supposed to cover the same territory as any protestant school district, the said catholic school district is not only wiped out, but its property and assets are vested in and belong to the other school district, which under the act becomes the public school district. But it is said that the catholics as a class are not prejudicially affected by this act. Does it not prejudicially, that is to say, injuriously, disadvantageously, which is the meaning of the word 'prejudicially,' affect them when they are taxed to support schools, of the benefit of which, by their religious belief, and the rules and principles of their church, they cannot conscientiously avail themselves, and at the same time by compelling them to find means to support schools to which they can conscientiously send their children, or in the event of their not being able to find sufficient means to do both, to be compelled to allow their children to go without either religious or secular instruction? In other words, I think the catholics were directly prejudicially affected by such legislation, but whether directly or indirectly, the local legislature was powerless to affect them prejudicially in the matter of denominational schools which they certainly did by practically depriving them of their denominational schools and compelling them to support schools the benefit of which protestants alone can enjoy." I do submit to your lordships that those passages do contain a powerful argument in favour of the views I am submitting.

Lord WATSON:—Do you understand the learned judge there to confine the nature and extent of the privilege? There is a great deal of that that does not raise any controversial matter. He says "There was at that time in actual operation or practice a system of denominational schools in Manitoba well established and the *de facto* rights and privileges of which were enjoyed by a large class of persons." I do not find he specifies anywhere what the privilege acquired then was which is infringed now, till he comes to the last part.

The ATTORNEY-GENERAL:—No.

Lord WATSON:—And that may be directly or indirectly. It may mean having the privilege of not paying for another. That is one view the learned judges take that that is directly invaded by the act of 1890. Another view is that they had certain rights and privileges before which were indirectly assailed by the fact of their having to pay.

The ATTORNEY-GENERAL:—Yes. The words "prejudicially affect" are certainly large words.

Lord SHAND:—I think when you read at length what the judges say who take that view of the case it is this:—You have prejudicially affected a right or privilege of exemption.

The ATTORNEY-GENERAL:—Certainly.

Lord SHAND :—That is what it comes to and the question is whether there is such a right of exemption.

The ATTORNEY-GENERAL :—And also prejudicially affect the schools which had been established, which were catholic schools and which are handed over to this board.

Lord SHAND :—I do not think that is made a point in the case at all—the taking over school buildings. I do not see any suggestion of that.

The ATTORNEY-GENERAL :—Sir William Ritchie refers to it most distinctly.

Lord WATSON :—If the learned chief justice had been of opinion that this was a privilege given by the first clause of exemption from payment of a rate towards the schools of another denomination when they were supporting their own it would not have been necessary for him to labour the point at all. It is clear that that privilege existed.

The ATTORNEY-GENERAL :—Would Lord Shand look at the bottom of page 90. It may be brief, but it is very distinct:—" Where, as in this case, a catholic school district is supposed to cover the same territory as any protestant school district the said catholic school district is not only wiped out but its property and assets are vested in and belong to the other school district which under the act becomes the public school district."

Lord SHAND :—Those assets and property were, as I understand it, taken up in the year 1889 or 1890, whereas the thing we have to deal with is the property in 1870.

The ATTORNEY-GENERAL :—But your lordship will permit me to point out that that 1890 property has been built up under the act of 1870.

Lord SHAND :—If the father and boy theory can be worked out, it comes to that.

Lord MACNAGHTEN :—The chief justice does contrast very strongly the position under the act of 1890 and under the act of 1881. That possibly may have more effect.

The ATTORNEY-GENERAL :—I have only argued it with reference to what were the rights existing in fact at the time of the passing of the act of 1870; but we must look at it as a growing system. It has growm up, as we believe, under the protection of the rights which existed in 1870 and I do not know that you can say it has become a different thing. Howev?r, I have sufficiently troubled your lordships on that. The case of Fearon *vs.* Mitchell was cited to your lordships, but we submit it has no application to this case at all. That was the case of a general act of parliament. The Markets Clauses Act, 1847, says that no markets shall be established that shall interfere with any rights and the right there supposed to be interfered with was the right of a butcher to sell meat. It is obvious that in a general statute of that character "rights" could not be construed in the same way as where we are dealing with a special class referred to, as in section 22. It applied to all towns, and of course "rights" there would be rights analogous to market rights —rights such as are supposed to be protected by a franchise or by grant or privilege of that kind. No authority is of any use to your lordships, but I will cite one or two, because my friend Mr. Ewart, who has given me great assistance, has been good enough to give me the cases. There are a number of cases in which a wider meaning has been given to the word "rights" under the Lands Clauses Act and although there was unity of ownership, "rights" have been held to include rights of way which would not be strictly and properly called rights of way unless over the property of another person. I would call attention to the language of Lord Blackburn in Musgrave *vs.* The Inclosure Commissioners, 9 Law Reports Queen's Bench, page 162, where the question was as to the right of pasturage. That was the case where under a general inclosure act the rights of pasturage which had been usually enjoyed by the lord of the manor and his tenants were to be specified and mentioned, and Lord Blackburn, referring to this language "a right of pasturage," said :—" By the technical rules of English law, when the owner of the fee simple of the dominant hereditament is also the owner of the waste ground in which the right of pasturage is exercised he can have, strictly speaking, no such right at all. In cases where the land has been parted with by the lord and so severed and then again attached in different portions, as where the lord buys back a farm, and instead of having it conveyed back to trustees, takes a conveyance to himself, he, *de facto*, as continually happens, loses the right of common. At the same time it is not an uncommon thing—and I take it to have been the case in the present instance—that the lord has farms on parts of the estates which have never been separated from the main estate, demesne farms that have always been his freehold, and which, therefore, never could strictly acquire the right of common. Nevertheless, that distinction not being recognized by those who practically managed these things in the days of old, the tenants of these demesne lands under the lord did enjoy the same rights of common over the wastes as those persons to whom lands had been conveyed; and they did *de facto* enjoy and use the rights of common just as if the freeholder of the demesne lands was not possessed of the freehold of the land over which the right of common was used. Looking at this enactment with a view to the existing *de facto* rights of that sort, I cannot construe the act of parliament, when it says 'right of pasturage which may have been usually enjoyed by such lord or his tenants' as meaning anything else than rights of pasturage and common which have been enjoyed by the lord and his tenants in such a manner as, if it were not for this technical rule—that the lord, being the freeholder of the dominant tenements and of the soil of the waste, too, cannot have a right to common —would prove an established right." Then Lord Blackburn speaks of them as *quasi* rights.

In the same way, Mr. Justice Chitty, in Bayley *vs.* Great Western Railway, 26 Chancery Division, where he was dealing with such words as "rights, numbers and appurtenances belonging to hereditaments" pointed out that where such enumeration was made, "rights" was meant to include benefits enjoyed as distinguished from rights in a secondary sense and something less than a legal sense. He actually uses that expression—"'rights' must be used in some secondary sense."

Sir RICHARD COUCH:—It has been applied in the case of right of way.

The ATTORNEY-GENERAL:—That was a right of way case, and in Barlow *vs.* Ross (24 Queen's Bench Division, p. 381), under the Artizans' Dwellings Act, the local authority were to purchase all rights or easements in or relating to such land, and they were to be extinguished, and the present chief justice said: "I admit that the words *prima facie* mean rights or easements actually existing, and it is true that under the Prescription Act a right or easement is gained only after the lapse of the particular time specified, and cannot be considered as existing before that period. All that must be conceded, and if we were dealing with an act the subject matter of which was different from that of the act now in question, and we could see that to give the words their *prima facie* effect would not defeat the scheme of legislation, we should interpret the words according to their ordinary meaning. But it is plain, if this contention were correct, the result would be that in many cases the objects of the act would be defeated." There we have got "rights and privileges" existing by practice—rights and privileges which the class of persons had by practice, and I submit that when you find the object being clearly to protect the Roman catholics and the protestants respectively, and the language being used of a general character, it is that class of legislation to which a wide meaning will be given, and not, as attempted by my learned friends, as we humbly submit, a narrow meaning. My lords, I do not hesitate to put before your lordships that, if this statute of 1890 had been attempted to be passed in the year 1871, upon the information before your lordships, it would have been regarded as being a breach of the conditions upon which Manitoba had consented to come in, and had asked to be brought into the union. It is only in consequence of it being what I may call the development of the educational system from the point of view of those who desire to divorce religion from education that such a statute can be forced or attempted to be forced upon Roman catholics, and they ordered to contribute to the cost of a purely secular education. I submit that however good may be the motives—no doubt they are excellent —of persons who hold those views, it was intended in the year 1870 to protect the privileges of Roman catholics, and to prevent their being prejudicially affected, and I do humbly submit to your lordships that a consideration of the provisions of that act of 1890 would lead your lordships to the conclusion that it does most prejudicially affect those rights, and that the unanimous judgment of the supreme court ought to be affirmed.

Mr. BLAKE :—My lords, in this case I need scarcely say I have a great deal of diffidence in addressing your lordships after the attorney-general and at the close of the third day that the case has been occupying the attention of your lordships. The first observation I was about to make was that which was stated by Lord Shand, that it is worthy of note that the nine judges in the court below all put, in language differing certainly the one from the other, our first ground or proposition, that is to say, that there are rights or there are privileges as was put by Mr. Justice Bain, at page 78: "I think that nothing in any law to be passed by the legislature relating to education was to prejudicially affect anything that any class of persons had been in fact and generally in the habit of doing with respect to denominational schools, with the acquiescence implied or expressed of the rest of the community." The whole of the nine judges concurred in that. Mr. Justice Dubuc (if your lordships care to take the page where he speaks of that) at page 61; Mr. Justice Bain at pages 78 and 80; Chief Justice Taylor, at pages 47 and 48; Mr. Justice Killam, at pages 33 and 34; Sir William Ritchie, in the same way, at pages 86 and 87; Mr. Justice Patterson, at pages 92 and 93; Mr. Justice Fournier, at pages 96 and 97; and Mr. Justice Taschereau, at pages 109 and 113, all concur in the conclusion that, notwithstanding the New Brunswick Act, there were rights in Manitoba, whether we call them rights or privileges—or there was a state of matters which it was intended should be preserved, and the point on which they differ is simply this: Six of the learned judges concluded that there was a prejudicial affecting of these rights and the other three came to the conclusion that these rights conceded to them were not prejudicially affected.

Now, my lords, I think it might perhaps be helpful, in answer to one or two of the statements made by your lordships in regard to the question of whether it would be possible to have any general system of school education in the province of Manitoba, just to call the attention of your lordships to our position in the province of Ontario and in the province of Quebec. There can be no doubt that a very large number, more probably in the province of Ontario, were very much in favour of having a general system of school education where all denominations, whether members of the church of England, Roman catholics, presbyterians, congregationalists or baptists, all could attend. There is no doubt whatever that the matter was bitterly, and very bitterly fought; the Honourable George Brown and the Honourable Alexander Mackenzie leading on the one side in favour of that, and the great benefits to arise from all the young of the country being educated in all general matters at the same schools, helping to efface to a large extent the bitterness which unfortunately sometimes does arise. Well, it was found that that could not be attained. The Roman catholics insisted that they would not have that. They made it a matter of faith. The leaders, whether they were right or whether they were wrong, insisted on the old-fashioned notion: Give me the child from the age of 5 to 15 and you may take the man after that and deal with him as you please; you cannot take from him the religion that we have saturated him with during the school period. A very great number of us thought it was most unfortunate, but still it exists, and it existed in these two provinces virtually of the dominion of Canada, representing four millions of inhabitants, as against the whole population of something under five millions. It was a matter that was well known. Persons who had gone to the province of Manitoba were from these two provinces. They knew perfectly well all these old fights, and knew perfectly well the way in which it had been resolved, and knew perfectly well that there was this right in each of these provinces that, if you choose to support either the protestant or the Roman catholic schools, you are absolved from any payment to the other schools. They knew perfectly well that these were the two divisions. They were divided into the Roman catholic and the protestant. To a large extent, although I quite admit that there were exceptions, the protestants generally ranged themselves on the side of the general education. All kinds of epithets were hurled—the godless schools and the godless colleges—and all through that war, which was well known, we passed. It had raised as much trouble as a few pence of ship money here or a few shillings of tithe in this land, and persons were all alert and were all alive to these questions.

Now, we in the province of Ontario cannot have, except in a very qualified way, any general system of education just because of that. A Roman catholic gives notice, and the result is that he is free from paying a cent to the assessment excepting so far as his own school is concerned. A protestant does the same. That is so in the province of Quebec; and that was a system which was introduced in 1865, and, when at the time of confederation it was thought reasonable to make another exertion and to introduce a system whereby there should be the general, or common, or national schools, then the arguments that took place in the confederation debate show that they submitted that was a matter that had been settled, and these very gentlemen I have referred to, though they were so very strongly wedded to the more general system of secular education, admitted in the confederation debate—that is the late Mr. George Brown and the late Mr. Alexander Mackenzie—that that had been settled and that they could not go back on that, and that they must accept the British North America Act with the introduction of those words that were to preserve these rights. I think, therefore, that perhaps it would be helpful for us to understand that in 1870 that was the position of matters; on the one side the protestant schools and on the other side the Roman catholic schools; a fierce and continued and lengthened war in favour of what a great many of us considered to be right, undenominational schools, but still the country had found in favour of the other. Therefore when they were dealing with Manitoba, this question was one that was well known to those persons, to a large extent a majority from these two provinces, who would know very well what had taken place in Ontario and in Quebec; perhaps as little knowing as to New Brunswick as perhaps many of the inhabitants of England would know about what might be the peculiar laws of the Channel Islands or some other place with which there may be as little commercial or other intercourse as between the islands of Guernsey and Jersey here.

Then that being so, I simply desire to call attention to one other matter in this book which was given yesterday to your lordships.

Lord MACNAGHTEN:—Before you pass from that, would you say that the act of 1890 would be unobjectionable if the catholics had been exempted from contributing to the school rate as they are in the Ontario Act?

Mr. BLAKE:—I think, my lord, that at all events a very great ground of objection would be removed.

Lord MACNAGHTEN:—That is the case in Ontario, is it not?

Mr. BLAKE:—Yes.

Lord MACNAGHTEN:—There is what you call undenominational education very much on the lines of the act of 1890 with this exception, that any person who contributes to a catholic school and gives proper notice is exempted from taxation.

Mr. BLAKE:—Quite so.

Lord MACNAGHTEN:—That is so.

Mr. BLAKE:—That is so, my lord.

Lord MACNAGHTEN:—There is no exemption in the act of 1890, but if there were that exemption in the act of 1890, you think it would remove a very great ground of objection?

Mr. BLAKE:—Yes.

Lord WATSON:—Under the Ontario act he must become a contributor to a catholic school which is approved of under the act?

Mr. BLAKE:—Yes.

Lord WATSON:—He must conform to a certain extent to the prescription of the act?

Mr. BLAKE:—Quite so, undoubtedly; but these acts from 1870 to 1890 are based very much upon our system in Ontario; that is to say, A gives a notice: I am a Roman catholic and I desire to support Roman catholic schools, and then the protestant collector cannot touch him or his property.

Lord WATSON:—Then he will not only get that relief, but participate in the government grant?

Mr. BLAKE:—Yes.

Lord MACNAGHTEN:—I was looking at the Ontario act, and I see that nothing in the act authorizing the levying of rates for public school purposes shall apply to the separate Roman catholic supported schools, and then there is a reference to the 48th Victoria. What act is that?

Mr. BLAKE:—That is the act which is consolidated. In our consolidations, for convenience, in following them they put in the clauses.

Sir RICHARD COUCH:—Show where they come from?

Mr. BLAKE:—Quite so; just as they do in the Manitoba Act they put the Ontario statute to show where it comes from, so that if there is a decision upon it they will be able to apply it at once to these clauses in the act.

Lord SHAND:—I feel the force of what you say, that on looking to the act of 1870 it is quite right and proper to see what is doing in all the different provinces, but am I not right in thinking that when the British North America Act of 1867 was passed there were clearly privileges and rights of Roman catholics under previous legislation which had to be preserved?

Mr. BLAKE:—Yes, in 1865.

Lord SHAND:—There was that distinction, that when you passed the act of 1867 you had clearly rights which must be preserved as they were under previous statutes. When you came to pass the act of 1870 you were in controversy whether there were any such?

Mr. BLAKE:—Quite so; but that would depend on whether when the representatives of these four provinces met they thought it would be too great a sacrifice to give up the right of having the general schools in favour of denominational schools. If they had stood by that they could not have had confederation at all, and it was then they said, as we made that sacrifice—and we consider it a great sacrifice—in 1865, we do not want to go back on that in 1867 and throw it down as a bone of contention to prevent confederation being carried out.

Then, I was going to make one other observation before going for a very few moments into details, and it was this: I argued the case before the supreme court, the judges of which seem to have been satisfied to allow the matter to be disposed of upon some of the grounds argued, but they did not pay so much attention to what I consider to be one of the principal points that was brought forward. We contended there that, as the judges in the courts below had found that we were entitled to the continuation of the state of matters that existed, modified as it might be by legislation that did not interfere with those—that as we had those, they could not be interfered with in any, at all events, of three ways. First, you cannot interfere with them by in any way altering our denominational schools; you must allow that to stand, you cannot compel us to support or sustain a school of another class. Second, because it takes away so much of the money that otherwise would have been expended in the sustainment of our own schools. But one point that I have thought of immense moment, and I put it in the foreground there, was this: You cannot stifle my conscientious religious convictions, and although I may be entirely wrong in the view of a vast number of persons, you cannot compel me to pay money to the support of a school that the head of my church says is a school which wanting the very foundation of all true education—wanting a religious training—should not be supported by you. My argument was that where you accord to persons rights in regard to denominational schools you cannot but interfere when you say under compulsion your money shall go to the support of that which you conscientiously believe to be doing a wrong in the community, and which the head of your church says is doing a wrong, and in respect of which, in the province of Quebec, if a Roman catholic were to attempt to send a child to a protestant school the rites of the church would at once be denied to that person.

Lord WATSON:—You suggest in other words, I think, that the object of the clause in the act of 1870 was to stereotype the relations to each other *inter se* of the two denominations, protestant and catholic, preserving to the legislature the right of regulating the kind of administration, the mode in which the funds should be raised and applied ——?

Mr. BLAKE:—Yes.

Lord WATSON:—And preserving throughout that relation of immunity of the one party paying for the other's schools?

Mr. BLAKE:—Helping each of these two denominations by making the rules so as to compel payments, and as to attendance, and in all the various ways in which it has been helped from 1870 to 1890, but not to affect that which was one of the matters that the Roman catholics had for a quarter of a century been absolutely insisting on, and had been a matter in respect of which there was very strong feeling from 1845, at all events up to this period of 1870.

Lord SHAND:—In other words, continuing denominational education for all time coming.

Mr. BLAKE:—I dare say that that may be the result of it. I dare say it may be the result. I, for one, deplore it in our own province of Ontario. I had a great deal rather it was not so. I was one of those who struggled against it. I was not a bit convinced.

Lord SHAND:—I do not say that it is not right, if the statute does it; but I want to see the result.

Mr. BLAKE:—Quite so; and your lordship will bear in mind that although we have a large protestant majority in Ontario, there is a very large—a much larger—Roman catholic majority in the province of Quebec, and one thing that solaced the protestants in Ontario was this: You want your rights protected in Quebec, do not you? Yes. Then we will award you in the same way protection there. So that it was a kind of compensating pendulum, the motion there—it equalized in both of the provinces, and made a great many people accept it that never would have accepted it in the province of Ontario. Their protestant friends wrote and communicated and urged: We are here at the mercy of Roman catholics, must not you think of us and not press too strongly to have a general school, although you may carry it in Ontario, because the evil results of it will be felt by us in the province of Quebec.

[Adjourned for a short time.]

Mr. BLAKE:—I was saying it was under these circumstances, and the matter being in a comparatively far off land, New Brunswick, creating the difficulty, that the questions were raised in 1869, of entering upon Manitoba, and your lordships will find in the blue book that my learned friend, Mr. McCarthy, gave in the day before yesterday, at page 73, the proclamation that was made when the country was in a state of rebellion. The governor general sends this proclamation, and on page 73, the 2nd paragraph, it says: "By her majesty's authority I do, therefore, assure you that on the union with Canada your civil and religious rights and privileges will be respected, your property secured to you, and that your country will be governed, as in the past, under British laws, and in the spirit of British justice." And your lordships will find that the then archbishop, who was at Rome, was cabled to come over and help in allaying the difficulty that had arisen in the province of Manitoba. It is part of the petition that is presented, the return to which, in the shape of the opinion of Sir John Thompson, was referred to, and I refer to pages 2 and 5 of that book in addition to the page that I have given. Then it was simply a question as between the protestants on the one side and the Roman catholics on the other. The principle of separate schools was the admitted principle introduced, as your lordships see, by the 93rd section of the British North America Act, and the protection afforded as much needed in the new land of Manitoba, as much demanded, they being in a state not willing to abandon any of their rights, and on the other side not in a position to make a demand against them, but on the contrary freely to accede almost anything in reason that was asked by the large body of Roman catholics in that province. Then it is to be observed also, I think, that the matter of education is the only one in respect of which there is special legislation and special restriction. There are various clauses as to what can be done, but in respect of this alone has the legislature deemed it necessary that there should be these especial clauses conferring these especial rights, and giving those limited powers of dealing therewith. It is also to be observed that the act of 1863, which was referred to, is an act to restore the Roman catholics in Upper Canada certain rights in respect to certain schools, and by section 14 of that act immunity from subscription to public schools is provided for. It is not a right which they had absolutely prior to that, and it is simply to show that the word "right" and that the word "privilege," and these words that are used in this enactment, as one of the judges in quotation said, *uti loquitur vulgus*, and not to be taken in any restricted or narrow signification. The general idea was that you have got a system of education, and that system of education is to be preserved, not to be interfered with prejudicially, and the same mode of dealing with the children is to be kept alive subsequent to the passing of this act as was in existence at the period previous to it. Your lordships will perceive that in the British North America Act it is called there a system of separate or dissentient schools, clearly referring to protestant and Roman catholic schools, from the second section, and I submit that in the same way this being, or the other act being, *in pari materia*, where we have "nothing in any such law shall prejudicially affect any right or privilege with respect to denominational schools which any class of persons have by law or practice," and the next section gives you the appeal shall lie affecting a right or privilege of the protestant or Roman catholic minority in the queen's bench. I do not think that it would be unfair to say that what is presented there is a system of education headed, on the one hand, by protestants, a system of education headed, on the other hand, by Roman catholics, and whatever may be the position—whatever may be the exemptions—whatever may be the benefits—nothing is to be taken from the one side and nothing is to be added to on the other. I would also ask your lordships' consideration of this in the Manitoba Act. I am reading of course from page 4 where the two are contracted. It is not merely that it shall not do away with the denominational schools at the date of the union but that the legislation shall be subject to and according to the following provisions. Therefore, there may be and it is intended to be legislation, but with this restriction, "That nothing in any such law shall prejudicially affect any right or privilege with respect to denominational schools which any class of persons have by law or practice." It is not that it shall be with reference to the denominational schools in existence, but there may be legislation—there may be a dealing with these schools, there may be additions made and there may be great improvements of these schools, and it is with that class of matters, which is the result of what was in existence at the time of the union, that I submit the Manitoba Act says is not to be interfered with. Then I say that the language of the act plainly deals with and intends to preserve certain rights: that, virtually, giving it the meaning of my learned friend on the other side, it is making it absolutely meaningless. It is not preserving to us any rights, for it never was questioned in our country but that you might, if you pleased, have your school supported by yourself. And as to the very far fetched idea that in Massachusetts the land of blue laws, they should not yet have forgotten them and added something of the kind, it can scarcely be an illustration to read I should think in the construction of our act. At that time there was no question whatever but that there was no thought in any person's mind but that you could have your school and could sustain your school. That was not the thought but the thought was: Can we have these separate or denominational schools? Can we have that system whereby, if we throw our money and our aid and our intelligence to the sustainment of those, and if we do carry them on, are we at liberty to do that fairly, and are we free at the same time from being charged with anything to the support of other schools? That, I submit, is what the position of matters, looking previous to the act, would reasonably be intended and desired, and that which is suggested, as a matter of fact, that might possibly be, is something that could not possibly be in the minds of those persons that either were asking for or passing this act. The one matter was one as to which no question had been raised. The other was one in respect of which all parties were very desirous of having the arrangement which had been found to work and which had been readopted at the time of confederation. That same thought pervaded the legislation in respect of the same subject matter.

Then, it is a fact not to be forgotten that by the confirmatory act, the Dominion parliament is not permitted to interfere on this subject at all. That is on page 31 and 32 of the collection of acts.

Now, what is meant by "any class?" It is, I submit, made very clear by those portions of the acts cited by the attorney-general, which referred to this subject matter from beginning to end. We have got nothing but on the one side protestants, and on the other side Roman catholics. It begins with that. They appoint a superintendent of the protostant school and one of the catholic to each section of the board, one being protestant and the other catholic. The districts are protestant districts and catholic school districts. Each is a section or class, and then the protestants resident in catholic districts, and the Roman catholics in the protestant, all through the very first act—it is nothing but the two classes. Then, when there are members appointed to the board, it is not that some shall be protestants and some church of England and the like, but twelve of whom shall be protestants and nine Roman catholics. Again, the board shall divide itself into two sections, protestant and Roman catholic, and the "selection by the catholic section of the board shall be subject to the approval of a competent religious authority." Then it certainly was very strong in a passage that was given. "The establishment of a school district of one denomination shall not prevent the establishment of a school district"—not of another, but—of the other denomination in the same place, and "a protestant and a catholic district may include the same territory in whole or in part." Two denominations, protestant and catholic. Again, "neither protestant nor catholic shall be assessed," and, again, the respective denominations are limited by the words that follow: "In no case shall a protestant ratepayer be obliged to pay for a catholic school, or a catholic ratepayer for a protestant school." And then again, it shall be the protestant or catholic school district. That is in the compilation of 1881. And again in the act of 1884, page 73 of the compilation, sub-section A: "The minority shall have power, by the action of their section of the board of education, to maintain their own district as it existed upon the incorporation of said city or town, or so to extend their district as to include members of their own denomination residing in the same vicinity where no school of the same denomination is in operation." So that I submit that, as that was expounded by the legislation that succeeded, the idea which I submit was present, as shown by the language of the act, is the preservation of these two classes identified here—the protestant on the one side, and Roman catholic on the other.

Therefore, I submit that by the language of the act—the confirmatory act—thereby the existing denominational schools were recognized, and that the legislature preserved matters in this respect *in statu quo*, and that nothing could be done by local or Dominion legislation to interfere with the state of matters.

I desire to say a word, my lords, upon the New Brunswick Act, on a point which was raised in the supreme court, but which they did not think it was necessary to dispose of, because they gave to the word "practice" such a signification that did not render it necessary. It will possibly be necessary for your lordships to consider it, and it is this: In the New Brunswick Act there was something for the words "by law" to operate upon, because there were schools established by law, but in the Manitoba Act there would be nothing for the words to operate upon—unless it is upon this state of matters that existed which has been described, and as there were the New Brunswick schools that had been established by act of parliament, and as there were also schools that existed grown out of those that were not established by act of parliament, they said: "As you have these two classes, and as it is established by law, we must hold it limited to those that come exactly under that language, and we cannot extend it." But I submit, with great deference to your lordships, that if there had been nothing for the words "by law" to operate upon, excepting such a state of matters as existed in Manitoba, the court would have come to the conclusion: "We must give some force to those words, and we cannot read them out of the acts." We must, therefore, allow to be preserved that which they have had, in strictly legal language, in existence and frequently spoken of as "That is my right or that is what I considered to be my position," and so on. I say there was no specific act as there is in the Manitoba Act, and their lordships read the language of the New Brunswick cases to cover the state of matters which did exist and were covered more strictly by the word "law" than by the other state of matters which, I submit, however, may also be covered by it, in view of other language in this Manitoba Act.

Now, I ask permission to emphasize what the attorney-general referred to—that in section 2 of the Manitoba Act: "An appeal shall lie to the governor-general in council from any act or decision of the legislature of the province or of any provincial authority." Now, in section 3 it says: "Where in any province a system of separate or dissentient schools exists by law at the union, or is thereafter established by the legislature," there may be the right, and, therefore, when they were dealing with the Manitoba Act they did not put in, "Where in any province a system of separate or dissentient schools exists by law," then there is to be liberty to appeal to the governor-general, but, knowing that that system may not have been exactly inaugurated or subsisting by law, they allow the appeal against anything that may be considered to be unreasonable, although there was no law to establish the schools. There must have been some reason for the omission of that—for the change in the language between the British North America Act and the Manitoba Act. Then the third, and that which the Chief Justice Ritchie, who, it is to be observed, was also chief justice in the New Brunswick court when the decision in the Renaud case was founded, lays stress on the enlarging of the language in the special act by the introduction of the word "practice" which, as Mr. Justice Taschereau refers to and is spoken of in the French as *par la coutume*, preserves that which exists by practice or custom in respect of denominational schools, that is, preserves as to the school in question, so that nothing injuriously affecting the same can be done because it says: "Nothing in any such law shall prejudicially affect any right or privilege with reference to denominational schools," not the school itself, as it then existed, but everythink connected with it—much wider, I submit, than the narrow construction that was put upon it by the learned judges in the court of Winnipeg—larger and wider. I submit, therefore, that upon that it was intended to preserve to the Roman catholics as a class and to the protestants as a class—that being the way in which, up to that time, they had been divided and had been dealt with—the enjoyment of the custom, of the practice of the system relevant to denominational schools as enjoyed at the date of the act of union, just as to these classes in the older provinces these rights were preserved. It is not pretended that there was any urging that there should be a further cutting up under the Manitoba Act than existed under the Ontario and Quebec Act.

Then, I have referred to the reasons which existed for promoting such a class as spoken of by the chief justice of the supreme court and Mr. Justice Fournier—the state of matters in the province—the not procuring the consent of the French Canadian Roman catholics, and the impossibility of procuring this consent, without agreeing to the preservation of the existing state of matters as to Roman catholic education. The situation was virtually controlled there, and it was necessary to exhibit a spirit of toleration in order to prevent the recurrence of a state of rebellion. This legislation would then, my lords, be on the same lines—would carry out the same thought, and would afford to both the parties in this new province those rights which they had struggled for, and which had been reasonably settled between them in these two provinces. Then, if the system of school education was by this act preserved to the Roman catholics of Manitoba, can it be said that it has not been partially interfered with? I should have referred, although the attorney-general did also, just in that view to reiterate it, that the only evidence that we have in this case upon this point is the evidence of Professor Bryce. Of course, I, personally, do not know anything about the other case. We have not got the affidavits and they were not before the supreme court, because the case was not launched until after the disposition of this present case and, therefore, the only evidence that we have is that which has been referred to, the archbishop of St. Boniface, and then Professor Bryce says at page 21: "That the presbyterians are thus able to unite with their fellow Christians of other churches in having taught in the public schools (which they desire to be taught by Christian teachers) the subjects of a secular education." They can all join. He is not claiming that the presbyterians stand in a different position to the members of the church of England, but they can all join in that, treating them as one body and not making the separation that has been indicated in the argument. They now seem to think this was not enough and so seem to have put in that further affidavit in the Logan case.

Then, my lords, the archbishop says that according to the view, not of himself individually, but, of the church, that each school is virtually to be a propaganda institution. Religion is not to be a matter to be divorced from general education, but it is to be a central point, and it is to be taught not merely through the catechism, but it is to be taught in history; it is to be taught in philosophy or whatever else may be taught in the school. It is to be pervaded by religion. In fact religion is to pervade everything from the moment the school opens until it closes. Anything less than this dethrones religion from its true position and degrades it, and in order to accomplish the better these views, persons skilled in the religion of the church must be appointed under the direction of the church, and so Roman catholic teachers are the only ones fit to carry on this work. It is not simply by Roman catholics that that is strongly felt, because the late Lord Justice Thesiger put it more strongly than I have ever seen it put by any person in an address by him, that where you have the best education without religion, you simply make a man a skilled villain. I thought at the time the language was very strong, but it shows that it is not merely the Roman catholics that have a strong opinion upon that matter.

Now then, my lords, what is asked to be done is that Roman catholics shall stifle their religious convictions by payment to the support of a system to which they are utterly and conscientiously opposed. Certainly they could not be compelled to do that before 1870. It is not merely a matter of education. Although it is not a matter of education, but the religious education—this denominational education, this particular class of school which is referred to here, their rights or privileges or position in respect of that is one, which strikes me, and always did, as one of the most vital points. It has been grievously attacked by the legislation. Their money is taken to support a system in competition with their denominational schools, thus weakening their ability to sustain their schools, and by their money strengthening the schools obnoxious to them; because it is not merely that their money is taken, but the schools that are obnoxious are, by their money, strengthened. The protestant schools are, partly through the money of Roman catholics, made free schools in opposition to their own denominational schools, in which fees are charged. That other class or body may have their free schools if they please, nobody objects, but it is submitted that before October, 1870, there was no right to have these denominational schools, or class of virtually protestant schools at the expense of Roman catholics. Then, there is the temptation to the poor Roman catholics to go to a free school, rather than to the paid schools of Roman catholics, and this again to some extent is the result of the Roman catholics' money, involuntarily taken. Then what was considered by Mr. Justice Taschereau is a very strong point; it is that the very school houses and places of education of the Roman catholics are taxed in order to give a free education through this other system. A free school to which a Roman catholic could not send his children may be started in the centre of a Roman catholic district, where the poor will be tempted to send their children, made free by their money. Then that it is an act of confiscation, which was the language which was used by Mr. Justice Taschereau, I think appears reasonably plain from the language of the section referred to by the attorney-general, and it is based upon this argument: that under the Manitoba Act there may be legislation, but it is "according to the following provisions." There has been legislation according to these provisions, and the result of the denominational school of 1870 is that in and through that legislation you have property, you have assets, it is the outcome of it, and it is now represented in 1890 by property that is dealt with by clause 179; that is, the denominational school which was nursed and sustained by this legislation has resulted in a school which is at present (we will call it at Z) in existence, the work all carried on under this, which is the denominational school referred to, I submit, in this Manitoba Act. That is to cease and all the assets of such catholic district shall belong to, and all the liabilities be paid by the public school district. It was on that argument that Mr. Justice Taschereau considered that there was virtually a confiscation of the rights which, existing in 1870, were moulded by the legislation up to 1889—that which existed in and through the various evolutions from 1870 to 1890. That is to cease to exist. That is blotted out and the assets of it are handed over to this other body.

It is not pretended but that the Roman catholic schools fully answer all the purposes of the state in their idea of educating the children. It is not pretended that there is any need for an act on that ground. And then, as to the many matters that can be done, Mr. Justice Patterson refers to those, and the amendments of the nineteen years show how much could be done, not as a matter of compromise, but exercising the absolute right and with the restriction referred to of making laws in relation to education. All their books are done away with—their teachers—their schools are confiscated, and their apparatus, and everything which is a result of the denominational school of 1870. All that ends. When a denominational or a separate school was referred to it means that system which is in existence at the time of the Manitoba Act.

This, it is to be observed, my lords, is not an act which compels attendance at the schools, although it has been claimed to be a necessary act for the furtherance of this most important matter of the general education of the people of the land. I dare say the Roman catholics would consent as much as the protestants to such a law being passed. As to the compulsory assessment, I presume the Roman catholics would not object to that so long as the money raised went in the two-fold channel--that from protestants to support their schools, and that from Roman catholics to support their schools. But I submit, my lords, that this is an act which prejudicially affects this class of persons in organizing the catholic schools and gives them corporate powers. Then, though it is not prejudicially affecting, it helps them, therefore, this legislation comes exactly within the terms of the act.

I submit, therefore, in closing, my lords, that this is an act which does prejudicially affect this class of persons as to their conscientious convictions—as to their pockets—and in relation to their church, all of which was covered by that system which was in existence in 1870, and in the most important matter of secular and religious education of their young. It is in most marked contrast to the spirit of conciliation displayed in the act of 1870, and in those which deal with these rights, and to the wise spirit of toleration which is displayed in the enactments that follow for twenty-one years. I submit that it offends against the spirit and against the letter of the act which defines the rights of these persons, and that therefore it will be held unconstitutional.

Mr. Ram:—My lords, on behalf of Mr. Logan, I have presumed, inasmuch as it was arranged that the two cases—Barrett's case and Logan's case—should be taken together, that any remarks that I have to make to your lordships should be limited to the point which has been asserted, that Mr. Logan's case differs to that of Mr. Barrett's, and that although Mr. Barrett may rightly claim to be here before your lordships, Mr. Logan has no such right.

The position of Mr. Logan is somewhat peculiar. The learned attorney-general has repeatedly and strenuously disavowed any connection with him at all, or any relation to him. On the other hand his claim has been received with some favour by his nominal opponent as represented by Sir Horace Davey.

The learned attorney general indicated in some ways that he thought and suggested that Mr. Logan's was not a *bona fide* claim. I am sure he would not have made a suggestion unless he felt there was good ground for it, but I may point out to your lordships there is no sort of evidence at all before you to invalidate, in any way, or cast the slightest suspicion on the claim so made by Mr. Logan, and more, that his claim rests for its principal foundation upon the affidavit made by the bishop of the diocese, that the affidavit so made by him would be regarded by your lordships as free from any taint of suspicion or *mala fides* whatever.

Therefore, my submission to your lordships will be this, that Mr. Logan is in the same position as Mr. Barrett; that he is, in other words, one of a class of persons having by practice in the province rights or privileges with reference to the denominational schools which have been affected by the act of 1890.

My lords, that question, namely, whether the denomination must be confined only to the broad details of Roman catholic and protestant, has already been decided in the supreme court of New Brunswick in the case already cited to your lordships of *exparte* Renaud, from which case no appeal was brought to your lordships' bar.

Mr. McCarthy:—Yes.

Mr. Ram:—It was confirmed here. I am obliged to my friend. I meant to say no appeal ——

Lord Shand:—It was this point.

Mr. Ram:—It was this point, disputing the ruling of the court below with regard to the point which I am now urging. The words of the learned judge below, at page 464 of that case, were as follows: "It is contended in this case that the words 'denominational schools' were not used by the legislature"——

Lord Watson:—I should like to know what you say is the effect of this point. You both complain that it is a hardship to you to have to pay for others. Mr. Barrett, who is a catholic, complains that a part of what he contributes goes to the education of English protestant children, and you complain that part of yours goes elsewhere.

Mr. Ram:—Yes, my lord.

Lord Watson:—Your allegation is made in such a manner, and in the strongest possible manner, that part of your money may go to them, but you do not shut out the alternative that the larger portion of their money comes to you. If so, where is your prejudice? One side or other may be prejudiced. You frame the particular allegation in such a way as to make it clear that they are prejudiced. More money goes to the protestants than protestant money to the others, but your client does not make his averment in such a fashion as to lead to that conclusion, necessarily.

Mr. Ram:—I think the averment made on behalf of Mr. Logan is certainly much less than that made on behalf of Mr. Barrett.

Lord Watson:—They are so less that there may be no prejudice except in this fact, that you send 1s. and get 2s. 6d. back.

Mr. Ram:—I submit, my lord, that Mr. Logan's contention is this: He complains not only with regard to the distribution of the money, because it may be that there is little or no loss to him on that, but he complains, that while he sends his boy to a school other than the public school, which is established by law, he has to pay for that public school. He is forced to do so, although at the same time to satisfy his conscience he sends his boy to the other school.

Lord Watson:—He says: "The tax by which I am compelled to contribute for the support of schools not under the control of the church of England, prejudicially affects my rights as a member of the church of England."

Mr. Ram:—"And if compelled to pay such tax, I and others, members of the church of England, are less able to support schools in which religious exercises and teachings in accordance with our form of worship could be conducted."

Lord Watson:—As to his other claim. That is the one he complains of—the other consists of this claim, "I claim the right to have my children taught religious exercises in school according to the tenets of the church of England." What school? Where? How maintained and how managed?

Mr. Ram:—I presume, my lord, one of the schools referred to in the affidavit.

Lord Watson:—It is a claim of a totally different kind. Does it mean one of the schools under the act? I think that is what it means.

Mr. Ram:—I confess I read it otherwise, I read it to mean one of the schools referred to in the affidavit.

Lord Watson:—Do you mean that he claims to be allowed to found and support a school at which his children shall be taught? Does he base his right on one of the public schools established by the act, and if so, where?

Mr. Ram:—I suggest to your lordship that the complaint that he makes is that he is prevented from doing what he was doing before the year 1870, namely having his child taught in a school where the child was taught the tenets of the church of England.

Lord Watson:—I confess at this moment I am entirely in ignorance of what he complains either one way or the other. Will you explain?

Lord Shand:—I see that in the application where you find what he says he complains of and requires the order to be quashed upon the following grounds:—"That by the said by-law the amount to be levied for school expenditure is levied upon members of the church of England and all other religious denominations alike," and, "that it is illegal to assess members of the church of England for the support of schools which are not under the control of the church of England and in which they are not taught religious exercises prescribed by that church," and I rather read that as meaning that he, just as much as a Roman catholic, says he objects to be taxed for this at all and insists upon maintaining his own school and being relieved from taxation.

Mr. RAM:—That is what I am endeavouring to put to your lordships. That is therefore the same as the Roman catholics, although the claim is worded with much less precision in Mr. Logan's affidavit.

Lord MORRIS:—I do not know that there is any want of precision. He says I claim so and so.

Lord WATSON:—They are both of the city of Winnipeg. The other makes a distinct averment and they are both under the very same assessment. Barrett's statement is that each Roman catholic will have to subscribe more than if he were assessed for Roman catholic schools alone.

Lord SHAND:—I understand you do not complain about the question of amount at all, "I do not care about the Roman catholics or anybody else. I object to pay a single penny because I have to maintain my own school." It is not a question of division. It is a question of exemption.

Mr. RAM:—Of exemption, my lord.

Lord SHAND:—It does not satisfy him that money is to be paid.

Mr. RAM:—As your lordship sees, he has to pay a general tax to maintain the general schools.

Lord WATSON:—Where is the school he wishes his children to go to?

Mr. RAM:—He does not say any school.

Lord MORRIS:—He is claiming the right to have his children taught religion in school, and I put the question to you, where?

Mr. RAM:—He does not say where. He says a school where they teach the tenets of the church of England, and, reading that with the next paragraph of his affidavit, he goes on to say what he desires to have.

Lord WATSON:—He is taking it, I infer, to the school established under the act.

Mr. RAM:—No.

Lord MACNAGHTEN:—"I want to have a school on a religious basis."

Lord SHAND:—"And we shall provide that for ourselves." He means to have them taught in a school of his own and wants to be free to do it.

Mr. RAM:—That is how I read it, my lord. Then in the affidavit of Mr. Hayward, in support of Mr. Logan, the question of the school is perhaps more accurately defined. That is on page 12, my lords, of Logan's Record, paragraph 10. He there states what he does as a matter of fact with regard to his boys. "I have one boy of school age, namely, the age of 13 years, and although I am compelled by the said by-law and by the Public Schools Act to contribute to the support of the said public schools, established under the Public School Act——"

Lord SHAND:—That illustrates it exactly.

Mr. RAM:—"I send him to a school established by the rector of the English church parish of All Saints, in the said city of Winnipeg."

Lord SHAND:—That just illustrates what the other man means. It is very clear.

Mr. RAM:—"And under the control and management of the said rector, where he receives religious instruction according to the tenets of the said church of England in addition to ordinary school instruction and I voluntarily pay fees for his tuition at said school, and I do not send him to any of the said public schools. There are many other boys in the said city of Winnipeg sent by their parents, who are resident ratepayers of the city of Winnipeg and members of the church of England, to the said All Saints school, which I verily believe are similar to my own."

Lord MORRIS:—Is there any statement in the petitions that it is contrary to the belief of the episcopalian church?

Mr. RAM:—I think so, I will refer your lordship to page 7 of the Record in Logan's case. Your lordships will kindly allow me to read the 17th paragraph—the last sentence of it: "With the great majority of the bishops and clergy of the church of England, I believe that the education of the young is incomplete, and may even be hurtful if religious instruction is excluded from it."

Lord MORRIS:—So far from that being an affirmative answer, it is a negative to what I asked, because if it is only the majority it is only the opinion of the majority—it is not the belief amongst them. Where is it stated that it is the belief of the church of which he is a member? If there is anybody who takes a different view, he *ipso facto* ceases to be a member.

Mr. RAM:—I think I can put it a little higher, if I may read paragraph 19.

Lord WATSON:—19 and 20 are very distinct, and amount to this, that a sufficient moral training is not given in the public schools, according to the views of the church, and that it will be necessary for the church to re-establish their own parish schools.

Mr. RAM:—In the 19th paragraph, your lordship will see he says: "And is not in accordance with the views of the church of England," and further down in the 21st paragraph: "I have no doubt that if religious training is excluded from the public schools, as is threatened," that is the re-establishment of separate schools, "this will be the policy in future of the church of England and myself. The re-establishment of our parish schools is merely a question of means and time."

Lord WATSON:—Is it quite as distinct as the other?

Mr. RAM:—I submit, my lord, that it is so, that he as distinctly asserts that his position is the same.

Lord MORRIS:—If a person says that it is the opinion of the majority of the members of his church, so and so, does not he imply that there is a minority of the church still who hold the reverse?

Mr. RAM:—I submit on that that even if there were a minority——

Lord MORRIS:—I do not think that is the same at all as the statement that it is the opinion of the church altogether.

Mr. RAM:—It does say that it is not in accordance with the views of the church of England.

Lord MORRIS:—Paragraph 17 states the majority believe one thing and the minority believe another. Is that the same as the statement of the archbishop of the Roman catholics that there is no minority at all, but it is the opinion of the whole?

Lord HANNEN:—I think there is a doctrine of the church of England, and that if a man ceases to hold that doctrine he ceases to be a member.

Mr. RAM:—If that minority forms itself and becomes a class it would also be within the purview of this fourth section.

Lord WATSON:—There are some points of doctrine upon which they have not all agreed.

Mr. RAM:—My lords, I was about to refer to the judgment of the case of *exparte* Renaud, and there the learned judges discussed the question as to whether——

Lord MORRIS:—I do not think there is anything in that.

Mr. RAM:—I was about to refer your lordships to the judgment in the case *exparte* Renaud. The learned judges say: "It is contended in this case, that the words 'denominational schools' were not used by the legislature, and should not be construed by us in their ordinary grammatical sense and meaning, but should have a much broader interpretation. While freely admitting that, though the general rule is that every word must be understood according to its legal meaning, in construing an ordinary, as opposed to a penal enactment, where the context shews that the legislature has used it in a popular or more enlarged sense, courts will so construe the language used." The learned judges discuss the sub-sections of the British North America Act put in parallel columns in the Record and they say, "But we are at a loss to understand why sub-sections 2 and 3 should be held to control or in any way limit or affect a previous distinct enactment, couched in plain and unambiguous language, and which, by quite as clear and unequivocal terms, has relation to all classes of persons or denominations, and to all the provinces of the Dominion; or why, because separate and dissentient schools, as between protestants and Roman catholics, not only in Ontario and Quebec, but in any province in which they may exist at the union, or be thereafter established, are provided for and protected, therefore, we must necessarily infer therefrom that, in using the term 'denominational schools' in sub-section 1, the legislature intended to legislate only as between Roman catholics and protestants, and then also as to schools not necessarily denominational in the ordinary acceptation of the term. We think that the term 'denomination' or 'denominational,' as generally used, is in its popular sense more frequently applied to the different denominations of protestants, than to the church of Rome; and that the most reasonable inference is, that sub-section 1 was intended to mean just what it expresses, viz: that 'any,' that is, every 'class of persons' having any right or privilege with respect to denominational schools, whether such class should be one of the numerous denominations of protestants, or Roman catholics, should be protected in such rights. If it had been intended that the clause was to be limited in its application to Roman catholics and protestants only, as dissentient one from the other, and apply to schools other than those usually understood as denominational schools, is it not fair to presume that the legislature would have used some expression in the sub-section itself indicating such a particular sense, especially as we have seen there were at the union, in this province at any rate, strictly denominational schools, both protestant and Roman catholic, to which such a clause would be applicable; and for the very reason also, that when dealing with schools as between protestant and Roman catholic, in sub-sections 2 and 3, the language clearly confines it to those bodies respectively?"

Lord Morris:—If any class with respect to denominational schools in sub-section 1 was not really protestant or Roman catholic, but was intended to apply to some infinitesimal body, why was not there an appeal left to them under sub-section 2?

Mr. Ram:—I venture to think that under sub-section 2 what was contemplated was this, that apart from any question of *ultra vires* or not, if a minority said, "I am oppressed," that was the party who had to come under that sub-section 2 and appeal to the government.

Lord Hannen:—It has a right to appeal against any act of the legislature.

Lord Shand:—Even *intra vires.*

Lord Watson:—It is a curious thing that if there were other denominations, there has been recognition, and nobody has said a word; I have not heard even of the existence of anybody who could not be ranked under the class either of a Roman catholic or a protestant, and then we come to the sub-section which has already been pointed out, and it would be a very singular thing if, after giving the privilege to a certain class, it should select a sub-class only, who have the right of appeal under that. In questions of this kind, apparently, nobody ever heard of any denomination except protestant and Roman catholic.

Lord Morris:—In all this legislation in Canada, in the Confederation Act and all the acts in Manitoba and all the other acts, is there any other denomination spoken of?

Lord Watson:—The acts of 1871 and 1882 were a grievous intrusion on the rights and privileges of these denominations. Why have they been silent for the 19 years between 1871 and 1890 and are silent at this moment?

Mr. Ram:—I think there is one section in the act of 1881 which does so protect the rights of what one of the noble lords has called an infinitesimal number of persons. It is the 30th section of the Manitoba School Act of 1881. Your lordships have already had it read to you, but in response to what has been put to me I venture to draw your attention to it again. It is at page 48 of the Statutes. "The ratepayers of a school district, including religious, benevolent or educational corporations, shall pay their respective assessment to the schools of their respective denominations, and in no case shall a protestant ratepayer be obliged to pay for a catholic school or a catholic ratepayer for a protestant school."

Lord Watson:—That is the two denominations. If there was such a thing as a third denomination, what was to become of them?

Mr. Ram:—That is what is aimed at in the concluding words of that section. If there is a denomination who have got a school, then a ratepayer who belongs to that denomination is to pay to the school of that denomination; but if there is a denomination so small that they have not got a school, in that case the protestant is to be relieved from payment to what may be the only alternative in that case.

Lord WATSON:—Do you mean to suggest that the respective denominations mean anything but protestant and catholic?

Lord HANNEN:—You say the last part would only be repeating it in different words.

Mr. RAM:—The last part would be redundant.

Lord WATSON:—The first part merely directs where he is to pay and then it goes on to say that is to be the only payment.

Mr. RAM:—The section would be complete if it ended with the semi-colon.

Lord WATSON:—If that first part of the clause included other denominations than protestant and catholic, the plain inference would be that that other ratepayer might be called upon to pay as well.

Lord MORRIS:—Is there any act of parliament of the whole series, not only of Manitoba but of the Canadian provinces from the time that they were confederated in 1867, or before, that ever in words or in any reasonable intendment contemplates any sub-division of protestant sects?

Mr. RAM:—I must say candidly that I do not find any such.

Lord MORRIS:—Is not that one of the strongest arguments?

Mr. RAM:—It seems to me that in this act of 1890, it may be, because there was no such division that these exceptionally wide words "of any class" are used. Had there been the rights of smaller denominations preserved in subsequent acts it may be that no such wide words would be necessary and it may be in consequence of those rights not being specially and exceptionally reserved that, therefore, so wide a phrase is used as "any class of persons."

Lord WATSON:—"The ratepayers of a school district, including religious, benevolent or educational corporations, shall pay their respective assessment to the schools of their respective denominations." If you go back to section 12*a* it is, "The establishment of a school district of one denomination shall not prevent the establishment of a school district of the other denomination,"—speaking of them as two. Then it goes on, "And a protestant and a catholic district may include the same territory in whole or in part."

Mr. RAM:—May I point out on that, that that only precludes the establishment of a school district otherwise than protestant or Roman catholic?

Lord WATSON:—The words are "shall pay to the schools of their respective denominations," and the only two kinds of schools authorized by the act are protestant schools and catholic schools.

Lord MORRIS:—And only two classes are authorized by any act.

Lord WATSON:—If there is the third denomination referred to in section 30, the act provides no school for which he is to pay.

Mr. RAM:—May I submit that the act provides for districts of two denominations and that one of those districts may contain in it schools of other sub-denominations, if I may use the word, if it is a protestant district; in that district there may be a church of England or presbyterian school. If so, then comes in section 30, which says that the ratepayer is to pay to the school of his respective denomination.

Lord WATSON:—A man of that third denomination would be obliged to pay either to the protestant or the catholic school. He might be sending his children to the school of his own denomination.

Mr. RAM:—He might, because that school would be maintained by the funds collected in common.

Lord WATSON:—He is to be left out in the cold, unquestionably, in the acts of 1871 and 1881—quite as clearly left out as your client is in the act of 1890.

Lord SHAND:—What is your interest in struggling against this? You get catholics and you get protestants and you concede that those are the two great bodies referred to, but if protestants happen to be divided into five or six different classes, is not that enough for your case?

Mr. RAM:—I think it is.

Lord SHAND:—If you are a class that had the privilege and your class has been injured, is not that enough for your purpose?

Lord WATSON:—The third denomination appears to me to be a perfect myth.

Lord SHAND:—It is a class of protestants. One of those classes is represented by this gentleman.

Lord WATSON:—That is not disputed, but Mr. Ram is maintaining that there are more denominations than protestant and catholic.

Mr. RAM:—I was rather induced to go into that argument, perhaps a mistaken one, in consequence of your lordship putting to me the section, and endeavoured to show that this section was not fatal to me, and to that effect only I talked about another denomination. The matter on which I should rely is that indicated by Lord Shand, which I put a short time ago; but if I am a class I do come within the wide words, I come within the first sub-section.

Lord SHAND:—That is all you want.

Mr. RAM:—I think so. I venture to think, if I prove that, then Mr. Logan stands on the same footing as Mr. Barrett and therefore I am entitled to pray in aid all the arguments which have been so forcibly urged before your lordships which I could not attempt to repeat on behalf of Mr. Barrett.

I only desire to draw attention to one other matter, which is this, that this question was also discussed before the learned judges from whom an appeal is brought to your lordships to-day. In the judgment both of Mr. Justice Dubuc and Mr. Justice Bain the matter is discussed.

Lord MORRIS:—The appeal is brought from the supreme court.

Mr. RAM:—That is so, Mr. Justice Bain gave a judgment which has been read before your lordships to-day.

Lord MORRIS:—Mr. Justice Bain held that the Roman catholic party had no claim.

Mr. RAM:—He did.

Lord MORRIS:—He was reversing that and he thought this would go in with it.

Mr. RAM:—I think not; I think Mr. Justice Bain in his judgment, at page 77, dealt with this as a separate matter.

Lord MORRIS:—He thought this went in with the judgment in Barrett's case.

Mr. RAM:—Yes.

Lord MORRIS:—That is what I said. He considered that the judgment of the supreme court would rule Logan's case.

Mr. RAM:—Yes, he did.

Lord MORRIS:—He said if Barrett's case is good, Logan's ought to be so too.

Mr. RAM:—It is not in Logan's case that he gives this judgment but in Barrett's case.

Lord SHAND:—Anticipating some point of this kind?

Mr. RAM:—Yes, at page 77 he says "It is to be observed too that in this sub-section 1." [Reading down to line 40 of page 77.] "Whether such class should be one of the numerous denominations of protestants or Roman catholics should be protected in such rights."

Lord WATSON:—He says you are not to inquire very nicely into what a man's religious views are, but if he is in the habit of resorting either to the catholic or protestant school then he should have the same right.

Lord MORRIS:—Is the chief justice, whom Mr. Justice Bain is quoting in that case, the same chief justice who decided this case in the supreme court?

Mr. RAM:—Yes, Mr. Justice Bain goes on to quote the archbishop's affidavit, which says that some of the schools which are denominational schools have been controlled by the Roman catholic church and others by various protestant denominations. I submit that that, as a matter of fact, establishes before your lordships that there was the existence at the time of the union of such classes and that Mr. Logan as representing such a class is entitled to be heard before your lordships and to maintain his case.

Mr. MCCARTHY:—My learned friend, Sir Horace Davey, was not present during the argument, and with your lordships' permission I will reply.

I desire in the first place to point out that the clauses which have been referred to as the confiscating clauses, do not fairly bear the meaning which the learned attorney-general has given to them. I refer to clauses 178 and 179, which transfer, it is true, the then existing Roman catholic schools and all their property to the public schools. I think they can be justified on public grounds and as just and fair in view of the whole scheme of legislation. But is it not sufficient to point out that Barrett has no right to complain? He had no interest in any school which has been confiscated, if they were confiscated; he has no right to come and complain of anything more than the imposition of the tax. It is the by-law of the municipality which he applied to quash and it is the by-law which has in effect been quashed by a judgment of the supreme court. Now, it might well be, though I do not concede that it is so, that sections 178 and 179, in transferring the property of the Roman catholics, were in contravention and in prejudice of their particular rights in respect of schools. But who is to complain of that? Not Mr. Barrett; his complaint and the only complaint is, that he objects to a by-law which imposes a tax upon him because under the taxing clause of the act it is *ultra vires*, and as to that alone. Your lordships perhaps will remember, and therefore it is needless for me to repeat, the explanation that was given of these two clauses. At the time when this act was brought into force in the year 1890, there were public schools throughout the whole province. The major number of these schools were connected with the protestant section. The legislature appears to have assumed—because no particular clause is to be found—that these would be the schools that would be continued. But there were in some few cases, not many cases, localities where both protestant and catholic schools existed and the question arose what was to be done with those schools? Now, they were not private property, they were public property; schools that had been built and established and maintained under the act of 1881 and not under the act of 1871. These schools had therefore to be disposed of, the property had to be disposed of; and the scheme, and the disposition was that they are to be valued—assets and liabilities. A liability would be in connection with the debenture debt for the establishment or building of the school or the purchase of school apparatus or matters of that kind.

Lord WATSON:—I suppose they had been chiefly erected by a public rate.

Mr. McCARTHY:—Altogether, as far as we know.

Lord WATSON:—Or money borrowed on the security of debentures.

Mr. McCARTHY:—Yes.

Lord MACNAGHTEN:—Is it clear that there were no private schools existing before?

Mr. McCARTHY:—Quite clear. The scheme was to put the assets on the one side and the liabilities on the other. If the assets exceed the liabilities, to that extent the Roman catholics are to be exempt, those who have contributed to that excess of assets over liabilities are to be exempt until that excess is worked off. Could anything be fairer? Schools had to be dealt with; could anything be fairer than saying, the property being taken over for that purpose, the one is to be placed against the other and credit is to be given and a provision is to be made, not in favour of the protestant section but of the Roman catholic section in case their assets exceeded their liabilities.

Lord WATSON:—That was all in winding up under the act of 1881.

Mr. McCARTHY:—They had to make some provision for them or else these schools would have become useless. They were the property of the public and if they had not been taken over in that way and exemption given for their value the Roman catholic ratepayers would have been so much the worse off.

There was another provision of the act, and that was as to the application of the provincial grant to which objection was also made upon similar grounds. Perhaps that has not been very clearly understood. A subsidy is granted to all the provinces of the Dominion—the subsidy that was granted to Manitoba was not merely in consideration of Manitoba surrendering its right to levy the customs duties, but as a part of the whole scheme of the federation, that a definite sum based upon population and upon the liability for debts and so on, should be granted yearly by the Dominion to the province. That and the power of direct taxation, and the right to obtain an indirect tax by licensing—exacting a fee for licenses, and so on, forms the provincial fund, and that provincial fund is subject, of course, to the legislative control of the province. Now, your lordships will see the far reaching nature of objection which has been put forward in this appeal that the provincial legislature cannot assist a public school system by the distribution of a portion of the consolidated fund of the province.

Very briefly then, going back to the question which is chiefly in dispute between the other side and the side that I represent, I have to quarrel with my learned friend the attorney general's construction of this word "denominational." Your lordships see, it is, "Nothing in any such law shall prejudicially affect any right or privilege with respect to denominational schools which any class of persons have by law or practice." I was going to read to your lordships that which has been read by my learned friend who last addressed you, the case of *exparte* Renaud, but is it possible to cut down the plain, simple, ordinary meaning of the word denominational, the rights which any class of persons have in respect of denominational schools, to say that means only the two leading divisions into which Christians are divided—Roman catholic and protestant?

Lord SHAND:—Can you explain to me what you think is the importance of that, for I have not been able to to see it?

Mr. McCARTHY:—The importance of that is this, and it appears to have a good deal of importance in this way——

Lord SHAND:—If Logan is one of a class of protestants, is not he just as good as if he were specially named in the act?

Mr. McCARTHY:—No, not as it affects the provincial power. Logan comes here and says, I claim not merely to be a protestant, but I claim to be a protestant connected with the church of England, and my claim is that I cannot be taxed for any scheme of education embracing all protestants, I have a right to insist that if I am to be taxed at all, if I have not an immunity from all taxation, I can only be taxed for a school in which the docrines of the church of England and the tenets of the church of England are taught. So a presbyterian can come, so a methodist can come, and so we say that the result of all this is, taking it most strongly against ourselves, all we can do, is to establish the four systems of schools, Roman catholic, presbyterian, methodist, church of England, which existed in 1871. The most we can do is to do that, and if we are compelled to do that, if that is our limited power, then, in point of fact, in a country like Manitoba, where the farmers live upon sections a mile or a half a mile square it would be utterly impossible to establish a system of schools at all. That is the great importance of it in a provincial point of view.

Lord HANNEN:—Is there any proof that there were in 1870 any methodists and so on established and having rights?

Mr. McCARTHY:—The only proof is in these general words in the archbishop's affidavit, at page 14, section 2, he says: "Prior to the passage of the act of the dominion of Canada, passed in the thirty-third year of the reign of her majesty Queen Victoria, chapter 3, known as The Manitoba Act, and prior to the order in council issued in pursuance thereof, there existed in the territory now constituted the province of Manitoba a number of effective schools for children. These schools were denominational schools, some of them being regulated and controlled by the Roman catholic church, and others by various protestant denominations."

Your lordships will have observed, the judges, of course, are familiar with it. I have the history of Manitoba here, if I was at liberty to refer to it, and I do not know why I should not in an important case of this kind, because it would be a thousand pities if it should turn on a question of that kind, and should require to go back for a fuller statement of facts. The facts are not really in dispute. There were church of England schools, presbyterian schools, Roman catholic schools and, just within a year or two of the union, a methodist school had been started. Now, if the "rights and privileges" are as the other side contend, how is it possible to say that that means the rights of the protestants as a whole, and not the rights of these classes of persons—all the various sects or denominations into which the protestant church is divided? If the other view was intended, why did they use the word "any?" Either would have been a much more appropriate term to use—"either denomination," but the phrase is "any class of persons." My learned friend, the attorney-general, seemed to base the argument on the fact that, as a matter of history, the struggle hitherto in the older provinces had been between protestants and catholics. That, no doubt, is true—not, perhaps, quite in the sense in which the learned attorney-general referred to it, but in the larger sense, no doubt, it is correct to say that. But I point, in answer to that, to the clear distinction that is made in the British North America Act between the word "denominational" and the word "separate." We have in the three sub-sections here the term "denominational school" used, and instead of that being repeated again, we have in the second section, the words "separate schools," and we have again in the third section the words "dissentient or separate schools." Now, is it possible to say that the word "denominational," which is a word of well known signification, which the archbishop uses himself as applicable to the protestants, and which the chief justice of the court of New Brunswick thought could be more properly applied to protestant denominations than it would be to the Roman catholic denomination—is it possible, I say, not to note that these words have a separate and distinct signification, and that they ought to have their proper meaning? That is more clear when you come to look at the use of the word "separate," which I think it is not perhaps too much to say might be treated as a word of art. The Separate School Act of Ontario —not the first—will be found in the Consolidated Statutes of Upper Canada, chapter 65, and it is headed: "An Act respecting Separate Schools."

Lord WATSON:—For which province?

Mr. McCARTHY:—For the old province of Upper Canada. That was before the days of confederation. It is an act of the old province of Canada, and it deals with merely the upper portion of the province. Now, the privilege that is given here is a very peculiar one, to which, perhaps, sufficient attention has not already been directed, that if the teacher of a public school, although the school is conducted under school regulations, was a Roman catholic, that fact gave the right to any twelve protestants to demand that they should be associated together into a separate school, and it also gave the right to the coloured people of the province to have a separate school, not as a denomination at all, but merely as a coloured race they have the right by this clause to have their separate schools.

Lord WATSON:—They may be very good protestants.

Mr. McCARTHY:—They may be catholics and protestants.

Lord WATSON:—I suppose that *inter se* these denominations have the privilege of selecting the persons they admit to the schools?

Mr. McCARTHY:—No, I think not.

Lord WATSON:—I am talking of the privilege before the act. As regulated by statute, it may not be so—that is a different question, but I suppose there can be no doubt that the privilege existing in Manitoba of having a school meant as many separate schools as they chose.

Mr. McCARTHY:—The privilege was the existing privilege at the time, we say, and the existing privilege was to have private schools. As I have already mentioned to your lordships yesterday, such a thing as a separate school was unknown in the territory. There is no evidence that there was such a thing as a separate school. There was simply a private school at Kildonan, St. Boniface, St. John's and one or two other places—parish schools, as they are perfectly well understood in this country.

Lord WATSON:—I suppose, if you say, "parish schools as they are perfectly well understood in this country," the conditions are not quite the same. As far as I can gather, in Canada a parish school meant originally the school that sprang up alongside of the church or chapel.

Mr. McCARTHY:—I think so, my lord.

Lord WATSON:—It was really a denominational school in connection with a place of worship—at least chiefly.

Mr. McCARTHY:—I think so. At all events in Manitoba that was the real meaning of it.

Lord WATSON:—That seems to have been so according to the evidence on both sides.

Mr. McCARTHY:—That is so. I do not think there is any question that every school in Manitoba was in connection with some one or other of the denominations, but the presbyterians had their own school, although they lived not very far from the place where the bulk of the people of the church of England resided. Now, apply this condition of the law to the province of Upper Canada. "All powers, privileges and duties," says the second section, "at the union by law conferred and imposed in Upper Canada on the separate schools and school trustees of the queen's Roman catholic subjects, shall be, and the same are hereby extended and made applicable to the province of Quebec," but "where in any province a system of separate or dissentient schools exists by law at the union, or is thereafter established by the legislature of the province, an appeal shall lie to the governor general in council from any act or decision of the provincial authority," and so on. Now, the schools of the coloured people are protected by that clause, and also the right of twelve protestants to form a separate school, if the teacher is a Roman catholic, and although he has passed the public school examination, although he has a better certificate, and although he is bound to teach in accordance with the provisions of the general school law, still they have got that right preserved to them by sub-section 3. I submit, therefore, still, with confidence, and with deference to the attorney-general's argument, that there is a distinction in the statute between the denominational and the separate schools, and I mention to your lordships, though I do not give you the statute, that in the establishment of the North-west Territories Act, where parliament, having sole control over the North-west Territories, had, as I think, to deal with the subject of schools, in giving the constitution to the North-west Territories they expressly provide for separate schools, and in these terms. Your lordships will find the act consolidated in the Revised Statutes of Canada, cap. 50, section 14. This was a consolidation of the acts which gave power to the North-west Territories to deal with various subjects, but on the school matter the power is limited in this way: "The lieutenant-governor in council shall pass all necessary orders with respect to education, but it shall therein always be provided that the majority of the ratepayers of any district or portion of the territories, or in any less portion or sub-division thereof, by whatever name the same is known, may establish such schools therein as they think fit, and make the necessary assessment and collection of rates therefor, and also that the minority of the ratepayers therein, whether protestant or Roman catholic, may establish separate schools therein, and in such case the ratepayers shall be"——

Lord WATSON:—I do not think there is any wide divergence between the two sides of the bar as to the fact or as to the statutes; the controversy chiefly is as to the construction to be put upon them, and as to the construction bearing it appears to me on one point only, and it all comes back to that. The light we have got from both sides is all directed as far as I can see to this: You admit there was a privilege in certain persons with respect to denominational schools in Manitoba; the real controversy between you is this: Was it a natural or implied incident of that privilege that the persons enjoying it were to be exempt from any taxation for the maintenance of national schools?

Mr. McCARTHY:—That of course is really what the argument resolves itself into.

Lord SHAND:—I understand you to qualify that by saying that the only privilege they had was that of having their own schools.

Mr. McCARTHY:—Yes.

Lord SHAND:—And if that is not the privilege, then they had no other and there was no privilege to which these words would apply.

Mr. McCARTHY:—I do not desire to abandon the point I put forward before, that it is not necessary absolutely to find that these words had any application.

Lord SHAND:—You say these words may be put there just to cover any possible privilege and we may find there was none.

Mr. McCARTHY:—Yes, and when your lordship sees that the whole scheme of the establishment of the provinces by the Dominion parliament, which was in that sense made the mother of these younger states, is simply to preserve such vested rights as they have, and when it would be fettering a legislative body, which, although at that time it only had a territory containing a population of 15,000, might before long hope to have a population of one or two millions, as the population of Ontario is. If I may venture to say so, it is dangerous to fetter and restrict, beyond what is absolutely necessary to preserve vested rights, the exclusive power to deal with the vast and great subject of education, which is exclusively conferred on the province.

Lord MORRIS:—But if you put that limitation on the privilege, that it was only the privilege to have their own schools; one of the judges says that that is the same privilege as to eat bread or drink water. I feel great difficulty in putting myself in the attitude to bring to the consideration of the case what I think proper and right to bring to bear on the subject. When considering the legislation, I think it perfectly right to put yourself as far as possible, and to regard as far as possible, the position of the parties who were asking for admission to the union on these terms; and even then, after you have done all that, the question will come back to be what they have meant by what they have said.

Mr. McCARTHY:—Will your lordship allow me to correct your statement? Manitoba was not like the other provinces. Manitoba was part of the Hudson's Bay territory which had been acquired by the dominion of Canada.

Lord MORRIS:—All that I think we are agreed upon.

Mr. McCARTHY:—And as to which the dominion of Canada had had to make no bargain. When British Columbia came in, as your lordships will find by the orders in council, a bargain had to be made between the province of British Columbia and the Dominion, which was carried out by orders in council and approved of here; but when Manitoba came in, it was part of that great territory which belongs to the Dominion and which the Dominion is daily or hourly in expectation of making new provinces of, and this was the first. But there was no bargain. It was merely the Dominion parliament itself applying to a portion of its own territory, which it thought fit to constitute into a province and to give provincial rights to, such laws as would protect whatever vested institutions they might have.

Lord MORRIS:—But although Manitoba may not have existed before, surely the dominion of Canada, that called it into existence, bargained with it the sort of existence it was going to have.

Mr. McCARTHY:—There was nobody to bargain with.

Lord MORRIS:—I beg your pardon, it bargained with the future Manitoba.

Mr. McCARTHY:—Of course they legislated for it.

Lord MORRIS:—Yes, I call that a bargain.

Mr. McCARTHY:—I draw a distinction between a bargain which is made with a new province and a bargain which is made with an existing province.

Lord WATSON:—I do not know how to get to the mind of the Dominion on the subject.

Sir HORACE DAVEY:—Except by understanding the words they have used.

Mr. McCARTHY:—That is what I am asking your lordships to do.

Lord WATSON:—The mind of the Dominion seems to have been that it had better not deal with the subject. It has left it to the province to deal with. That, I think, seems to have been their mind.

Mr. McCARTHY:—I think your lordship has struck the key-note of the question.

Lord WATSON:—It is a thorny question to be dealt with by anybody, demanding a certain power of moderation.

Mr. McCARTHY:—I was only desiring in that observation to answer the appeal that the learned attorney general made to this board as to the legislation that had passed during the earlier period. Surely a province which is to be, we hope, a great province, is not to be fettered by what 15,000 or 16,000 people did between 1871 and 1881.

Lord WATSON:—If I were to speculate on the subject at all, I would say that the legislative power relative to educational subjects was a power that the province desired to possess for themselves; and that the Dominion was quite willing to let them have it.

Mr. McCARTHY:—That, of course, is the scheme of the first act. It was one of those things which was exclusively assigned to the province, but, owing to the difficulties that had arisen, the power of the province was cut down, and there is no reserved power in the Dominion to deal with it. It is not a matter as to which there is any reserved power to pronounce as to the power that there is, and if it does not rest with the province it is not to be found anywhere.

My learned friend, Mr. Blake, pressed before your lordships a new contention—new, at all events, as not appearing in the judgments before, and not having been advanced by the attorney general—and that is the conscientious right which he claimed against contributing to a system of education which the Roman catholics disapproved of; but, with great respect to my learned friend, is not he confounding a private right with that? That was not a right of a class of persons, but a private right. It is not a private right that is preserved, but it is the right of the class of persons. I think that seems to be the answer to that. There only just remains now to be said that what we contend for is this——

Lord SHAND:—Does the archbishop, in his affidavit, carry it the length which was contended for?

Mr. MCCARTHY:—No.

Lord SHAND:—I do not think he does. I think he puts it entirely on this, that they were obliged to pay for two sets of schools.

Mr. MCCARTHY:—As an historical fact, I may say that he is one of the members of the present advisory board.

Lord MACNAGHTEN:—One of the last board; is he one of the advisers of the present?

Mr. MCCARTHY:—I was mistaken—I was misinformed. It was the bishop of Rupert's Land.

Lord MORRIS:—I was startled at that. I think he puts himself in a very dangerous position, because I think if he had become a member of the board he would have become rather outlawed.

Mr. MCCARTHY:—I do not know that he would. One of the very distinguished prelates of the church of Rome has recently, with the sanction of the holy see itself, permitted the attendance of the Roman catholics at the public schools in the adjoining states.

Mr. BLAKE:—In case of absolute necessity.

Mr. MCCARTHY:—In case of absolute necessity, that is true, but still it is not a matter of conscience to that extent, because the bishop recently appealed to Rome to know whether, considering the difference of country and the difficulty of establishing parish schools, the children of his diocese might not attend at the public schools, and permission was given. And as another fact, I may say that many of the Roman catholics all through the Dominion attend the public schools even when they have separate schools.

Lord MORRIS:—They may do that. As I said before, I was in college with the present bishop of Ontario, who was an old fellow pupil of mine. What particular Roman catholics do does not prove anything.

Mr. MCCARTHY:—Only there cannot be said to be any conscientious scruples about it in that sense, because in many cases they attend public schools even when they have established separate schools.

Lord MORRIS:—It is not what the individuals may do.

Lord HANNEN:—There would appear to be no doctrine of the church against it. It seems to be a matter of discipline in particular cases.

Mr. MCCARTHY:—That is what I think it is, more correctly speaking. Now, the immunity that may be claimed is surely not an immunity against contributing to a public school system. The immunity that they enjoyed was, what? The immunity was that each individual of the class—because you cannot find out the immunity of the class without seeing what the immunities of the individuals composing it were—that they were bound to contribute nothing, or only just so much as they pleased. How can that be called an exemption, or a privilege, or a right? There was the right to their schools. Any law which said they could not have the denominational schools would be beyond the power of the legislature. Any law which prejudiced that right would be beyond the power of the legislature.

Lord WATSON:—Yes, but the legislature might by positive enactment grant an exemption which would be recognized as a privilege. It is perfectly true that no government can bind its successor by granting an exemption. That exemption may be repealed.

Mr. MCCARTHY:—Yes, my lord.

Lord WATSON:—But suppose there is a standing statutory exemption, would not that have enured to their right?

Mr. MCCARTHY:—Unquestionably.

Lord WATSON:—I say, if there had been a statutory exemption before 1870, would not that have enured?

Mr. MCCARTHY:—Undoubtedly, my lord.

Lord WATSON:—The question is whether, no exemption having been enacted, there can be any circumstances here sufficient to raise an implied exemption?

Mr. MCCARTHY:—Undoubtedly. It just comes back to the question of fact.

Lord WATSON:—Are there any circumstances which imply it, or is there anything in this case which, there being no enacted exemption, warrants the supposition of one? As I understand the judges of the supreme court, the latter is the view they have taken.

Mr. MCCARTHY:—Undoubtedly, that is their view.

Lord WATSON:—They contended that the legislature by that recognition of the rights and privileges, meant to agree to recognize it as an existing exemption, although it was not a legal exemption.

Mr. MCCARTHY:—That undoubtedly is the view they have taken. That, of course, is the view that we contend against here, but your lordships will not forget that the two French judges, Mr. Justice Taschereau and Mr. Justice Fournier, take it on the ground that there was a system of separate schools. Now, if in fact there was no system of separate schools, then it is quite clear that those learned judges have erred in the conclusion that they have drawn from the facts which existed at the time of the union.

Lord WATSON:—Is not it part of the constitution of a separate school that this immunity should accompany it?

Mr. MCCARTHY:—It is.

Lord WATSON:—It is essential to the definition of the word.

Mr. MCCARTHY:—Precisely, and therefore if the legislature proposed to say they shall have separate schools, or if parliament proposed to say they shall have separate schools——

Lord WATSON:—Of course the learned judges do not mean to say that the one is as plain a case as the other, but they say, taking into account what the legislature must have meant to do, and what the two parties before them were—they did not use the word contracting, but were really arranging, this must have entered into it.

Mr. MCCARTHY:—I desire just to add one word with regard to the question as to whether the schools established by the act of 1890 are in fact denominational schools.

Lord SHAND:—I have already drawn attention to the fact that at page 8 the counsel in their pleadings expressly say that they are not denominational.

Mr. MCCARTHY:—Yes, and they put that forward as a ground why the archbishop——

Lord SHAND:—But I understood you to say that most of the judges took that view also.

Mr. MCCARTHY:—They all do. There is not a single judge of the court, out of the nine judges, who does not take, so far as he has expressed any view at all, the view that these schools were non-denominational and non-sectarian.

Lord SHAND:—Schools under the act of 1890?

Mr. MCCARTHY:—Yes, schools under the act of 1890. Of course if you put forward the view that every school that a Roman catholic cannot attend is a denominational school, then there may be some foundation for the argument, but look at where it leads to.

Lord WATSON:—I rather think the original idea of denominational schools is a school of a sect of people who are desirous that their own religion should be taught in it, and taught in their own way—a doctrinal religion; and not only taught because religion is taught in a non-sectarian school, but, in the view of those who founded denominational schools originally, the theory was that their views of religion and teaching of their religion should permeate and run through all the education given in the school—that, whether it were rudimentary science or anything else, there should be an innoculation of the youthful mind with particular religious views.

Mr. McCarthy:—History and philosophy, as the archbishop puts it, at all events are embraced within this view. He puts it so in his affidavit.

Lord Watson:—That is their theory of what the teaching ought to be. In fact the essence of denominational views is that secular instruction and religious instruction ought not to be made separate matters.

Mr. McCarthy:—Then these may be in a sense secular schools, but they certainly cannot be called denominational schools.

Lord Watson:—I take it that the word may come to mean this: a school to which the denomination does not object, but that is not the primary signification of the word.

Mr. McCarthy:—If your lordships will just look at what this conclusion leads to. No model school—your lordships have heard what a model school is——

Lord Shand:—What is it?

Mr. McCarthy:—It is a model school under the act for the training of teachers —no normal school, which is a school of a somewhat similar character; no-provincial university——

Lord Morris:—Do not provincial universities come within this act?

Mr. McCarthy:—I think they do.

Lord Morris:—Under the act of 1890?

Mr. McCarthy:—Yes, and they would be denominational schools. There was in point of fact something in the nature of a provincial university.

Lord Morris.—You must have a peculiar mode of description in Manitoba if you describe a university as a school. It may be a school in one sense, as the school of Plato, but a university can hardly be called a school.

Mr. McCarthy:—Originally, in the province of Manitoba, there was something in the nature of a university, but there is not one leading denomination which has not a university of its own, and I think I am not going too far in saying that more importance is attached to the university education in a denominational sense than even to the earlier education.

Lord Morris:—Not necessarily from the Roman catholic point of view. I do not think the archbishop would have made an affidavit that it was contrary to the practice and rules and tenets of the Roman catholic church for a Roman catholic to go to a university.

Mr. McCarthy:—If I may use contemporary and current history, I have always understood there is a great controversy in Ireland on the very fact that the Roman catholics had not university education according to the Roman catholic faith.

Lord Morris:—They wish it, but there is no objection to any Roman catholic going to Trinity college.

Mr. McCarthy:—Because at present it is undenominational.

Lord Morris:—Very well.

Mr. McCarthy:—But what I say is that these words are not to be a fetter.

Lord Watson:—There was a great deal of controversy at one time in the country about a Roman catholic university in Ireland.

Mr. McCarthy:—It is not dead yet.

Lord Watson:—There was a great deal of controversy at one time, but I always understood that it was limited to the education of priests for the service of the church.

Mr. McCarthy:—It was only the other day that I read a statement of one of the Roman catholic prelates in Ireland pointing out how unfairly their people were treated because they had to go to the university school, which, although undenominational, was under the teaching of members of the church of England.

Lord Morris:—I was only saying, when you were saying that you considered there was even a stronger objection to a Roman catholic going to a non-denominational university than there was to going to a primary school, I do not agree with that, because I think it is the converse of that; there is a much greater objection to going to a non-denominational primary school than to a university, for the very reason that is given there, that in the one you are feared, and in the other you are supposed to be so invulnerable that you cannot be led astray.

Mr. McCARTHY:—I am speaking of the fact, and I am submitting—and that is the point of the argument—that if the schools cannot be narrowed down to training schools or early schools, they must embrace every class of school, and I am unable to see why that word would not cover colleges or so-called universities. The result is, as I say, that if this judgment is upheld, practically the educational power granted by the legislature would be practically stifled.

Lord SHAND:—Would not it be very much what it is in the other provinces if this decision is confirmed? We are told in the other provinces that you have nothing but denominational education

Mr. McCARTHY:—In two out of seven, my lord. In New Brunswick they have got no denominational schools, except in the sense only that they read the Douay Bible.

Lord MORRIS:—It is so in the two important ones—Ontario and Quebec. New Brunswick has been always different.

Mr. McCARTHY:—Of course the reason as to Ontario and Quebec is that each had its own special history. It is owing to the large French population, and the province of Quebec formed a part of the old province of Canada. It was they who insisted on imposing the separate schools on the upper provinces. It was done against the will of the majority of the people of the upper provinces and against their voting, but when they got in one legislature, it was imposed on them, and they also imposed at the time of the confederation that it should be made perpetual, but the people who go out to the new provinces want to be free.

Lord MORRIS:—What are the five where there is none?

Mr. McCARTHY:—Nova Scotia, New Brunswick, British Columbia, Prince Edward Island, those four are perfectly free, and then there is one in Manitoba, which is the fifth. Then the other two provinces make seven, and the North-west Territories have not yet any act, but talk is now going on in parliament as to the question of schools in the North-west Territories.

Judgment reserved.

FURTHER RETURN

(33*b*)

To an ADDRESS of the HOUSE OF COMMONS dated the 6th February, 1893, for a copy of the judgment of the Judicial Committee of Her Majesty's Privy Council in the appealed case of Barrett *vs.* the City of Winnipeg, commonly known as the "Manitoba School Case;" also copy of factums, reports and other documents in connection therewith.

By order.

JOHN COSTIGAN,

Secretary of State.

OTTAWA, 20th February, 1893.

RECORD OF PROCEEDINGS

Before the Judicial Committee of the Privy Council, and the cases of the Appellants and Respondent in "Barrett *vs.* the City of Winnipeg" (the Manitoba School Case), and Record of Proceedings and the Appellants' and the Respondent's cases in Logan *vs.* the City of Winnipeg.

CONTENTS.

PAGE.

Barrett *vs.* City of Winnipeg:

Factum of the Appellant 3
Factum of the Respondents 7
Factum of Case on Appeal 9
Order of Supreme Court of Canada allowing appeal 9
Registrar's Certificate verifying Transcript Record 10
Case of the Appellants 11
Case of the Respondent 15

Logan *vs.* City of Winnipeg:

Case of the Appellants 19
Case of the Respondent 23
Record of Proceedings 26, 27

IN THE PRIVY COUNCIL

ON APPEAL FROM THE SUPREME COURT OF CANADA.

BETWEEN

THE CITY OF WINNIPEG - - - - - - *Appellants,*

AND

JOHN KELLY BARRETT - - - - - - *Respondent.*

RECORD OF PROCEEDINGS.

"B."

IN THE SUPREME COURT OF CANADA.

In the Matter of an Application to quash By-laws 480 and 483 of the City of Winnipeg.

APPELLANT'S FACTUM.

John Kelly Barrett (Applicant) - - - - *Appellant,*

and

The City of Winnipeg (Respondents) - - - *Respondents.*

1. The question at issue upon this appeal is whether the Manitoba Public School Act, 53 Vict., c. 38, 1890, is void, as offending against the following provision in the Constitutional Act of Manitoba, 33 Vict., c. 3 (Dom. 1870), "Nothing in any such law shall prejudicially affect any right or privilege with respect to denominational schools which any class of persons have by law or practice in the province at the union."

The appellant contends that the school law offends against this provision in its effects on the Roman catholics of Manitoba. The question arises upon an application in the court of queen's bench to quash certain assessment by-laws of the city of Winnipeg made under the school law. Mr. Justice Killam dismissed the application; and the full court in term confirmed his judgment, Mr. Justice Dubuc dissenting.

2. In attempting to construe the provision in question, it is proper to compare it with the provision *in pari materia* of "The British North America Act, 1867," and to examine into the history of the legislation.

See "Rex *vs.* Loxdale," 1 Burr, p. 447.

"When there are different statutes *in pari materia*, though made at different times, or even expired, and not referring to each other, they shall be taken and construed together as one system, and as explanatory to each other."

See also "Hawkins *vs.* Gathercole," 6 De G. M. and G. 1.

See also "Maxwell on Statutes," 40, 41.

See also "Wilberforce on Statutes" 260–4.

3. For convenience there are set out below in parallel columns the corresponding paragraphs of "The British North America Act, 1867," and "The Manitoba Constitutional Act."

BRITISH NORTH AMERICA ACT.

In and for the province the legislature may exclusively make laws in relation to education, subject and according to the following provisions:—

(1.) Nothing in any such law shall prejudicially affect any right or privilege with respect to denominational schools which any class of persons have by law in the province at the union.

(2.) All powers, privileges, and duties at the union by law conferred and imposed in Upper Canada on the separate schools and school trustees of the queen's Roman catholic subjects shall be and the same are hereby extended to the dissentient schools of the queen's protestant and Roman catholic subjects in Quebec.

(3.) Where in any province a system of separate or dissentient schools exists by law at the union, or is thereafter established by the legislature of the province, an appeal shall lie to the governor-general in council from an act or decision of any provincial authority affecting any right or privilege of the protestant or Roman catholic minority of the queen's subjects in relation to education.

(4.) In case any such provincial law as from time to time seems to the governor-general in council requisite for the due execution of the provisions of this section is not made, or in case any decision of the governor-general in council on any appeal under this section is not duly executed by the proper provincial authority in that behalf, then, and in every such case, and as far only as the circumstances of each case require, the parliament of Canada may make remedial laws for the due execution of the provisions of this section and of any decision of the governor-general in council under this section.

MANITOBA ACT.

In and for the province the said legislature may exclusively make laws in relation to education, subject and according to the following provisions:—

(1.) Nothing in any such law shall prejudicially affect any right or privilege with respect to denominational schools which any class of persons have by law or practice in the province at the union.

(2) An appeal shall lie to the governor-general in council from any act or decision of the legislature of the province or of any provincial authority affecting any right or privilege of the protestant or Roman catholic minority of the queen's subjects in relation to education.

(3.) In case any such provincial law as from time to time seems to the governor-general in council requisite for the due execution of the provisions of this section is not made, or in case any decision of the governor-general in council on any appeal under this section is not duly executed by the proper authority in that behalf, then and in every such case, and as far only as the circumstances of each case may require, the parliament of Canada may make remedial laws for the due execution of the provisions of this section and of any decision of the governor-general in council under this section.

4. Some years prior to 1867, when "The Britsh North America Act" was passed, the parliament of the late province of Canada had passed a separate school law for Upper Canada, which was understood to be a final settlement of a long standing subject of contention. The understanding preceding the addresses on which "The British North America Act" was passed, was, that the privileges granted by this separate school law to the Roman catholic minority of Upper Canada should be secured to them, and that like privileges should be granted and secured to the protestant minority of Lower Canada. It had been intended that the latter privileges should be granted by legislation of the provincial parliament before confederation, and that the privileges so granted to the minorities in both Upper and Lower Canada should be secured by an identical process in the Confederation Act. The suggested provincial legislation failing, the clauses of "The British North America Act" above set out were moulded to accomplish the desired object by means of that act itself.

5. It will be observed that sub-section 1 of the clause of "The British North America Act" deals only with rights or privileges had by law at the union. Shortly after confederation a question arose as to the effect of this provision when applied to the state of things existing in New Brunswick at the union. In the session of the New Brunswick legislature of 1869 a school bill was introduced by the government of the day; and it was reintroduced in 1870, and debated at great length in March and April of that year, the Roman catholic minority of New Brunswick asserting that the privileges which in practice the Roman catholics had before the union in connection with denominational schools were theirs by law within the meaning of "The British North America Act," and therefore could not be, as it was alleged they were being, violated by the proposed legislation; while the protestant majority asserted, and the proposed legislation was based on, the view that such privileges were not had by law, but only by practice, and therefore were not protected from infringement by the provision.

6. It was under these circumstances that "The Manitoba Constitutional Bill" was, on the 2nd of May 1870, introduced into the Canadian house of commons, and it became an act on the 12th of that month. The appellant contends that the addition in the Manitoba Act to the words "by law" of the words "or practice" contained in the definition of the protected rights or privileges must be taken to have regard to the existing state of things in the territory then being formed in the province of Manitoba, and to the difficulties likely to arise there, as developed by the controversy in New Brunswick; and that the obvious object of the parliament of Canada, to be if possible effectuated by the courts, was to extend the security for privileges so as to cover the *status quo*, whether that *status quo* existed under the authority of law or that of practice only.

7. What, then, was the *status quo?* The affidavit of Archbishop Taché shows that:—

"Roman catholic schools have always formed an integral part of the work of the Roman catholic church. That church has always considered the education of the children of Roman catholic parents as coming peculiarly within its jurisdiction. The school, in the view of the Roman catholics, is in a large measure the children's church, and wholly incomplete and largely abortive if religious exercises be excluded from it. The church has always insisted upon its children receiving their education in schools conducted under the supervision of the church, and upon them being trained in the doctrines and faith of the church. In education, the Roman catholic church attaches very great importance to the spiritual culture of the child, and regards all education unaccompanied by instruction in its religious aspect as possibly detrimental and not beneficial to children. With this regard the church requires that all teachers of children shall not only be members of the church, but shall be thoroughly imbued with its principles and faith; shall recognize its spiritual authority and conform to its directions. It also requires that such books be used in the schools with regard to certain subjects as shall combine religious instruction with those subjects, and this applies peculiarly to all history and philosophy."

This affidavit further shows that:—

"Prior to the passage of the act of the dominion of Canada passed in the thirty-third year of the reign of her majesty Queen Victoria, chapter 3, known as the Manitoba Act, and prior to the order in council issued in pursuance thereof, there existed in the territory now constituting the province of Manitoba a number of effective schools for children. These schools were denominational schools, some of them regulated and controlled by the Roman catholic church, and others by various protestant denominations.

"The means necessary for the support of the Roman catholic schools were supplied to some extent by school fees paid by some of the parents of the children who attended the schools, and the rest was paid out of the funds of the church, contributed by its members.

"During the period referred to, Roman catholics had no interest in or control over the schools of the protestant denominations, and the members of the protestant denominations had no interest in or control over the schools of Roman catholics.

There were no public schools in the sense of state schools. The members of the Roman catholic church supported the schools of their own church for the benefit of the Roman catholic children, and were not under obligation to and did not contribute to the support of any other schools.

"In the matter of education, therefore, during the period referred to, Roman catholics were as a matter of custom and practice separate from the rest of the community, and their schools were all conducted according to the distinctive views and beliefs of Roman catholics as herein set forth."

8. Shortly after the passing of "The Manitoba Constitutional Act" in the year 1871, the local legislature of Manitoba passed a school law, by which and its amendments educational matters were, so far as the questions now in issue are concerned, substantially regulated until 1890, when the act now impeached was passed. The question whether this intermediate law violated the rights of the Roman catholics was never tested in the courts. But its bearing is described by Mr. Chief Justice Taylor in his judgment in the present case, as follows:—"Under that earlier law there was one board of education, which for certain purposes acted as a united board, but which was also divided into two sections, a protestant section, consisting of all the protestant members, and a Roman catholic section, consisting of the Roman catholic members. The school districts throughout the province were divided into protestant and catholic. The protestant schools were under the control of the protestant section of the board, and the trustees of these schools were elected by the protestant ratepayers. The Roman catholic section of the board had in like manner entire control of the catholic schools, and the catholic ratepayers elected the trustees. There was also one superintendent of education for the protestant schools and another for the catholic schools. The law also provided for levying the taxes for the support of schools in protestant school districts upon the property of protestants alone, and in Roman catholic school districts upon Roman catholics only. Provision was also made for apportioning taxes derived from the property of corporations, or of persons who could not be considered to belong to either body. The grant made annually by the legislature for educational purposes was apportioned between the two sections of the board for distribution among the schools under the charge of each respectively."

9. By the School Law of 1890, now attacked, all the former statutes were repealed. Its practical effect may be said to be to abolish all provisions for Roman catholic schools, and to continue the former protestant schools under the name of public schools; for while some changes in methods of government are provided for, the new schools are substantially identical with those formerly established by protestants under the repealed law. Such inadequate provision as is made for religious exercises requires (as the divisions of protestants into numerous denominations necessitates) that the exercises should be of an unsectarian character, and it is thus diametrically opposed to the principles and practice of the Roman catholic church. This provision being accepted by the protestants, and satisfactory to them as a whole, the schools may be not unfairly described as protestant schools, in the sense that they conform to the protestant, and do not conform to the Roman catholic principles and practices in education.

10. These schools, being the only ones established under and recognized by the law, are to be maintained under that law at the cost of the whole population, Roman catholic as well as protestant; and the assessment by-laws, which are objected to, provide for the levying of rates upon the whole population, including the Roman catholics, for the maintenance of such schools in Winnipeg. The Roman catholic church, as shown by the eighth paragraph of the affidavit of Archbishop Taché, "Regards the schools provided for by 'The Public Schools Act' as unfit for the purpose of educating their children, and the children of Roman catholic parents will not attend such schools. Rather than countenance such schools Roman catholics will revert to the system of operation previous to the Manitoba Act, and will establish, support, and maintain schools in accordance with their principles and faith as before mentioned."

11. Under these circumstances it is that the appellant contends that the school law of 1890 does prejudicially affect rights or privileges in respect to denomina-

tional schools, which the class of persons called Roman catholics had by law or practice in the province at the union. At the union, Roman catholics had by practice the right to support their own denominational schools, at their own charge, for the purpose of instructing their own children, separate from those of the other denominations in the community, free from all charge in respect of the support of schools for or used by any other denomination. At the union, Roman catholics were in practice enjoying and acting upon these rights. By the law impeached, the Roman catholics are compelled to bear a ratable share of the charge for the schools thereunder established, schools which are not denominational, not Roman catholic, not separate, and of which Roman catholics cannot conscientiously avail themselves; while these schools are under the name of "public," substantially protestant, and are at any rate accepted and used by, and satisfactory to, the various denominations of protestants:

12. The Roman catholics being obliged to re-establish and maintain separate and denominational schools according to the practice at the union, are thus prejudicially affected by the change, in being compelled first of all to pay the whole cost of those denominational schools, and secondly, to bear a ratable proportion of the charge for the so-called public schools of which they can and do make no use. This change does not merely prejudicially affect the Roman catholics in their purse, but (tending, as it must, to increase very greatly the burden of Roman catholics in connection with education, while it diminishes those of the protestant denominations) difficulties are thrown in the way of efficient and wide-spread Roman catholic denominational education in schools most prejudicial to that body. It is therefore obvious that they are prejudicially affected within the meaning of the provision.

For these reasons the appellant contends that the appeal should be allowed and the by-laws quashed, with costs.

JOHN S. EWART,
Counsel for Appellant.

"C."

IN THE SUPREME COURT OF CANADA.

Appeal from the Court of Queen's Bench for Manitoba.

In the Matter of an Application to quash By-laws 480 and 483 of the City of Winnipeg.

RESPONDENTS' FACTUM.

John Kelly Barrett (Applicant) - - - *Appellant*

and

The City of Winnipeg (Respondents) - - - *Respondents.*

This is an application to quash two by-laws of the city of Winnipeg, numbered 480 and 483, on the ground "That, because by the said by-laws, the amounts to be levied for school purposes for the protestant and Roman catholic schools are united, and one rate levied upon protestants and Roman catholics alike for the whole sum."

The application is made under section 258 *et seq.*, of "The Municipal Act" of 1890, of the province of Manitoba, and raises the question as to the legality, or illegality, of "The Public Schools Act," chapter 38 of 53 Vict., Statutes of Manitoba.

The first legislation in Manitoba, for the establishment of a public school system, was passed in the year 1871 (34 Vict., c. 12), whereby a board of education, composed of not less than 10 nor more than 14 persons, was established, one-half of whom were protestants and one-half catholics. Each section of the board had a separate superintendent, and, amongst other powers, had under its control and management the "discipline" of the schools of the section, and the proscribing of such books as had reference to religion or morals. The moneys appropriated by the legislature for common school education were, after deducting the expenses of the board, and superintendents' salaries, to be "appropriated to the support and maintenance of common schools, one moiety thereof to the support of protestant schools, and the other moiety to the support of the catholic schools" (section 13).

By subsequent legislation, enacted at various times up to the passage of "The Public Schools Act" (53 Vict., c. 38), the powers of the protestant and catholic sections of the board of education were enlarged, whereby the entire control and management of the schools, their general government and discipline, were delegated to the section of the board to which the school belonged. Each section had power to select all the books, maps, and globes to be used in the schools under its control, and to approve of the plans for the construction of school houses, "Provided, however, that in the case of books having reference to religion and morals, such selection by the catholic section of the board shall be subject to the approval of the competent religious authority." *See* Man. Stat., 34 Vict., c. 12; ditto, 36 Vict., c. 22; ditto, 39 Vict., c. 1; ditto, 42 Vict., c. 2; ditto, 44 Vict., c. 4.

By the act respecting the department of education (53 Vict., c. 37) and by "The Public Schools Act" (53 Vict., c. 38), all prior legislation as to schools and education in Manitoba was repealed, and a department of education created, to consist of the executive council or a committee thereof, which, with an advisory board. to be elected in the manner prescribed by the act, practically replaced the old board of education. It was further provided that all public schools in the province were to be free schools (section 5), that all religious exercises in the public schools should be conducted according to the regulations of the advisory board (section 6), and that, except as above, no religious exercises were to be allowed in the schools which were declared to be "entirely non-sectarian" (section 8).

Power was given to municipalities to levy on the taxable property in each school district the sum required by such district, in addition to the legislative and municipal grants (section 90), and in cities, towns, and villages the municipal councils are to "levy and collect upon the taxable property within the municipality, in the manner provided in this act and in the municipal and assessment acts, such sums as may be required by the public school trustees for school purposes" (section 92), and it was declared that the taxable property in a municipality for school purposes was to include all property liable to municipal taxation, and also all property exempt by the council from municipal and not from school taxation (section 93).

"The British North America Act, 1867," enacted, section 92, "In each province the legislature may exclusively make laws in relation to matters coming within the classes of subjects next hereinafter enumerated, that is to say . . . . (2.) Direct taxation within the province in order to the raising of a revenue for provincial purposes . . . . (8.) Municipal institutions in the province"; and by section 93, "In and for each province the legislature may exclusively make laws in relation to education, subject and according to the following provisions:—(1) Nothing in any such law shall prejudicially affect any right or privilege with respect to denominational schools which any class of persons have by law in the province at the union."

By the 22nd section of the Manitoba Act, "In and for the province the said legislature may exclusively make laws in relation to education, subject and according to the following provisions:—(1) Nothing in any such law shall prejudicially affect any right or privilege with respect to denominational schools which any class of persons have by law or practice in the province at the union."

Prior to the province of Manitoba entering confederation, the schools then in existence were purely private schools, and were not in any way subject to public control, nor did they receive public support. No school taxes were levied or collected by any authority, and whatever contributions were made for the support of said schools were purely voluntary. *See* affidavit, Alexander Polson, affidavit, John Sutherland, and affidavit, Archbishop Taché.

The respondents submit that the words "law or practice," as used in sub-section 1 of section 22 Manitoba Act, can only mean some binding rule or obligation to which the inhabitants of the province were at the date of the union committ'ed. There is no evidence showing such to have been the case. *Exparte* Renaud, 1 Pugsley, N. B. R., 273; S. C., 2, Cart., Cas. 445.

The "right or privilege" with respect to denominational schools at the date of the union was, according to the affidavit of his grace Archbbishop Taché, the right to establish denominational schools supported by private contributions of parents or by the funds of the church. This right has in no way been interfered with by "The Public Schools Act." Roman catholics are still entitled, notwithstanding the abolition of separate schools, to establish and maintain denominational schools the same as before the union.

The Manitoba Act (section 22) contemplated the establishment of a system of free undenominational public schools, and the maintenance of the same by grants of provincial funds or by direct taxation, or both. The enactment of "The Public Schools Act" was therefore within the powers granted to the provincial legislature by the Manitoba Act, and was not an interference with the rights and privileges with respect to "denominational" schools.

The respondents contend that the provincial legislature was intended to have power to provide against popular ignorance as an evil, and for that purpose to expend the public moneys, and, if necessary, to levy taxes. That certain individuals in the community, who voluntarily contribute to and maintain denominational schools would have to pay the rates imposed by the legislature for the support of free schools, is too indirect and remote an effect to bring it within the act as an invasion of their rights and privileges thereunder.

The establishment and maintenance of private denominational schools by certain individuals or classes in the community, prior to and at the time of the union, was not a "right or privilege" within the ordinary meaning of these words as used in the Manitoba Act. "Bac. Abrid.," Vol. 8, p. 158; Com. Dig. (*Sic.*); "McKeddy's Roman Law," Section 189; "Campbell *v.* Spottiswoode," 3 B. and S., 769; "Fraser *v.* Mitchell," L. R. 7, Q. B., 690. *See* definitions in "Bouvier's Law Dictionary"; ditto "Browne's Law Dictionary"; ditto "Wharton's Law Lexicon"; ditto Imperial and Webster's Dictionaries.

"A."

IN THE SUPREME COURT OF CANADA.

FACTUM OF CASE ON APPEAL TO THE SUPREME COURT OF CANADA

NOTE.—*See Sessional Paper No. 63b*, 1891.

D.

ORDER OF SUPREME COURT OF CANADA ALLOWING APPEAL, DATED 28TH OCTOBER, 1891.

E.

REASONS OF JUDGES OF THE SUPREME COURT OF CANADA.

NOTE.—*See Sessional Paper No.* 46, 1892.

IN THE SUPREME COURT OF CANADA.

REGISTRAR'S CERTIFICATE VERIFYING TRANSCRIPT RECORD.

In the Matter of an Application to quash By-laws 480 and 483 of the City of Winnipeg.

Between

John Kelly Barrett (Applicant) - - - *Appellant.*

and

The City of Winnipeg - - - - *Respondents.*

I, Robert Cassels, registrar of the supreme court of Canada, hereby certify that the printed document annexed hereto marked A is a true copy of the original case filed in my office in the above appeal; that the printed documents also annexed hereto marked B and C are true copies of the factums of the appellant and respondents respectively deposited in said appeal; and that the document marked D, also annexed hereto, is a true copy of the formal judgment of this court in the said appeal; and I further certify that the document marked E, also annexed hereto, is a copy of the reasons for judgment delivered by the judges of this court when rendering judgment, as certified by George Duval, Esq., the official reporter of this court.

Dated at Ottawa, this 28th day of December, A.D. 1891.

(Seal.) ROBERT CASSELS,

Registrar.

IN THE PRIVY COUNCIL

ON APPEAL FROM THE SUPREME COURT OF CANADA.

BETWEEN

THE CITY OF WINNIPEG - - - - - - - - - - - *Appellants*

AND

JOHN KELLY BARRETT - - - - - - - - - - - *Respondent.*

CASE OF THE APPELLANTS.

1. This is an appeal from a judgment of the supreme court of Canada pronounced on the 28th October, 1891, reversing a judgment of the court of queen's bench for the province of Manitoba pronounced on the 2nd February, 1891.

2. The respondent, John Kelly Barrett, applied to a judge of the court of queen's bench for Manitoba, under section 258 of the Manitoba Municipal Act (53 Vict., cap. 51), to quash two by-laws of the appellants, the city of Winnipeg, being by-laws numbered 480 and 483, for "illegality," and upon the ground, "That because by the said by-laws the amounts to be levied for school purposes for the protestant and Roman catholic schools are united, and one rate levied upon protestant and Roman catholics alike for the whole sum."

3. The application was heard before Mr. Justice Killam, who dismissed it, his reasons for doing so being reported in 7 "Manitoba Law Reports," page 273, and also printed in the Record.

4. From this judgment the respondent appealed to the court of queen's bench for Manitoba. The appeal was heard before the full court, consisting of the chief justice, Mr. Justice Bain, and Mr. Justice Dubuc, and was dismissed by that court, Mr. Justice Dubuc dissenting, the reasons of their lordships being reported in the same number of the Manitoba Law Reports, commencing at page 304, and also printed in the Record.

5. From this judgment the respondent appealed to the supreme court of Canada, and the appeal was allowed by that court, and an order made quashing the said by-laws, the reasons for the judgment of their lordships being printed in the Record.

6. The two by-laws in question were passed for levying a rate for municipal and school purposes in the city of Winnipeg for the year of 1890. The principal by-law, viz., by-law 480, recited amongst other matters the aggregate amount necessary to be raised to meet the interest for debentures and for the ordinary current municipal and school purposes without distinction and the total value of the ratable property in the city as shown by the last revised assessment rolls, and enacted that there should be raised, collected, and levied a rate of 2 cents on the dollar upon the whole assessed value of the real and personal property in the city according to such rolls for meeting the expenditure mentioned. The by-law is set out in full in the Record.

7. By-law 483 amended the former by-law. It recited that the property of certain corporations was liable only for school rates, and that it was desirable to distinguish the rates providing for city schools, but so that the total several rates should not exceed 2 cents on the dollar, and it amended the former by-law so as to make the rate 15⅔ mills on the dollar for interest on debentures and for the ordinary current municipal expenditure for the year, and 4⅓ mills for school purposes also for the year.

8. The substantial question in the appeal is whether the Public Schools Act, passed by the legislature of the province of Manitoba in 1890 (53 Vict., cap. 38,

Manitoba), under the authority of which the said by-laws were passed, is within the power of that legislature to enact. This act established one system of public schools throughout the province and abolished all the laws regarding public schools which had theretofore been passed and were then existing. The respondent contends that the act is *ultra vires*, and that the by-laws in question which levied a rate for school purposes pursuant to it on all the ratepayers alike are consequently illegal, his ground for so contending being that the act, as he alleges, offends against the following provision contained in "The Manitoba Act," under which the province was admitted into confederation (33 Vict., cap. 3, Dominion, 1870):—

"21. In and for the province the said legislature may exclusively make laws in relation to education, subject and according to the following provisions:

"(1.) Nothing in any such law shall prejudicially affect any right or privilege with respect to denominational schools, which any class of persons have by law or practice in the province at the union."

9. The respondent filed, in support of the application, his own affidavit, which stated that he was a ratepayer and a resident of the city of Winnipeg, and a member of the Roman catholic church, and that the effect of these by-laws was that one rate was levied upon all protestant and Roman catholic ratepayers, in order to raise the amount required for school purposes, and he claimed that the result to individual ratepayers was "that each protestant will have to pay less than if he were assessed for protestant schools alone, and each Roman catholic would have to pay more than if he were assessed for Roman catholic schools alone."

10. An affidavit of his grace the archbishop of St. Boniface was also filed by the respondent, and several affidavits in answer were filed on behalf of the appellants. The material facts relied upon by the respondent are set out in the affidavit of the archbishop as follows:

"(*a*) Prior to the passing of the Manitoba Act, and prior to the order in council issued in pursuance thereof, there existed in the territory now constituting the province of Manitoba a number of effective schools for children.

"(*b*) These schools were denominational schools, some of them being regulated and controlled by the Roman catholic church, and others by various protestant denominations.

"(*c*) The means necessary for the support of Roman catholic schools were supplied, to some extent, by school fees, paid by some of the parents of the children who attended the schools, and the rest were paid out of the funds of the church, contributed by its members.

"(*d*) During the period referred to Roman catholics had no interest in or control over the schools of the protestant denominations, and the members of the protestant denominations had no interest in or control over the schools of the Roman catholics. There were no public schools in the sense of state schools. The members of the Roman catholic church supported the schools of their own church for the benefit of the Roman catholic children, and were not under obligation to and did not contribute to the support of any other schools.

"(*e*) The Roman catholic schools were all conducted according to the distinctive views and beliefs of Roman catholics."

11. The affidavits filed by the appellants, the city of Winnipeg, showed that prior to the province of Manitoba entering confederation the schools then in existence were merely private schools, and were in no way subject to public control, and did not receive public support; that no school taxes were levied or collected by any authority, and whatever contributions were made for the support of said schools were purely voluntary.

12. The province of Manitoba became one of the provinces of the dominion of Canada on 15th July, 1870, under the following circumstances:

(*a*) Prior to the union the district comprised in the province of Manitoba was a portion of Rupert's Land, and was a part of the territory granted to the Hudson's Bay Company on 2nd May, 1670, by King Charles II.

(*b*) Prior to 1870 a number of white settlers and half-breeds had established themselves along the banks of the Red and Assiniboine rivers, in what was known as the Red River Settlement, all of which was included in the new province.

(*c*) By the British North America Act (Imperial Statute 30 and 31 Vict., cap. 3) the old provinces of Upper and Lower Canada, Nova Scotia and New Brunswick were confederated into the dominion of Canada.

(*d*) On the 23rd of June, 1870, an imperial order in council was passed admitting Manitoba into confederation, the same coming into force on the 15th July, 1870, from which last mentioned date Manitoba has been one of the provinces of the Dominion.

(*e*) The Dominion Statute (32 and 33 Vict., cap. 3) commonly called "The Manitoba Act," provided for the government of the new province, and declared that the provisions of the British North America Act should, except as to those parts thereof which were in terms made or by reasonable intendment might be held to be specially applicable to or only affect one or more but not the whole of the provinces then comprising the Dominion, and except as the same might be varied by that act, be applicable to the province of Manitoba. This act was confirmed by the imperial act (34 and 35 Vict., cap. 28.)

(*f*) By the British North America Act it is enacted (section 92): "In each province the legislature may exclusively make laws in relation to matters coming within the classes of subjects next hereinafter enumerated, that is to say:

"(2) Direct taxation within the province, in order to the raising of a revenue for provincial purposes."

"(8) Municipal institutions in the province." And by section 93: "In and for the province the legislature may exclusively make laws in relation to education, subject and according to the following provisions:

"(1) Nothing in any such law shall prejudicially affect any right or privilege with respect to denominational schools which any class of persons have by law in the province at the union."

(*g*) The provisions of section 93 of the British North America Act were varied in and by the provision hereinbefore set out in full in paragraph 8 of this case. And in addition the section 22 in sub-section (2) provides somewhat more generally for an appeal to the governor-general in council from any act or decision of the provincial legislature or authorities affecting any right or privilege of the protestant or Roman catholic minority of the queen's subjects in relation to education. The provisions contained in section 92 of the British North America Act and above referred to are not altered, and apply to Manitoba.

13. The act known as the Public Schools Act, the validity of which is in question, enacts that all public schools in the province are to be free schools (section 5); that all religious exercises in the public schools shall be conducted according to the regulations of the advisory board, which is provided for (section 6); but in case the guardian or parent of any pupil notifies the teacher that he does not wish such pupil to attend such religious exercises, then the pupil shall be dismissed before the religious exercises take place, the time appointed for such religious exercises being just before the closing hour. All public schools are non-sectarian, and no religious exercises shall be allowed therein except as above provided. The act is not compulsory; no parent or guardian is compelled to send his child to a public school.

14. The question involved in this appeal turns largely upon the effect of the words "by law or practice" contained in section 22 of the Manitoba Act (33 Vict., cap. 3). The law in force prior to the union in the territory which now forms the province of Manitoba was the law of England as at the date of the Hudson's Bay Company's charter, viz., 2nd May, 1670, in so far as such law was applicable to the country. Roman catholics did not therefore possess any right or privilege with respect to denominational schools by law in the province at the union. The "right

or privilege" with respect to denominational schools existing by practice at the date of the union was, as shown by the affidavits, merely the privilege to establish and maintain private schools which were supported by fees paid by the parents or guardians of the children who attended them, supplemented, it may be, by those who belonged to the Roman catholic church. This right has in no way been interfered with or "prejudically affected" by the Public Schools Act of 1890. Roman catholics are still entitled to establish and maintain denominational schools in the same manner as before the union.

15. The appellants petitioned your majesty in council for special leave to appeal from the judgment of the said supreme court, dated the 28th October, 1891, and by an order dated the 9th May, 1892, leave to appeal was granted.

16. The appellants submit that the judgment of the supreme court of Canada should be set aside, and the judgment of the court of queen's bench for Manitoba reinstated, with their costs in the courts below, for the following amongst other

REASONS:

(1) Because the reasons of Killam, J., Taylor, C.J., and Bain, J., are right in law and fact.

(2) Because the provincial act respecting public schools does not affect any right or privilege with respect to denominational schools which the respondent or any class of persons had by law or practice in the province prior to the union.

(3) Because the respondent had not, nor had the Roman catholics of the province, prior to the union any right or privileges by law in relation to the Roman catholic denominational schools.

(4) Because the respondent had not, nor had the Roman catholics of the province, prior to the union any right or privileges by practice respecting denominational schools other than that of establishing and maintaining private schools in which the tenets of the Romish church were taught, which is in nowise interfered with by the act in question.

(5) Because in any view the School Act does not prejudically affect any right or privileges which the Roman catholics had respecting denominational schools in the sense in which these words have been judicially interpreted.

(6) Because the respondent has not shown that the School Act interferes with any right or privileges which were locally enjoyed in the part of the province which is now within the limits of the city of Winnipeg.

HORACE DAVEY,
D'ALTON McCARTHY.

IN THE PRIVY COUNCIL

ON APPEAL FROM THE SUPREME COURT OF CANADA

BETWEEN

THE CITY OF WINNIPEG - - - - - - - - - *Appellants*

AND

JOHN KELLY BARRETT - - - - - - - - - - *Respondent.*

CASE OF THE RESPONDENT.

1. This is an appeal by special leave of her majesty in council from a judgment of the supreme court of Canada ordering that certain by-laws of the city of Winnipeg should be quashed. The question at issue, which is one of great importance, is whether the Public Schools Act, 1890, (Manitoba Statute) is within the power of the provincial legislature of Manitoba. The judges of the supreme court reversing the decision of the court of queen's bench of Manitoba, unanimously held that it was not.

2. Manitoba joined the union in 1870, upon the terms of the Constitutional Act of Manitoba, 1870, 33 Vict., c. 3 (Dominion Statute). Section 22 of that act is as follows :—

" 22. In and for the province (*i. e.*, of Manitoba) the said (*i. e.*, provincial) legislature may exclusively make laws in relation to education, subject and according to the following provisions :—

> " (1) Nothing in any such law shall prejudicially affect any right or privilege with respect to denominational schools which any class of persons have by law *or practice* in the province at the union :
>
> " (2) An appeal shall lie to the governor-general in council from any act or decision of the legislature of the province or of any provincial authority affecting any right or privilege of the protestant or Roman catholic minority of the queen's subjects in relation to education :
>
> " (3) In case any such provincial law as from time to time seems to the governor-general in council requisite for the due execution of the provisions of this section, is not made, or in case any decision of the governor general in council on any appeal under this section is not duly executed by the proper provincial authority in that behalf, then, and in every such case, and as far only as the circumstances of each case require, the parliament of Canada may make remedial laws for the due execution of the provisions of this section, and of any decision of the governor-general in council under this section."

3. The first sub-section of the above section, upon which the question in this case mainly turns, is identical in terms with section 93 sub-section 1 of the British North America Act, 1867, with the exception that the words " or practice " printed above in italics do not appear in section 93 sub-section 1 of the British North America Act, 1867. The two sections above mentioned are collocated for comparison in the Record.

4. At the date of union in 1870 there was not, nor ever had been, any state system of education in Manitoba, nor any compulsory rate or state grant for purposes of education. There was, however, and for many years previously had been, an established and recognized system of voluntary denominational education. There were in particular throughout Manitoba a number of effective Roman catholic (hereinafter called catholic) schools, at which the children of catholics attended, and where the education was under the control of the catholic church. These schools were supported partly by school fees and partly by voluntary contributions from catholics.

In a similar way the various protestant sects supported schools of their own, which were also exclusively under their control.

5. In 1871 the legislature of Manitoba passed an act, 34 Vict., chapter 12, establishing a state system of education in the province, and in subsequent sessions other enactments dealing with the subject were passed. The legislation on the subject was codified and extended by 44 Vict., chapter 4, and subsequent modifications were introduced by 45 Vict., chapters 8 and 11; 46 and 47 Vict., chapter 46; 47 Vict., chapters 37 and 54; 48 Vict., chapter 27; 50 Vict., chapters 18 and 19; 51 Vict., chapter 31; 52 Vict., chapters 5 and 21.

6. By virtue of this legislation a board of education was established in the province appointed by the lieutenant-governor in council, of whom a certain specified proportion were protestants and a certain specified proportion were catholics. This board was divided into two sections, protestant and catholic, each section being exclusively composed of the members professing these faiths respectively, and the control of protestant schools was exclusively vested in the protestant section, while the control of the catholic schools was (subject as regards the selection of books relating to religion and morals to the control of competent catholic religious authority) exclusively vested in the catholic section. The acts then provided for the division of the province into school districts, which were styled respectively protestant and catholic school districts. It was further provided that the establishment of a school district of one denomination at a particular place should not prevent the establishment of a school district of another denomination at the same place. Provision was made for the election of school trustees of each school district, the electors being the ratepayers within such district of the religious denomination which such district bore, and the school trustees, when elected, became a corporation under the name of "The School Trustees for the Protestant (or Catholic, as the case may be) School District of ." The school trustees had power under certain conditions to levy compulsorily a rate within their district, for school purposes, but only upon ratepayers of of the religious denomination of the particular district, so that no protestant was under liability to contribute to a catholic school nor a catholic to a protestant school. Provision was further made for the division of such grants as were made by the state in aid of education between the various catholic and protestant district schools in proportion to population.

7. In 1890 (53 Vict.) the legislature of Manitoba passed two statutes relating to education. By chapter 37 a state department of education was established, together with an advisory board consisting of seven members, all appointed without reference to their creed, of whom four were appointed by the department of education and three by the teachers of the province. The advisory board so appointed was substituted for the protestant and catholic sections of the board of education previously existing, which was abolished. By chapter 38, which is the act the validity of which is now in question and which was entitled "The Public Schools Act," 1890, the previous legislation relating to public education was repealed. It was provided that existing protestant and catholic school districts should become subject to the provisions of the act, and that religious exercises in the public schools should be conducted according to the regulations of the advisory board, it being on the one hand optional upon the school trustees of each district whether any religious exercises should take place, and upon the other optional upon any parent or guardian to refuse to allow his child to attend such religious exercises. It was further provided that the schools should be entirely non-sectarian and no religious exercises should be allowed except as above provided. Subject to the control of the advisory board, the management of the school was vested in school trustees who were to be elected by the ratepayers without distinction of creed. The act further provided for the assessment by the municipal authorities upon all ratepayers within the municipality of such rates as should be necessary for the maintenance of the public schools therein. In the rural districts the amount to be assessed was a fixed sum for each school, while in the cities, towns and villages the municipal authorities were required to raise such sum as might be required by the school trustees of the district. It was provided that amongst other persons any

clergyman should be a school visitor within the place where he had pastoral charge and might examine the pupils and give advice to the teachers and pupils. Section 179 further provided that in all cases where, before the coming into operation of the act, catholic school districts had been established such catholic districts should cease to exist, and all the assets of such catholic schools should belong to and all the liabilities thereof be paid by the public school district.

8. It appeared by an affidavit of the archbishop of the Roman catholic ecclesiastical province of St. Boniface, that it was in the view of members of that church an essential element in the education of children that such education should be a religious education, and should be conducted under the supervision of the church. He stated (and it was not substantially disputed) that the schools provided by the Public Schools Act would be regarded by catholics as unfit for the education of their children, and that they could not conscientiously permit their children to attend them, and would consequently have to establish throughout the province fresh voluntary schools, conducted in accordance with the principles of their faith, and to support and maintain such schools. It would appear on the other hand that schools conducted as specified in the Public Schools Act would have the approval of certain protestant denominations in Manitoba and among others of the presbyterians, and it appears probable that such schools would be conducted mainly for the benefit of these denominations, and would be in effect their schools.

9. On the 14th and 28th July, 1890, the appellants, the corporation of Winnipeg, passed two by-laws, nos. 480 and 483, sanctioning the raising of a large sum of money for the purpose, amongst others, of defraying the amount required for school expenditure under the Public Schools Act, 1890, for the public schools within the district. The amount of the said rate which was required for this purpose was a sum of 77,550 dollars, made up of a sum of 75,000 dollars, required for school purposes by the trustees of a public school within the municipality called the school trustees for the protestant school district of Winnipeg, no. 1, in the province of Manitoba, and a sum of 2,550 dollars required for similar purposes by the school trustees for the catholic school district of Winnipeg, no. 1.

10. For the purpose of obtaining a decision upon the question of the validity of said act, the respondent obtained a summons calling on the appellants to show cause why the said by-laws should not be quashed for illegality upon the ground that the amounts levied for protestant and catholic schools were therein united, and that one rate was levied upon protestants and catholics alike for the whole sum. A rate so levied would be invalid according to the education acts in force at the time of the passing of the Public Schools Act, 1890.

11. The application was heard before Killam, J., who dismissed the summons. His formal order appears at p. 23, and his reasons at pp. 24 to 38 of the Record. He held that the rights and privileges referred to in the act were those of maintaining denominational schools of having children educated in them, and having inculcated therein the peculiar doctrines of the respective denominations. He regarded the prejudice effected by the imposition of a tax upon catholics for schools to which they were conscientiously opposed as something so indirect and remote that he could not take it to be within the act.

12. The respondent appealed to the court of queen's bench of Manitoba in *banc*, composed of three judges who, after argument, dismissed the appeal, Dubuc, J., dissenting. The formal judgment appears at p. 83, the reasons of Taylor, C. J., at p. 39, of Dubuc, J., at p. 52 and of Bain, J., at p. 73 of the Record.

13. Taylor, C. J., thought that the "rights and privileges" included moral rights, and that parliament intended in fact that whatever any class of persons was, at the time of the union, in the habit or custom of doing in reference to denominational schools, should continue and should not be prejudicially affected by provincial legislation, but he held that none of these rights or privileges were in any way affected by the act. Bain, J., delivered a separate judgment but, substantially on the same grounds. Dubuc, J., held that the right or privilege existing by practice at the date of the union, and intended to be protected, was the right of each denomination to have its denominational school with such teaching as it might think fit, and the privilege of not being compelled to contribute to other schools of which

members of such denominations could not in conscience avail themselves, and that this right or privilege was invaded by the Public Schools Act, 1890, which was consequently *ultra vires*.

14. The respondent then appealed to the supreme court of Canada, which court, composed of five judges, after taking time for consideration, unanimously allowed the appeal. The formal order of the court appears at p. 84 of the Record, the reasons of Ritchie, C. J., with which Strong, J., agreed at pp. 85 to 91, those of Patterson, J., at pp. 91 to 96, those of Fournier, J., at pp. 96 to 108, those of Taschereau, J., at pp. 108 to 113 of the Record.

15. Ritchie, C. J., held that as catholics could not conscientiously continue to avail themselves of the public schools as carried on under the system established by the Public Schools Act, 1890, the effect of that act was to deprive them of any further beneficial use of the system of voluntary catholic schools which had been established before the union and had thereafter been carried on under the state system introduced in 1871. Patterson, J., pointed out that the words "injuriously affect" in sec. 22, sub-section 1, of the Manitoba Constitutional Act, would include any degree of interference with the rights or privileges in question, although falling short of the extinction of such rights or privileges. He held that the impediment cast in the way of obtaining contributions to voluntary catholic denominational schools by reason of the fact that all catholics would under the act be compulsorily assessed to another system of education amounted to an injurious affecting of their rights and privileges within the meaning of the sub-section. Fournier, J., pointed out that the mere right of maintaining voluntary schools if they chose to pay for them and causing their children to attend such schools could not have been the right which it was intended to reserve to catholics or other classes of persons by the use of the word "practice," since such right was undoubtedly one enjoyed by every person or class of persons by law, and took a similar view to that taken by Patterson, J. Taschereau, J., gave judgment in the same sense, holding that the contention of the appellants gave no effect to the word "practice" inserted in the section.

16. The respondent submits that the judgment appealed from is correct and should be affirmed for the following amongst other

REASONS.

1. Because the provisions of the Public Schools Act, 1890, prejudicially affect the rights and privileges of catholics in the province as they existed by law or practice at the date of the union with respect to denominational schools.
2. Because catholics cannot conscientiously permit their children to attend the public schools as constituted and carried on under the said act.
3. Because by reason of the compulsory rate levied upon catholic ratepayers in support of the public schools, material impediments are cast in the way both of subscribing and of obtaining subscriptions in support of catholic denominational schools, and of setting up and maintaining the same, and the rights and privileges of catholics in reference thereto are thereby prejudicially affected.
4. Because by the operation of the said act catholics are deprived of the system of catholic denominational schools as they existed at the date of the union, or are prejudicially affected in reference to such system.
5. Because the public schools as constituted by the said act are or may be protestant denominational schools, and catholic ratepayers are by the said act compelled to contribute thereto.
6. Because the judgments and reasons of Dubuc, J., and of the several judges of the supreme court of Canada are correct.

RICHARD E. WEBSTER.
JOHN S. EWART.
FRANCIS C. GORE.

IN THE PRIVY COUNCIL

ON APPEAL FROM THE COURT OF QUEEN'S BENCH OF THE PROVINCE OF MANITOBA.

BETWEEN

THE CITY OF WINNIPEG - - - - - - - - *Appellants,*

AND

ALEXANDER LOGAN - - - - - - - - - *Respondent.*

CASE OF THE APPELLANTS.

1. This is an appeal from a judgment of the court of queen's bench for the province of Manitoba, dated the 19th day of December, 1891.

2. The respondent, Alexander Logan, applied to the chief justice of the court of queen's bench for Manitoba under section 258 of the Manitoba Municipal Act (53 Vict., cap. 51), to quash a by-law of the appellants, the city of Winnipeg, being bylaw numbered 514, " for illegality," upon the grounds, "That by the said by-law the amount estimated to be levied for school expenditure is levied upon members of the church of England and all other religious denominations alike.

"That it is illegal to assess members of the church of England for the support of schools which are not under the control of the church of England, and in which there are not taught religious exercises prescribed by said church, and upon grounds appearing in affidavits and papers filed."

3. The application was by consent referred to the full court in term, and the court after argument quashed the by-law on the ground that the case could not be distinguished from the decision of supreme court in the case of Barrett *vs.* Winnipeg, which is now under appeal to her majesty in council. This case is reported in Manitoba Law Reports, vol. 8, p. 3, and the judgments are printed in the Record.

4. The substantial question in the appeal is whether the Public School Act, passed by the legislature of the province of Manitoba in 1890 (53 Vict., cap. 38, Manitoba) is within the powers of that legislature to enact. This act established one system of public schools and abolished the protestant and Roman catholic separate public schools theretofore existing. The respondent claims that the act is *ultra vires*, and that the by-law in question which levied a rate for school purposes, pursuant to the act, upon all ratepayers alike is consequently illegal, his ground for so contending being that the act, as he alleges, offends against the following provision contained in the act under which Manitoba was admitted into confederation (33 Vict., cap. 3, sec. 22, Dominion of Canada, 1870) :—

"In and for the province the said legislature may exclusively make laws in relation to education, subject and according to the following provisions:

"Nothing in any such law shall prejudicially affect any right or privilege with respect to denominational schools which any class of persons have by law or practice in the province at the union."

5. The by-law in question was passed for levying a rate for municipal and school purposes in the city of Winnipeg for the year 1891. It recited the aggregate amount necessary to be raised to meet interest for debentures and ordinary current municipal and school purposes, the total value of the ratable property in the city as shown by the last revised assessment rolls, and enacted that there should be raised, collected, and levied a rate of $15\frac{3}{10}$ mills on the dollar upon

the whole assessed value of the real and personal property in the city according to such rolls for meeting the interest on debentures accruing due and for ordinary municipal expenditure, and a rate of $4\frac{2}{10}$ mills on the dollar on all ratable property for school expenditure for the year 1891.

6. The respondent filed in support of the application his own affidavit, which stated that he was a ratepayer and a resident of the city of Winnipeg; that he was born in 1841 within what are now the city limits, and had continuously resided therein since, is a member of the church of England, and has several children within school age.

7. Affidavits of the bishop of Rupert's Land, and of Robert Henry Hayward, also a ratepayer of Winnipeg, who objected to the public schools system, and who sent his children to a church school unsupported in any way by public funds, were also filed by the respondent; and several affidavits in answer were filed on behalf of the appellants. The material facts relied upon by the respondent are set out in the affidavit of the bishop as follows:—

(*a*) Prior to the passing of the act of the dominion of Canada, passed in the thirty-third year of her majesty Queen Victoria, chapter 3, known as the Manitoba Act, and prior to the order in council issued in pursuance thereof, there existed in the territory now constituting the province of Manitoba a number of effective schools for children.

(*b*) These schools were denominational schools, most of them being regulated and controlled by the church of England, and others by the Roman catholic church and the presbyterians. The system of schools controlled by the church of England is efficient.

(*c*) The means necessary for the support of schools were supplied to some extent by school fees paid by some of the parents of the children who attended the schools, and the rest was paid out of the funds of the churches.

(*d*) There were no public schools in the sense of state schools.

(*e*) The clauses of the Public Schools Act of 1890, prohibiting religious instruction and limiting religious exercises in the schools as therein provided, are unsatisfactory to the bishop.

8. The affidavits filed by the appellants, the City of Winnipeg, showed that prior to the province of Manitoba entering confederation the schools then in existence were:

Purely private schools.
In no way subject to public control.
Did not receive public support.
No school taxes were levied or collected by any authority, school board or otherwise.

There was no government or municipal grant of any kind made to schools, and whatever contributions were made for the support of said schools were purely voluntary.

9. The province of Manitoba became one of the provinces of the dominion of Canada on the 15th July, 1870, under the following circumstances:

(*a*) Prior to the union the district comprised in the province of Manitoba was a portion of Rupert's Land, and was part of the territory granted to the Hudson's Bay Company on 2nd May, 1670, by King Charles II.

(*b*) Prior to 1870 a number of white settlers and half-breeds had established themselves along the banks of the Red and Assiniboine rivers, in what was known as the Red River Settlement, all of which was included in the new province.

(*c*) By the British North America Act (Imperial Statute, 30 and 31 Vict., cap. 3) the old provinces of Upper and Lower Canada, Nova Scotia, and New Brunswick were confederated into the dominion of Canada.

(*d*) On the 23rd June, 1870, an imperial order in council was passed admitting Manitoba into confederation, the same coming into force on 15th

July, 1870, from which last-mentioned date Manitoba has been one of the provinces of the Dominion.

(*e*) The Dominion Statute (32 and 33 Vict., cap. 3), commonly called the Manitoba Act, provided for the government of the new province, and declared that the provisions of the British North America Act should, except as to those parts thereof which were in terms made or by reasonable intendment might be held to be specially applicable to or only affect one or more but not the whole of the provinces then comprising the Dominion, and except as the same might be varied by that act, be applicable to the province of Manitoba. This act was confirmed by the imperial act (34 and 35 Vict., cap. 28).

(*f*) By the British North America Act it is enacted (section 92): "In each province the legislature may exclusively make laws in relation to matters coming within the classes of subjects next hereinafter enumerated, that is to say:

"(2) Direct taxation within the province in order to the raising of a revenue for provincial purposes.

"(8) Municipal institutions in the province." And by section 93: "In and for each province the legislature may exclusively make laws in relation to education, subject and according to the following provisions:

"(1) Nothing in any such law shall prejudicially affect any right or privilege with respect to denominational schools which any class of persons have by law in the province at the union."

(*g*) The provisions of section 93 of the British North America Act are altered by section 22 of the Manitoba Act, the words 'or practice' being inserted after the words 'by-law' in the sub-section last above cited. In addition to this, the said section 22 in sub-section 2 provides somewhat more generally for an appeal to the governor-general in council from any act or decision of the provincial legislature or authorities affecting any right or privilege of the protestant or Roman catholic minority of the queen's subjects in relation to education. The provisions contained in section 92 of the British North America Act and above referred to are not altered, and apply to Manitoba.

10. In the year 1890 the legislature of the province of Manitoba passed two acts in reference to education. One is the act respecting the department of education (53 Vict., cap. 37), and the other is the Public Schools Act (53 Vict., cap. 38). By these acts all prior legislation as to schools and education in Manitoba was repealed, and a department of education created, to consist of the executive council or a committee thereof, with an advisory board to be elected in the manner prescribed by the act. The Public Schools Act provides that all public schools in the province are to be free schools (section 5); that all religious exercises in the public schools shall be conducted according to the regulations of the advisory board (section (6); but in case the guardian or parent of any pupil notifies the teacher that he does not wish such pupil to attend such religious exercises, then such pupil shall be dismissed before such religious exercises take place, the time appointed for such religious exercises being just before the closing hour. All public schools by the act are to be entirely non-sectarian, and no religious exercises shall be allowed therein except as above provided.

11. The act is not compulsory. No parent or guardian is compelled to send his child to a public school.

12. The only "right or privilege" with respect to denominational schools existing by practice at the date of the union was, as shown by the affidavits, a right or privilege of establishing private schools of a denominational character, supported by fees paid by parents and by voluntary contributions. This right has in no way been interfered with or "prejudicially affected" by the Public Schools Act of 1890. Members of the church of England are still entitled to establish and maintain denominational schools in the same manner as before the union.

13. The appellants petitioned your majesty in council for special leave to appeal from the judgment of the court of queen's bench for Manitoba, dated the 19th day

of December, 1891, and by an order dated the 9th day of May, 1892, special leave to appeal was granted.

14. The appellants submit that the judgment of the court of queen's bench for Manitoba should be set aside with costs for the following amongst other

REASONS.

1. Because the judgment of the supreme court of Canada in Barrett *vs.* Winnipeg, on which the judgment of the court of queen's bench is founded, is erroneous.
2. Because the respondent has not established that he is one of a class of persons possessed of any right or privilege with respect to denominational schools in the province at the union which has been prejudicially affected by the Public Schools Act, or the by-laws complained of.
3. That the words "by law or practice" refer only to some binding rule or obligation, if there were any such, to which the inhabitants of the province were at the date of the union committed, and no such rule or obligation existed.
4. None of the rights or privileges which members of the church of England had at the union with respect to denominational schools have in any way been interfered with by the act complained of.

HORACE DAVEY,
D'ALTON McCARTHY,
ISAAC CAMPBELL.

IN THE PRIVY COUNCIL.

ON APPEAL FROM THE COURT OF QUEEN'S BENCH FOR MANITOBA.

BETWEEN

THE CITY OF WINNIPEG - - - - - - - - - - *Appellants,*

AND

ALEXANDER LOGAN - - - - - - - - - - *Respondent.*

THE CASE OF THE RESPONDENT.

---

1. This is an appeal from the decision of the court of queen's bench for the province of Manitoba unanimously quashing by-law 514 of the city of Winnipeg the appellants.

2. The said by-law provided for the levying of a rate of $15\frac{3}{10}$ mills in the dollar to pay interest on the debentures of the appellants and ordinary current expenditure during the year 1891 and $4\frac{3}{10}$ mills in the dollar for school expenditure for that year, these rates being levied upon all the ratable property in the city of Winnipeg and the school-rate being levied upon persons of all religious denominations alike.

3. The respondent obtained a rule *nisi* to quash the said by-law for illegality on the following grounds:—

(*a*) That by the said by-law the amount to be levied for school expenditure is levied upon members of the church of England and all other religious denominations alike.

(*b*) That it is illegal to assess members of the church of England for the support of schools which are not under the control of the church of England and in which there are not taught religious exercises prescribed by that church, and upon grounds appearing in affidavits and papers filed.

4. The respondent established by the affidavits filed the following facts about which there is no dispute.

(*a*) That he is a resident ratepayer of the city of Winnipeg and a tax-payer to a large amount.

(*b*) That he has always been a member of the church of England; that he was born in the territory now comprised in the city of Winnipeg and has always lived there, and that he was married and had children at the time of the union of the province of Manitoba with Canada.

(*c*) That at the time of the union there was a parochial denominational school of the church of England in the territory now comprised in the city of Winnipeg, which school was conducted by teachers appointed by the church of England bishop of the diocese and in which religious exercises in accordance with the tenets of the church of England were taught.

(*d*) That the said school was the only public school at the union in the territory now comprised in the city of Winnipeg.

(*e*) That there was at the union and for some time previously thereto a complete system of schools established in the province by the church of England, all of which were under the control of the bishop and clergy of that church and were purely denominational schools in which religious exercises were conducted in accordance with the tenets of the church of England.

(*f*) These schools were supported partly by the funds of the church, partly by voluntary subscription and partly by fees charged to the parents of the children, but no child was excluded by reason of poverty.

(*g*) The respondent objected to the manner in which religious exercises are conducted in schools under the Public Schools Act and claimed the right of having his children given religious instruction in schools according to the tenets of the church of England.

5. The Public Schools Act passed by the legislature of the province of Manitoba in 1890 (53 Vict., c. 38 Man.) established one system of free public schools for the support of which all religious denominations alike should be taxed and in which no religious exercises should be taught except those prescribed by the advisory board of the department of education.

6. The respondent claimed that this act was not within the powers of the legislature of the province to enact by reason of the following provisions contained in the statute under which Manitoba was admitted into confederation, being 33 Vict., c. 3, Dominion:—

"In and for the province the said legislature may exclusively make laws in relation to education, subject and according to the following provisions:—

"(1) Nothing in any such law shall prejudicially affect any right or privilege with respect to denominational schools which any class of persons have by law or practice in the province at the union.

"(2) An appeal shall lie to the governor-general in council from any act or decision of the legislature of the province or of any provincial authority affecting any right or privilege of the protestant or Roman catholic minority of the queen's subjects in relation to education.

"(3) In case any such provincial law as from time to time seems to the governor-general in council requisite for the due execution of the provisions of this section is not made or in case any decision of the governor-general in council on any appeal under this section is not duly executed by the proper provincial authority in that behalf, then and in every such case and so far only as the circumstance of each case require, the parliament of Canada may make remedial laws for the due execution of the provisions of this section and of any decision of the governor-general in council under this section." (33 Vict., c. 3 sec. 22.)

7. Upon hearing the argument of the rule *nisi*, which was heard before the full court of queen's bench for Manitoba, that court (consisting of Taylor, C.J., Dubuc, J., and Bain, J.,) gave judgment ordering the said by-law to be quashed upon the grounds taken, the court being unanimous. The reasons of their lordships are reported in 8 Manitoba Law Reports, page 3, and are printed in the Record.

8. The respondent submits that the judgment of the court of queen's bench for Manitoba should be affirmed and that this appeal should be dismissed with costs for the following amongst other

REASONS.

1. Because the judgments of the said judges of the court of queen's bench are right in law and fact.
2. Because the members of the church of England had at the union rights or privileges with respect to denominational schools by law or practice which are prejudicially affected by the Public Schools Act and by the by-law in question.
3. That the respondent and all other members of the church of England have the right to have religious instruction given to their children in schools in accordance with the tenets of that church.

4. Because the members of the church of England had at the union a system of schools in the province in which religious instruction was given according to the teachings of their church and the Public Schools Act in effect precludes them from now having such by compelling them to pay taxes to support non-sectarian schools from which religious instruction is practically excluded.
5. Because the provisions contained in the first sub-section of section 22 of the Manitoba Act (33 Vict., c. 3 Dominion) and above set out were specially framed to protect the rights of all classes of persons having denominational schools at the union, and the respondent belongs to one of such classes.
6. The respondent has not acquiesced in the legislation by the provincial legislature in regard to schools.
7. Acquiescence by individuals in legislation that is *ultra vires*, or tacitly submitting thereto, cannot make such legislation good.

W. E. PERDUE.

IN THE PRIVY COUNCIL

ON APPEAL FROM THE COURT OF QUEEN'S BENCH FOR MANITOBA.

BETWEEN

THE CITY OF WINNIPEG - - - - - - - - - - *Appellants,*

AND

ALEXANDER LOGAN - - - - - - - - - - - *Respondent.*

RECORD OF PROCEEDINGS.

INDEX OF REFERENCE.

Description of Document.	Number of Document.
Rule *nisi* to show cause why an order should not be made quashing the by-law 514 of the city of Winnipeg......	1
Affidavit of service of copy rule	2
Affidavit of the Most Reverend Robert Machray, the bishop of Rupert's Land....................	3
Affidavit of Alexander Logan (the respondent)............	4
By-law no. 514 of the city of Winnipeg...........	5
Affidavit of Robert Henry Hayward	6
Certified copy regulations of the advisory board regarding religious exercises in the public schools.	7
Affidavit of Alexander Polson.......................	8
Affidavit of George Bryce.........	9
Affidavit of Edmund M. Wood......	10
Affidavit of Thomas Dickey Cumberland	11
Affidavit of Hector Mansfield Howell.......	12
Judges' reasons, viz.:—	
The chief justice of the court of queen's bench..............	13
Mr. Justice Bain..	13
Rule absolute quashing by-law 514..............................	14
Order granting leave to appeal to her majesty in council..	15
Prothonotary's certificate of correctness of transcript record..	16

IN THE PRIVY COUNCIL

ON APPEAL FROM THE COURT OF QUEEN'S BENCH FOR MANITOBA.

BETWEEN

THE CITY OF WINNIPEG - - - - - - - - - - - - *Appellants*

AND

ALEXANDER LOGAN - - - - - - - - - - - - - *Respondent.*

RECORD OF PROCEEDINGS.

No. 1.

Rule Nisi to show cause why an Order should not be made quashing the By-law No. 514 *of the City of Winnipeg, dated 5th December,* 1891.

In the Queen's Bench.

In the Matter of the Application to quash by-law 514 of the City of Winnipeg.

Upon the application of Alexander Logan, a resident ratepayer of the city of Winnipeg, and upon hearing read a copy of said by-law certified under the hand of the clerk of the said city and under the corporate seal of the said city, and also the affidavits of the said Alexander Logan and the affidavits of the Right Reverend Robert Machray and R. H. Hayward, and the exhibits therein referred to, and upon hearing the attorney for the applicant;

I do order that the attorney or agent for the corporation of the city of Winnipeg attend before the presiding judge in chambers at the court house in the city of Winnipeg on the 17th day of December instant, at the hour of half past ten o'clock in the forenoon, or so soon thereafter as the matter can be heard, and show cause why an order should not be made quashing the said by-law for illegality because of the following among other grounds:—

1. That by the said by-law the amount estimated to be levied for school expenditure is levied upon members of the church of England and all other religious denominations alike.

2. That it is illegal to assess members of the church of England for the support of schools which are not under the control of the church of England and in which there are not taught religious exercises prescribed by said church; and upon grounds appearing in affidavits and papers filed.

Dated at chambers this 5th day of December, A. D. 1891.

T. W. TAYLOR,
Chief Justice.

Certified a true copy of the rule *nisi* on the above application.

G. H. WALKER,
Prothonotary.

"A."

This is Exhibit "A" referred to in the affidavit of Daniel Coyle, sworn before me this 5th day of December, A. D. 1891.

J. O'REILLY,
A Commissioner.

No. 2.

Affidavit of service of Copy Rule, sworn 5th December, 1891.

In the Queen's Bench.

In the Matter of the Application to quash by-law 514 of the City of Winnipeg.

I, Daniel Coyle, of Winnipeg in the county of Selkirk, clerk, make oath and say:—

That I did on the 5th day of December, 1891, serve C. J. Brown with a true copy of the rule marked exhibit "A" hereunto annexed by delivering such copy to and leaving the same with the said C. J. Brown.

DAN. COYLE.

Sworn before me at Winnipeg, in the county of Selkirk, this 5th day of December, 1891.

J. O'REILLY,
A Commissioner for taking Affidavits in B.R., &c.

Certified a true copy of the affidavit of Daniel Coyle filed on the above application

G. H. WALKER,
Prothonotary.

No. 3.

Affidavit of the Most Reverend Robert Machray, Bishop of Rupert's Land, sworn 3rd December, 1891.

In the Queen's Bench.

In the Matter of the Application to quash By-law 514 of the City of Winnipeg.

I, the Most Reverend Robert Machray, doctor of divinity, of the city of Winnipeg, in the province of Manitoba, the bishop of Rupert's Land, make oath and say:—

1. In the year 1865 I was appointed by the crown, on the recommendation of the archbishop of Canterbury, under the sign manual of the queen, bishop of Rupert's Land.

2. The diocese of Rupert's Land in 1865 covered the whole of the North-west Territories of Canada, the district of Keewatin, the present province of Manitoba, and that portion of the westerly part of the province of Ontario lying westerly of the height of land and running between Rat Portage and Port Arthur.

3. Subsequently the diocese was subdivided into eight bishoprics, one of which, still known as Rupert's Land, consists of the province of Manitoba and that portion of the province of Ontario referred to above. The whole of the said original diocese of Rupert's Land is now called the ecclesiastical province of Rupert's Land, of which I am the metropolitan, and I am also bishop of the smaller diocese of Rupert's Land last above described.

4. I have continued to be bishop of the old diocese of Rupert's Land first above described and of the smaller diocese last above described ever since my appointment in 1865.

5. Upon my arrival in the diocese in 1865, I found there existed a great want of schools for the education of the youth, and I at once set about reorganizing St. John's college, and in 1866 I opened it for higher education and it has so continued ever since, and I commenced as soon as I could the reorganization of the system of primary schools of which I found most vacant.

6. I endeavoured to start at least one parochial school in each parish where there was a missionary of the church of England, and I so far succeeded in this

work that with the assistance of the church missionary society of the church of England there were under my care in 1867, 14 common parochial schools within the Red River Settlement, as well as schools at the missions in Manitoba outside the settlement and missions in the interior.

7. In the year 1869 there were 16 schools regularly organized for the teaching of boys and girls in the different parishes in the said Red River Settlement, inclusive of the Westbourne and Scanterbury.

8. I find that in my address to the synod of Rupert's Land, delivered on the 29th day of May, 1867, I used the following language with reference to the schools, viz.—"Passing now from the college to the common schools, I rejoice to say that there has been during the past half-year a full opportunity for learning the elements of education—reading, writing, and arithmetic—from the extreme end of the Indian Settlement up to Westbourne, with the single exception of the small parish of St. Margaret's at the High Bluff; and in that parish a very creditable subscription was promised towards the salary of a master, so that I trust by another year even that blank may be supplied. And I believe the distances to be travelled to these schools are not greater than are frequently performed in our home parishes in England and Scotland. Excluding the school at Westbourne, which remains on the church missionary list, being about 35 miles beyond the settlement, we must look to the maintenance of 14 schools. Of these, eight have hitherto been supported by the church missionary society at a cost of 285*l*. a year. The society said, some time ago, that this help must at once cease."

And in my charge to the synod of Rupert's Land on the 24th day of February, 1869, I used the following language:—"Schools have been established in every parish, but the effort to maintain them has been a difficult one, from the larger amount now required to obtain the service of a schoolmaster, and from frequent resignations. The whole question must, however, soon be grappled with. There must be some distinct regulations laid down, defining the conditions under which grants from the diocesan fund are to be given, and some plan of diocesan inspection will be necessary. But before we can obtain all we could wish with our schools, I feel we must be able to provide still larger salaries and have trained teachers. How to secure such a training has been a good deal in my mind, but I do not yet see the way to the accomplishment of what I wish." And the statements therein made by me on those two occasions are, I believe, true in substance and in fact, and are given in the reports of the synod published at the time.

9. The schools which were established as above set forth, continued until the establishment of public schools by the laws of Manitoba hereinafter referred to.

10. The teacher in each of these schools was under the control of the vestry and the clergyman of each parish, and in some cases there were two and even three parochial schools in one parish. The schools were opened and closed with forms of prayer, and the teacher of each of these schools was required to instruct the school every day in the Holy Scriptures, and he was required to teach the children the English church catechism. The missionary in each parish was expected to look after such religious training and to teach the children or see that the children were taught according to the tenets of the church of England, and the said schools were denominational schools belonging to and supported by the religious denomination of the church of England.

11. The teachers were paid a salary, part of which was paid through me to the parish clergyman, as I was treasurer of the synod, and specially looked after the funds for the support and maintenance of these various schools.

12. The money for the payment of the school teachers and for the maintenance of the schools was procured partly from the funds of the church, partly from voluntary subscriptions, and partly from fees charged the parents of the children attending the parochial schools; but, as far as my knowledge goes, no child of any English church parents was prevented from attending these schools by reason of poverty.

13. The schools above described were purely denominational schools, the teachers were members of the church of England. I do not remember in my time any instance of a teacher who was not a member of our church, with one exception.

14. At the time of the union of this province with Canada there were estimated to be, and I believe there were, about 12,000 Christians residing in this province. Of these over 6,000 were Roman catholics, and nearly 5,000 were members of the church of England, the rest were chiefly presbyterians, with a few of other denominations.

15. The Christians residing in this province as above set forth resided in what was known as the Red River Settlement, and would practically be included in an area not exceeding 60 miles from the city of Winnipeg.

16. In the year 1871, when the first Public Schools Act of Manitoba was passed, I joined heartily with the provincial executive in endeavouring to carry into effect the school law then enacted, believing that under that act public schools could be carried on giving such religious instruction as would be satisfactory to the members of the church of England and to myself.

17. But many of the members of the protestant section of the board of education did not hold the same views as myself as regards, for example, the necessity of not only reading but teaching the Bible, so that the religious instruction given in the schools was never satisfactory to me; but there was nothing in the act preventing a more satisfactory amount of religious teaching when the members of the section became favourable to this, so I always looked forward to securing some day more satisfactory provision. With the great majority of the bishops and clergy of the church of England, I believe that the education of the young is incomplete, and may even be hurtful if religious instruction is excluded from it.

18. The Public Schools Act passed by this province in the year 1890 has so limited religious exercises that it is doubtful if under it there can be any religious teaching given in the schools, so that the public schools to-day are not, as regards religious teaching, as I hoped and expected they would be when the first act was passed.

19. The religious and moral training given to children in the public schools of this province, under sanction of the laws of this province, is not in accordance with my views or wishes, and is not in accordance with the views of the church of England; and consequently the present law, in taxing all members of the church of England, and giving no aid from the state to denominational schools, prejudicially affects the rights and privileges of the people belonging to the church of England with respect to the denominational schools which they had by practice, and were lawfully exercising, before and at the union of this province with Canada.

20. Before the union, I, with the advice of my synod, controlled the religious training of children of persons belonging to the church of England in their education in the parochial schools.

21. When the first school act was passed above mentioned, and when the first schools under that act were established, the various parish vestries, with my sanction, permitted schools to be established and to be carried on under that act in most, if not all, the schoolhouses in which the church of England parish schools had previously been carried on, and my sanction was given in the hope and belief that at least those public schools would still give a religious and moral training such as I thought it necessary for children to receive; but if I had known then that the public schools law would permit and allow schools under that act to be carried on without, or with as little, religious training as is now given in the public schools of this province, I should have done what I could to resist it, and if unable in our peculiar circumstances to continue those parochial schools, I should have encouraged the opening of such schools and the increasing of them as soon as it was permitted; and I have no doubt that if religious training is excluded from the public schools, as is threatened, this will be the policy in future of the church of England and of myself. The re-establishment of our parish schools is merely a question of means and time.

22. If separate schools are granted to any body of Christians because of rights secured owing to practice existing prior to the union, then I claim that the church of England is peculiarly entitled to such separate schools.

23. As far as I have had any influence, I have always endeavoured to influence public opinion and the legislature as much as I could to have provision made for the

religious training of youth, and by the Public Schools Act of 1890 I was deeply disappointed; and I believe that by that act, if separate schools do not receive state aid as well as the schools under the act, the children of parents of the church of England have been prejudicially affected.

24. Before the act of 1890 was passed I expressed my views on the schools question and on the rights of the people of the church of England, under the Manitoba Act, in my charge to the synod, given on the 29th day of October, 1889, in which I used the following language:—"Though we have not now any primary schools, it is not because, in view of the church, such schools are of small importance. The day was when we had a church primary school wherever we had a clergyman. That was our position when this province was transferred to Canada, and it seems probable that the Dominion intended to recognize such efforts in the past and to protect the school interests that then existed. But our church saw such advantages in a national system of schools, and such reason to have confidence in the administration of it, that it went heartily into it, trusting that the schools would be worthy of a Christian people and give an education in which the first, namely, the religious interests of the children, would not be lost sight of. And I may say that the only reason which has led me for so many years to give up time that I could ill spare to be a member of the board of education has been the hope that, by conciliatory action, I might help in securing a measure of religious instruction reasonably satisfactory at once to ourselves and the other religious bodies."

25. One of the schools conducted by the church of England as hereinbefore mentioned was situate in the parish of St. John's, which parish now forms a part of the city of Winnipeg, and said school was situate at the time of the union of this province with Canada in a territory which now forms part of the territory of the city of Winnipeg.

26. Said schools of the church of England were supported in part by funds of the church, in part by voluntary subscriptions, and in part by fees voluntarily paid by members of the church of England and by the parents and guardians of children attending such schools, and were in no way supported or aided by funds raised by general rates or taxation.

R. MACHRAY,
Bishop of Rupert's Land.

Sworn before me at Winnipeg, in the province of Manitoba, this 3rd day of December, A.D. 1891.

J. R. FULLERTON,
A Commissioner in B. R., &c.

Certified a true copy of the affidavit of Robert Machray, Bishop of Rupert's Land, filed on the above application.

G. H. WALKER,
Prothonotary.

No. 4.

Affidavit of Alexander Logan (the Respondent), sworn 3rd December, 1891.

In the Queen's Bench.

In the Matter of the Application to quash by-law 514 of the City of Winnipeg.

I, Alexander Logan, of the city of Winnipeg, in the province of Manitoba, esquire, make oath and say:—

1. I was born in the year eighteen hundred and forty-one, at Point Douglass, in the Red River Settlement in Rupert's Land, and I have always resided at the said Point Douglass, and still reside there.

2. The said Point Douglass is in the parish of St. John's, in the province of Manitoba, and is within the territorial limits of the city of Winnipeg, and I am a resident of the said city of Winnipeg and a ratepayer thereof to a large amount.

3. I am and always have been a member of the church of England.

4. At the time of the union of the province of Manitoba with Canada I was married and had two children.

5. At, and for many years prior to the said union, there was a parochial denominational school of the church of England within the said parish of St. John's, and within the territory now comprised in the city of Winnipeg, and the said school was a day school conducted by teachers appointed by the church of England bishop of Rupert's Land, in which, and in addition to the ordinary subjects taught in schools, the catechism of the church of England was taught,and the pupils in said school were instructed in religious subjects according to the tenets of the church of England.

6. The said school was continued up to and for some time after the union of the said province with Canada, and the same school still exists in a modified form, and I attended said school as a pupil before said union and received my primary education therein.

7. I was well acquainted with the said Red River Settlement before and after said union, and I say that at the time of said union there was established in each parish of the church of England throughout said settlement a parochial denominational school, and in some parishes more than one of such schools, and in all such schools teachings in religious subjects according to the church of England faith were conducted in a manner similar to the said school in the parish of St. John's, and the children of English church parents attend said schools and no other schools.

8. Save and except the said English church parochial school of the parish of St. John's and St. John's college, which also belonged to the church of England, and except a private school kept by the nuns on the property of the late William Drever, there was not at the time of said union any school or educational institution in existence within said territory now included in the city of Winnipeg.

9. The territory comprised in the city of Winnipeg covers an area of about 20 square miles.

10. The paper writing hereunto annexed and marked with the letter "A" is a certified copy of the above-mentioned by-law of the city of Winnipeg, no. 514, and said copy was received from the city clerk of the city of Winnipeg.

11. In and by said by-law a rate is levied for school purposes of four and two-tenths mills in the dollar upon all ratepayers alike, and upon persons of all religious denominations alike, and the moneys so raised are intended to be used in the support of public non-sectarian schools pursuant to the provisions of the Public Schools Act.

12. I have not yet paid my taxes for the year one thousand eight hundred and ninety-one, imposed under said by-law.

13. I have at the present time three children of school age, namely, one of the age of fourteen years, one of the age of eleven years, and one of the age of five years, and I claim the right to have my children taught religious exercises in school according to the tenets of the church of England, and I claim that such right was secured to me and other members of the church of England at the time of said union by the provisions of the Manitoba Act.

14. I do not approve of the manner in which religious exercises are taught in schools where they are so taught under the provisions of the Public Schools Act, and I claim that the tax for the support of schools imposed upon me by said by-law, and pursuant to said Public Schools Act, or by any other act of the legislature by which I am compelled to contribute for the support of schools not under the control of the church of England, prejudicially affects my rights as a member of the church of England, and if compelled to pay such tax I and other members of the church of England are less able to support schools in which religious exercises and teachings in accordance with our form of worship could be conducted.

ALEXANDER LOGAN.

Sworn before me, at the city of Winnipeg, in the province of Manitoba, this 3rd day of December, A.D. 1891.

R. H. HAYWARD,
A Commissionner in B. R., &c.

Certified a true copy of the affidavit of Alexander Logan, filed on the above application.

G. H. WALKER,
Prothonotary.

No. 5.

By-law No. 514 *of City of Winnipeg, dated* 13*th July*, 1891.

"A."

By-law No. 514.

A By-law to Authorize an Assessment for City and School Purposes in the City of Winnipeg for the current Municipal Year, A.D. 1891.

Whereas, it is expedient and necessary for city purposes to raise the sum of 389,327 dollars 19 cents, for interest on debentures and ordinary current municipal and district and school expenditure for the current year by a tax on all real and personal property appearing on the assessment rolls of the city of Winnipeg for the year 1891, except properties wholly or partially exempt;

And whereas, the amount of the whole ratable property of the city of Winnipeg as shown by the last revised assessment rolls of the said city of Winnipeg is 19,944,270 dollars;

And whereas, certain properties are exempt from all rates save for schools and school expenditure, and it will require a rate of $19\frac{1}{2}$ mills on the dollar on the amount of the said ratable property to raise the sum so required as aforesaid for interest on debentures now accruing due and for the ordinary current municipal and school expenditure for the year A.D. 1891, whereof the rate of $15\frac{3}{10}$ths mills on the dollar shall be for interest on debentures now accruing due, and for the ordinary current municipal expenditnre, and the rate of $4\frac{2}{10}$ths mills on the dollar shall be for school expenditure for the year 1891;

Therefore the council of the city of Winnipeg in council assembled enacts as follows: —

1. There shall be raised, levied, and collected a tax of $19\frac{1}{2}$ mills on the dollar upon the whole assessed value of the real and personal property in the city of Winnipeg, according to the last revised assessment rolls for the year 1891, of which the amount of $15\frac{3}{10}$ths mills on the dollar shall be to provide for the payment of interest on debentures now accruing due, and for the ordinary current municipal expenditure, and $4\frac{2}{10}$ths mills on the dollar shall be for the schools of the city for the year A.D. 1891.

2. Upon properties ratable for school expenditure only, there shall be levied and collected a rate of $4\frac{1}{5}$th mills on the dollar of assessment.

3. The sum of two dollars poll tax shall be levied and collected from every person residing within the city of Winnipeg, and being of the age of 21 years and upwards who has not been assessed upon the assessment roll of the city of Winnipeg, or whose taxes do not amount to two dollars, in which latter case a total tax of two dollars only shall be levied, which taxes shall be collected in the same manner as other taxes.

The taxes and rates hereby imposed shall be considered to have been imposed and to be due on and from the 14th day of July, A.D. 1891.

Done and passed in council assembled at the city of Winnipeg this 13th day of July, A.D. 1891.

A. McMICHEN,
Chairman.

C. J. BROWN,
City Clerk.

Certified true copy of by-law no. 514 of the City of Winnipeg, passed in council on the 13th day of July, A.D. 1891.

C. J. BROWN,
City Clerk.

Certified a true copy of the copy of by-law filed on the application to quash by-law 514.

G. H. WALKER,
Prothonotary.

No. 6.

Affidavit of Robert Henry Hayward, sworn 4th December, 1891.

In the Queen's Bench.

In the Matter of the Application to quash By-law 514 of the City of Winnipeg.

I, Robert Henry Hayward, of the city of Winnipeg, in the province of Manitoba, accountant, make oath and say :—

1. I am now and have been for the past 10 years a resident of the city of Winnipeg.

2. I am and have been for a number of years past a ratepayer of said city.

3. I am a member of the church of England.

4. The religious exercises conducted in the public schools of the city of Winnipeg at the present time are those prescribed by the advisory board of the department of education, pursuant to the provisions of the Public Schools Act, and such exercises consist of the reading, without note or comment, of certain selections from the authorized English version of the Bible, or the Douay version of the Bible, and the use of a form of prayer.

5. The said selections from the Scriptures are not taught, but are simply read without comment, and neither the catechism of the church of England nor any other catechism is taught in said schools, nor is any religious instruction given in said schools beyond the reading of said selections from the Bible, and the reading of said prayer.

6. The printed pamphlet now produced and shown to me and marked as exhibit "B" to this my affidavit, is a printed copy of the regulations of the said advisory board regarding religious exercises in public schools, and the said pamphlet was received from the department of education for the province of Manitoba.

7. I have read over the certified copy of the above-mentioned by-law, which is annexed to the affidavit of Alexander Logan, sworn to herein on the 3rd day of this present month of December, and which certified copy is now produced and shown to me at the time of making this affidavit, and is marked as exhibit "A" to this affidavit.

8. In and by the said by-law a rate is levied for school purposes of 4$\frac{2}{10}$ths mills in the dollar upon all ratepayers of the city of Winnipeg alike, and upon members of the church of England as well as upon members of all other religious denominations, no distinction being made in respect of religious denominations, and the moneys so raised are intended to be used in the support of public non-sectarian schools established pursuant to the provisions of the Public Schools Act.

9. The effect of said by-law is that members of the church of England are compelled to pay a tax for the support of public non-sectarian schools, in which there is not religious teaching according to the tenets of the church of England.

10. I have one boy of school age, namely, the age of 13 years, and although I am compelled by the said by-law and by the Public Schools Act to contribute to the support of said public schools established under said Public Schools Act, I send him to a school established by the rector of the English church parish of All Saints, in the said city of Winnipeg, and under the control and management of the said rector, where he receives religious instruction according to the tenets of the said church of England in addition to ordinary school instruction, and I voluntarily pay fees for his tuition at said school, and I do not send him to any of the said public schools.

11. There are many other boys in the said city of Winnipeg sent by their parents who are resident ratepayers of the city of Winnipeg and members of the church of England to the said All Saints school, for reasons which I verily believe are similar to my own.

R. H. HAYWARD.

Sworn before me, at the city of Winnipeg, in the county of Selkirk, this 4th day of December, A.D. 1891.

GHENT DAVIS,
A Commissioner in B. R., &c.

Certified a true copy of the affidavit of Robert Henry Hayward, filed on the above application.

G. H. WALKER.
Prothonotary.

No. 7.

Regulations of the Advisory Board regarding Religious Exercises in Public Schools, adopted 21st May, 1890.

Until further notice the religious exercises in the public schools shall be:—

(*a*) The reading, without note or comment, of the following selections from the authorized English version of the Bible or the Douay version of the Bible.

(*b*) The use of the following forms of prayer.

SCRIPTURE READINGS.

Part I.—*Historical.*

No.	Subject	Reference
1	The Creation	Gen. i., 1-19.
2	The Creation—cont.	Gen. i., 20-31.
3	The Fall of Man	Gen. iii.
4	The Deluge	Gen. viii., 1-22.
5	The Covenant with Noah	Gen. ix., 1-17.
6	The Trial of Abraham	Gen. xxii., 1-18.
7	Isaac Blesses Jacob	Gen. xxvii., 1-29.
8	Esau's Blessing	Gen. xxvii., 30-45.
9	Jacob's Vision	Gen. xxviii., 10-22.
10	Jacob's Return to Bethel	Gen. xxxv., 1-15.
11	Joseph and his Brethren	Gen. xxxvii., 1-22.
12	Joseph Sold into Egypt	Gen. xxxvii., 23-36.
13	Pharaoh's Dream	Gen. xli., 1-24.
14	Joseph's Interpretations	Gen. xli., 25-43.
15	Jacob's Sons' Visit	Gen. xlii., 1-20.
16	Jacob's Sons' Return from Egypt	Gen. xlii., 21-38.
17	The Second Visit to Egypt	Gen. xliii., 1-14.
18	Joseph and his Brethren	Gen. xliii., 15-34.
19	Joseph and his Brethren—cont.	Gen. xliv., 1-13.
20	Joseph and his Brethren—cont.	Gen. xliv., 14-34.
21	Joseph Discovers Himself to his Brethren	Gen. xlv.
22	Jacob and his Household go into Egypt	Gen. xlvi., 1-6, 28-34.
23	Jacob's Interview with Pharaoh	Gen. xlvii., 1-12.
24	Death of Jacob	Gen. xlviii., 1-21.
25	Burial of Jacob	Gen. l., 1-26.
26	Moses at the Burning Bush	Exod. iii., 1-20.
27	Grievous Oppression of the Hebrews	Exod. v.
28	The Passover	Exod. xii., 1-20.
29	The Israelites Escape through the Red Sea	Exod. xiv., 10-31.
30	The Song of Deliverance	Exod. xv., 1-22.
31	Giving of Manna	Exod. xvi., 2-35.
32	The Water from the Rock	Exod. xvii.
33	The Ten Commandments	Exod. xx., 1-17.
34	The Convenant with Israel	Exod. xxiv.
35	The Tabernacle	Exod. xl., 17-36.
36	Spies sent into Canaan	Num. xiii., 17-33.
37	The People Rebel at the Report of the Spies	Num. xiv., 1-30.
38	The Song of Moses	Deut. xxxii., 1-14.
39	The Death of Moses	Deut. xxxiv.
40	Joshua Succeeds Moses	Josh. i., 1-17.

41	The Covenant with Joshua	Josh. xxiv., 1-28.
42	The Call of Samuel	1 Saml. iii.
43	The Israelites Desire a King	1 Saml. viii., 1-20.
44	Samuel Anoints Saul	1 Saml. ix., 21-27, xi., 1-11.
45	Samuel Anoints David	1 Saml. xvi.
46	David and Goliath	1 Saml. xvii., 1-27.
47	David Overcomes Goliath	1 Saml. xvii., 28-54.
48	David and Jonathan	1 Saml. xviii., 1-16.
49	David instructed as to the Building of the Temple	1 Chron. xvii., 1-17.
50	David's Advice to Solomon	1 Chron. xxviii., 1-20.
51	David's Preparation for Building the Temple	1 Chron. xxix., 1-19.
52	Solomon's Wise Choice	1 Kings iii., 1-15.
53	Preparations for Building the Temple	1 Kings v.
54	Solomon's Prayer at the Dedication of the Temple	2 Chron. vi., 1-21.
55	Solomon's Prayer—cont	2 Chron. vi., 22-42.
56	Elijah	1 Kings xvii.
57	Elijah and the Prophets of Baal	1 Kings xviii., 1-21.
58	Discomfiture of the Prophets of Baal	1 Kings xviii., 22-46.
59	Elijah in the Wilderness	1 Kings xix., 1-13.
60	Elijah and Elisha	2 Kings ii., 1-15.
61	Naaman the Leper	2 Kings v., 1-19.
62	The Fall of Israel	2 Kings xvii., 6-24.
63	Public Worship of God Restored	2 Chron. xxix., 20-36.
64	Deliverance under Hezekiah	2 Kings xix., 1-19.
65	Deliverance under Hezekiah—cont	2 Kings xix., 20-39.
66	Rejoicing of the Israelites at the Restoration of Divine Worship	2 Chron. xxx.
67	Jerusalem taken by Nebuchadnezzar	2 Chron. xxxvi., 5-21.
68	The Golden Image	Dan. iii., 1-18.
69	The Fiery Furnace	Dan. iii., 19-30.
70	Daniel in the Lions' Den	Dan. vi.
71	The Temple Rebuilt	Ezra i., 1-6, and iii.

Part II.—*The Gospels.*

1	Christ the Word	John i., 1-18.
2	The Birth of Christ announced	Luke ii., 8-20.
3	The Visit of the Magi	Matt. ii., 1-12.
4	The Song of Simeon	Luke ii., 25-40.
5	Jesus in the Temple	Luke ii., 41-52.
6	The Baptism of Jesus Christ	Matt. iii., 1-17.
7	The Temptation of Our Lord	Luke iv., 1-15.
8	Testimony of John the Baptist	John i., 19-34.
9	The First Disciples	John i., 35-51.
10	Jesus at Nazareth	Luke iv., 16-32.
11	At Capernaum	Matt. iv., 13-25.
12	Sermon on the Mount	Matt. v., 1-12.
13	Sermon on the Mount—cont	Matt. v., 13-20, 33-37.
14	Sermon on the Mount—cont	Matt. v., 38-48.
15	Sermon on the Mount—cont	Matt. vi., 1-18.
16	Sermon on the Mount—cont	Matt. vi., 19-34.
17	Sermon on the Mount—cont	Matt. vii., 1-14.
18	Sermon on the Mount—cont	Matt. vii., 15-29.
19	The Miraculous Draught of Fishes	Luke v., 1-15.
20	The Healing of the Paralytic	Luke v., 16-26.
21	The Twelve Apostles sent forth	Matt. ix., 36-38, x., 1-11.
22	The Centurion's Servant. The Widow's Son	Luke vii., 1-17.
23	The Declaration concerning John	Matt. xi., 2-19.
24	The Feast in Simeon's House	Luke vii., 36-50.

25	Privileges and Responsibility	Matt. xi., 20-31.
26	The Sabbath	Luke vi., 1-11.
27	Parable of the Sower	Mark iv., 1-20.
28	Parable of the Tares, &c	Matt. xiii., 24-35.
29	Parable of the Tares explained, with other Parables	Matt. xiii., 36-52.
30	Children brought to Jesus. Condition of Discipleship	Mark x., 13-30.
31	Tribute to Cæsar. The Widow's Offering	Matt. xxii., 15-22; Mark xii., 41-44.
32	Christ Confessed	Matt. xvi., 13-28.
33	Christ feeding Five thousand	Mark vi., 30-41.
34	Christ Walking on the Sea	Matt. xiv., 22-23.
35	The Transfiguration	Matt. xvii., 1-13.
36	The Great Supper	Luke xiv., 7-24.
37	The Lost Sheep and Lost Piece of Silver	Luke xv., 1-10.
38	The Two Sons	Luke xv., 11-32.
39	The Pharisee and the Publican	Luke xviii., 9-17.
40	Blind Bartimeus. Zaccheus the Publican	Luke xviii., 35-43; xix., 1-10.
41	The Good Samaritan	Luke x., 25-37.
42	The Good Shepherd	John x., 1-18.
43	Christ One with the Father	John x., 22-42.
44	Humility	John xiii., 1-17.
45	The Death of Lazarus	John xi., 30-48.
46	The Triumphal Entry into Jerusalem	Mark xi., 1-11; Matt. xxi., 9-16.
47	Parable of the Ten Virgins	Matt. xxv., 1-13.
48	Parable of the Talents	Matt. xxv., 14-30.
49	The Judgment	Matt. xxv., 31-46.
50	Christ Comforts the Disciples	John xiv., 1-14.
51	The Holy Spirit Promised	John xiv., 15-31.
52	Christ the True Vine	John xv., 1-17.
53	Last Sayings of Jesus	John xvi., 1-15, 26-33.
54	The Prayer of Christ	John xvii., 1-26.
55	The Box of Precious Ointment	Matt. xxvi., 1-13.
56	The Last Supper	Matt. xxvi., 17-29.
57	The Agony in the Garden. Betrayal of Jesus	Matt. xxvi., 30-56.
58	Christ before Caiaphas and Peter's Denial	Matt. xxvi., 57-75.
59	Christ before Pilate	Matt. xxvii., 1-25.
60	The Crucifixion	Matt. xxvii., 26-43.
61	The Crucifixion—cont	Luke xxiii., 39-56.
62	The Resurrection	Mark xvi., 1-7; John xx., 3-18.
63	The Journey to Emmaus	Luke xxiv., 13-35.
64	Jesus Appears to His Disciples. The Doubts of Thomas	John xx., 19-29.
65	Jesus Appears again to His Disciples	John xxi., 1-23.
66	The Ascension	Matt. xxviii.

Form of Prayer.

Most merciful God, we yield thee our humble and hearty thanks for thy fatherly care and preservation of us this day, and for the progress which thou hast enabled us to make in useful learning; we pray thee to imprint upon our minds whatever good instructions we have received, and to bless them to the advancement of our temporal and eternal welfare; and pardon, we implore thee, all that thou hast seen amiss in our thoughts, words and actions. May thy good providence still guide and keep us during the approaching interval of rest and relaxation, so that we may be prepared to enter on the duties of the morrow with renewed vigour both of body and mind; and preserve us, we beseech thee, now and for ever, both outwardly in our bodies and inwardly in our souls, for the sake of Jesus Christ, thy Son, our Lord. *Amen.*

Our Father who art in heaven, hallowed be thy name. Thy kingdom come. Thy will be done on earth as it is in heaven. Give us this day our daily bread; and forgive us our trespasses, as we forgive them that trespass against us; and lead us not into temptation, but deliver us from evil.—*Amen.*

The grace of our Lord Jesus Christ, and the love of God, and the fellowship of the Holy Ghost, be with us all evermore.—*Amen.*

Certified a true copy of exhibit "B" to affidavit of Robert Henry Hayward filed herein.

G. H. WALKER,
Prothonotary.

No. 8.

Affidavit of Alexander Polson, sworn 12th December, 1891.

In the Queen's Bench.

In the Matter of the Application to quash By-law 514 of the City of Winnipeg.

I, Alexander Polson, of the city of Winnipeg, in the county of Selkirk, in the province of Manitoba, license inspector, make oath and say:—

1. That for a period of fifty years I have been a resident in the province of Manitoba.

2. That schools which existed prior to the province of Manitoba entering confederation, were, so far as the people were concerned, purely private schools, and were not in any way subject to public control, nor did they in any way receive public support. Attendance at such schools was voluntary, and only the parents or guardians who had children attending school paid any fees. There was no law or statute as to schools. The schools were under the direction of the clergy or the governing bodies of one of the three churches, the Roman catholic, the church of England, and the presbyterian.

3. No school taxes or rates were collected by any authority prior to the province of Manitoba entering confederation, and there were no means by which any person could be forced by law to support any of said private schools.

I think the only public revenue of any kind then collected was the customs duty of 4 per cent, but none of this was for schools. There were no municipal or school rates, and no direct taxes of any kind levied, whether by assessment on property, income tax, or otherwise.

ALEX. POLSON.

Sworn before me, at the city of Winnipeg, in the county of Selkirk, this 12th day of December, A.D., 1891.

CHAS. N. BELL,
A Commissioner in B. R., &c.

Certified a true copy of affidavit of Alexander Polson, filed on the above application.

G. H. WALKER,
Prothonotary.

No. 9.

Affidavit of George Bryce, sworn 11th December, 1891.

In the Queen's Bench.

In the Matter of an Application to quash By-law 514 of the City of Winnipeg.

I, George Bryce, of the city of Winnipeg, in the county of Selkirk, in the province of Manitoba, professor in Manitoba college, make oath and say:—

1. That I have been a resident of the province of Manitoba since the year 1871. That I am the minister of the presbyterian church longest resident in the province; that I have been in constant communication with the officers and councils of the church, having been the first moderator of the synod of Manitoba and the North-West Territories of the presbyterian church in Canada, and I am personally aware of the truth of the matters herein alleged.

2. That I am familiar with the opinions of the presbyterians of the province in the years immediately succeeding the entrance of Manitoba into confederation in 1870, and am aware that the presbyterians of this province did not claim to have the church schools, which had been previously voluntarily maintained by them or by the church for them, continued to them at cost to the general public, but were willing to support a public school system.

3. That in founding Manitoba college, in November, 1871, I took over the highest class of Kildonan school as the beginning of the college, which had thus far continued a purely church institution, and for which I never heard the claim advanced that we were entitled to any consideration under the Manitoba Act; indeed, I always considered the government schools as entirely different, and, up to 1871, unknown in the country, and for several years we did take younger students into our church college, who might have been educated in the government schools alongside.

4. That about the year 1876 a strong agitation took place in the province to have one public school system established, but this agitation failed to obtain effect in legislation.

5. The presbyterian synod of Manitoba and the North-west Territories, which represents the largest religious body in Manitoba, passed in May, 1890, a resolution heartily approving of the Public School Act of this year, and I believe it is approved of by the great majority of the presbyterians of Manitoba.

6. That the presbyterian church is most solicitous for the religious education of all its children. It takes great care in the vows required of parents at the baptism of their children, and in urging its ministers to teach from the pulpit the duty of giving moral and religious training in the family. It is most energetic in maintaining efficient Sunday schools, which have been called the "children's church," and in requiring the attendance of the children at the church services, which are made a great means of instruction. I think it is our firm belief that this system, joined with the public school system, has produced and will produce a moral, religious, and intelligent people.

7. I believe that the views of a large number of the presbyterians in this province are represented by the following extracts from a public address delivered by the Rev. J. M. King, D.D., principal of Manitoba college, on the 31st day of October 1889. After giving reasons in opposition to purely secular schools, Dr. King proceeds:—"At the opposite extreme there is a system of separate or denominational schools, such as to some extent now obtains in this province, a system under which not only is religious instruction given, but the distinctive doctrines and practices of individual churches are taught. Does the continuance and extension of this system promise a solution of the educational difficulty? By no means. Less injurious probably in its operation, it is even more indefensible in principle than the one which has been so freely criticised. First, it is in direct violation of the principle of the separation of church and state. It is unnecessary, indeed it would be quite irrelevant, to argue this principle here. It is that on which, rightly or wrongly, the state with us is constituted. I do not understand it to mean that the state may not have regard to religious considerations, such as it shows when it enforces the

observance of the Sabbath rest, or that it may not employ religious sanctions, as it does when in its courts of law it administers an oath in the name of God; but I do understand it to mean that the state is neither to give material aid to the operations of the church in any of its branches, nor to interfere with its liberties. Each, while necessarily influencing the other, has its own distinctive sphere, and must bear all the responsibilities of action within that sphere . . . . . . Second, the system of separate or sectarian schools operates injuriously on the well-being of the state. However useful it may be to the church or churches adopting it, enabling them to keep their youth well in hand and to preserve them from any danger to faith and morals which might result from daily contact with those of a different creed, it is in that measure hurtful to the unity and therefore to the strength of the state. It occasions a line of cleavage in society, the highest interests of which demand that it should as far as possible be one. It perpetuates distinctions, and almost necessarily gives rise to distinctions which are at once a reproach and a peril . . . . . . Surely the state should not, unless compelled to do so, lend the authority of law and the support of public moneys to a system of education which so injuriously affects its unity and therefore its stability and well-being . . . But if a purely secular system of education is deemed in the highest degree objectionable, and a denominational or sectarian system only less objectionable, what is it proposed to establish in their place? I answer, a system of public, unsectarian, but not non-religious schools. It is admitted on all hands that the main work of the school ought to be instruction in the various secular branches. Its primary aim is to fit those in attendance for the active duties of life. But as not inconsistent with this aim, rather as in a higher degree subservient to its attainment, it is desired that the religious element should have a definite place assigned to it in the life of the school; that it should be recognized to this extent at least, that the school should be opened and closed with prayer; that the Bible, or selections from it, should be read daily, either in the common, or in the Douay version as the trustees may direct; that the morality inculcated should be Christian morality, and that the teacher should be at liberty to enforce it, and should be encouraged to enforce it, and should be encouraged to enforce it by those considerations, at once solemn and tender, which are embraced in the common belief of Christendom. A system of public education of this kind, in which religion has a definite but at the same time strictly guarded place assigned to it, ought to be acceptable to the great majority of the people of this province. It has certainly much to recommend it. It has no sectarian features, and yet it is not godless. Religion is recognized in it in such form and degree as to make it possible to give a high tone to the life of the school, as to secure more or less familiarity with the contents of Scripture on the part of every child, and as to make available for the teacher those lofty and sacred sanctions which have in all ages been found the most effective instruments in the enforcement of morality."

GEORGE BRYCE,

Sworn before me, at the city of Winnipeg, in the county of Selkirk, this 11th day of December, A.D. 1891.

ALEX. HAGGART,

A Commissioner, &c.

Certified a true copy of affidavit of George Bryce, filed in above application.

G. H. WALKER,

Prothonotary.

No. 10.

Affidavit of Edmund M. Wood, sworn 10th December, 1891.

In the Queen's Bench.

In the Matter of the Application to quash By-law 514 of the City of Winnipeg.

I, Edmund M. Wood, of the city of Winnipeg, in the province of Manitoba, esquire, make oath and say:—

1. I am an officer employed by the government of Manitoba, and occupy the position of chief clerk in the department of municipal commissioner, and am also employed in the public works department, and know the facts herein deposed to be true.

2. Pursuant to chapter 25 of the statutes passed in this province in the fifty-second year of her majesty's reign, the government of the province of Manitoba erected a building to be used as the Manitoba deaf and dumb institution, the erection and completion of which building with its furniture cost over 18,000 dollars.

3. The government of the province of Manitoba have for several years past carried on at public expense a school for the teaching of the deaf and dumb, and that school is now being carried on at an annual cost of about 7,500 dollars.

4. This money is paid out of the general funds of the province, and the school is open to all classes of people of every creed and belief.

5. The school is purely non-sectarian, and is for the education in a purely secular way of all classes of children.

E. M. WOOD.

Sworn before me, at Winnipeg, in the province of Manitoba, this 10th day of December, A.D. 1891.

JOHN O. SMITH,
A Commissioner, &c.

Certified a true copy of affidavit of Edmund M. Wood, filed on the above application.

G. H. WALKER,
Prothonotary.

No. 11.

Affidavit of Thomas Dickey Cumberland, sworn 10th December, 1891.

In the Queen's Bench.

In the Matter of the Application to quash By-law 514 of the City of Winnipeg.

I, Thomas Dickey Cumberland, of the city of Winnipeg, in the province of Manitoba, barrister, make oath and say:—

1. I have examined the Dominion government census returns of the census of the province of Manitoba taken during the year 1886, and I find that the population of the said province shown by said census was 108,640.

2. From the said returns I find that the five leading religious denominations in the said province were, according to the said census, in number as follows, namely:—Roman catholic, 14,651; church of England, 23,206; presbyterians, 28,406; methodist, 18,648; and baptist, 3,296.

3. I have been a resident of the province of Manitoba since the year 1881.

4. I believe no material change has taken place in the relative numbers of the different denominations aforesaid since the year 1886 in Manitoba.

T. D. CUMBERLAND.

Sworn before me, at Winnipeg, in the province of Manitoba, this 10th day of December, A.D. 1891.

J. B. MORRICE,
A Commissioner, &c., in B. R.

Certified a true copy of affidavit of Thomas Dickey Cumberland, filed on the above application.

G. H. WALKER,
Prothonotary.

No. 12.

Affidavit of Hector Mansfield Howell, sworn 12th December, 1891.

In the Queen's Bench.

In the Matter of the Application to quash By-law 514 of the City of Winnipeg.

I, Hector Mansfield Howell, of the city of Winnipeg, in the province of Manitoba, esquire, make oath and say:—

1. I have resided in this province continuously for the last twelve years. I have travelled over large portions of this province, and am familiar with the general state of its settlement and the distribution of its population.

2. The chief city of the province is the city of Winnipeg, with a present population of about 25,000 people. There are two other towns with populations of about 4,000 each, and there is a large number of villages with populations ranging from 200 or 300 to 1,000 people.

3. According to the last census taken in this year, there is reported to be about 155,000 residents in the whole province, and in my opinion at least 50,000 of these reside in villages and in the towns and in the city of Winnipeg. The remainder of the population reside upon farms pretty evenly distributed over an area of country exceeding 23,000 square miles.

4. From my knowledge of the sparse settlement of this country, I verily believe that if separate schools are granted to the English church people and to the Roman catholics it will be very difficult to support any system of public schools except in the centres of population like towns and cities, and I verily believe that if three systems of schools were established, each system would be very defective and would be of little use towards general education.

H. M. HOWELL.

Sworn before me, at Winnipeg, in the province of Manitoba, this 12th day of December, A. D. 1891.

HEBER ARCHIBALD,
A Commissioner in B.R., &c.

Certified a true copy of the affidavit of Hector Mansfield Howell, filed in the above application.

G. H. WALKER,
Prothonotary.

No. 13.

Judges' reasons.—Judgment.

THE CHIEF JUSTICE.

This is an application made by a ratepayer, a member of the church of England, to quash the by-law no. 514 of the city of Winnipeg, for levying and raising the assessments for the year 1891, on the grounds :—

(1) That by the said by-law the amount estimated to be levied for school expenditure is levied upon members of the church of England and all other religious denominations alike.

(2) That it is illegal to assess members of the church of England for the support of schools which are not under the control of the church of England, and in which there are not taught religious exercises prescribed by that church. The affidavits filed in support of the application allege that at the time of the union with Canada of what is now the province of Manitoba, there were in operation a number of parochial schools, in which the distinctive principles and doctrines of the church of England were taught, and which were supported by members of that church, and out of the funds of the church. In the case of "Barrett *vs* Winnipeg," a Roman catholic ratepayer sought to quash two by-laws of the city, levying by assessment the amount required for the municipal and school purposes of the city for the year 1890. The ground upon which it was sought to quash these by-laws was that, by them the amounts levied for school purposes for the protestant and catholic schools were united, and one rate levied upon protestants and Roman catholics alike for the whole sum. The question involved in that case was whether "The Public Schools Act" of 1890, under the authority of which the city had acted, was one within the power of the local legislature to pass. The argument against its validity was that the Roman catholics had at the time of the union, denominational schools in this province, and therefore the act prejudicially affected a right or privilege which they, as a class of persons, then had by law or practice. The supreme court has decided this contention to be well founded, that the Public Schools Act is one which the legislature of this province had no power to pass, and has ordered the by-laws in question in that case to be quashed. If the facts alleged in the affidavits supporting the present application are correct, and no attempt has been made to contradict them, I do not see how it can be distinguished from "Barrett *vs* Winnipeg." The supreme court there decided a case in which the question was raised as here, by an individual member of the church. There can be no doubt that under the decision in that case the members of the church of England are also a class of persons who had, in the matter of education, a right or privilege by law or practice at the time of the union. In the New Brunswick case of *re* Renaud, the court in New Brunswick dealt with section 93 of the British North America Act. In that case the learned chief justice, now chief justice of the supreme court, held that the words of sub-section 1 were not intended to distinguish between Roman catholics on one hand and protestants on the other. The sub-section means, he said, just what it expresses, that "any," that is every "class of persons," having any right or privilege in respect of denominational schools, whether such class should be one of the numerous denominations of protestants or Roman catholics, should be protected. If that is the true reading of sub-section 1 of section 93 of the British North America Act, and I do not see how any other reading can be given to it, the same construction must be put upon the corresponding sub-section of the Manitoba Act. The words protestant and catholic are used in the British North America Act as in the Manitoba Act. That being so, there can, I think, be no doubt that under the decision of the supreme court in "Barrett *vs.* Winnipeg," the members of the church of England are a class of persons who had, at the time of the union, a right or privilege by law or practice, which is prejudicially affected. I cannot see that the argument can be urged of acquiescence on the part of the applicant. He may not, indeed he did not, move while the previous school acts were in force, but it is a public right he is now contending for, and I do not see that such a constitutional right can be waived. It may slumber, or not be

enforced, but it is there at the same time. If the members of the church of England have the right or privilege under the act, it is illegal to assess members of that church for the support of schools which are not under the control of that church, and as the by-law no. 514, now in question, levies one rate upon ratepayers of all denominations it is illegal and must be quashed. Mr. Justice Dubuc and Mr. Justice Bain both concurred.

Certified a true copy of the judgment of the chief justice of the court of queen's bench delivered on above application.

G. H. WALKER,
Prothonotary.

BAIN, JUSTICE.

I agree with the chief justice that the application should be allowed. In view of the decision of the supreme court reversing the judment of this court in "Barrett *vs.* Winnipeg," 7 M. R., 273, it seems to me that the only question that is open to us to consider is whether the applicant has shown that he is one of a class of persons who at the time of the union were maintaining denominational schools; the affidavits filed show that Mr. Logan was at the time of the union, and still is, a member of the church of England, and at the time of the union, the church of England was maintaining a number of schools, and that these schools beyond question were strictly denominational schools. Now, unless it can be held that sub-section 1 of section 22 of the Manitoba Act applies only to Roman catholics and protestants, and not to Roman catholics and the several protestant denominations or classes of persons who were maintaining denominational schools, the applicant here is in precisely the same position that Mr. Barrett was in in "Barrett *vs.* Winnipeg," and he has made out a much stronger case as regards the episcopalians than Mr. Barrett did as regards Roman catholics. What was shown in the Barrett case was, that the applicant was a ratepayer and a member of the Roman catholic church, and that the church prior to and at the time of the union had been maintaining denominational schools, and the supreme court holding that the Public Schools Act, 1890, prejudicially affected the rights of Roman catholics with respect to denominational schools, declared the act to be invalid, and quashed the by-law that the city of Winnipeg had enacted under its authority. As regards the application of sub-section 1, I agree with the chief justice that it applies not merely to protestants and Roman catholics, but to every class of persons who were maintaining denominational schools at the time of the union, and indeed, the decision in *ex parte* Renaud probably precludes any other view of its application.

I cannot distinguish the present case from "Barrett *vs.* Winnipeg," and I think the by-law must, therefore, be quashed.

Certified a true copy of the judgment of Mr. Justice Bain, delivered on the above application.

G. H. WALKER,
Prothonotary.

No. 14.

Rule absolute quashing By-law No. 514, *date* 19*th December*, 1891.

In the Queen's Bench.

In the Matter of the Application to quash By-law 514 of the City of Winnipeg.

Upon reading the rule granted herein on the 5th day of December, A.D. 1891, upon the application of the applicant, Alexander Logan, to quash the said by-law and the affidavit of service thereof, and upon reading the certified copy of the said by-law and the affidavits and papers filed in support of said rule, and the affidavits of the Reverend George Bryce, Alexander Polson, H. M. Howell, T. D. Cumberland, and

E. M. Wood, filed on behalf of the city of Winnipeg, and upon reading the order by the Honourable Thomas Wardlaw Taylor, chief justice of this court, referring the said rule to the full court, and upon hearing what was alleged by counsel for the said applicant, Alexander Logan, and for the city of Winnipeg and for the attorney-general of the province of Manitoba;

It is ordered that the said by-law 514 of the city of Winnipeg be and the same is hereby quashed.

And it is further ordered that the said city of Winnipeg do pay to the said applicant, Alexander Logan, the costs of and incidental to the said rule and application forthwith after taxation by the master of this court.

By the Court.

G. H. WALKER,
Prothonotary.

Certified a true copy of the rule absolute issued at the above application.

G. H. WALKER,
Prothonotary.

No. 15.

Order granting leave to appeal to Her Majesty in Council, dated 15*th January*, 1892.

In the Queen's Bench.

In the Matter of the Application to quash By-law 514 of the City of Winnipeg.

Upon reading the petition of the city of Winnipeg presented in this matter praying for leave to appeal from the judgment of this court given on the 14th day of December last past, and the affidavit filed in support thereof, and upon hearing counsel for all parties;

It is ordered that upon payment into this court to the credit of this matter of the sum of 2,000 dollars as security, that the city of Winnipeg will effectually prosecute this appeal, the said city be at liberty to appeal from the said judgment to her most excellent majesty the queen in council; and pending this motion the said sum of 2,000 dollars has been paid into this court in this matter by the city of Winnipeg.

It is further ordered that the same be taken as such security and that the said appeal of the city of Winnipeg to her most excellent majesty the queen in council be and the same is hereby allowed.

Dated at the city of Winnipeg this 15th day of January, A.D. 1892.

By the Court.

AUGUSTUS MILLS,
Deputy Prothonotary.

Certified a true copy of the rule absolute issued on the above application.

G. H. WALKER,
Prothonotary.

No. 16.

Prothonotary's Certificate of Correctness of Transcript Record, dated 28th January, 1892.

In the Queen's Bench.

In the Matter of the Application to quash By-law 514 of the City of Winnipeg.

I, Geoffrey Henry Walker, of the city of Winnipeg, in the province of Manitoba, prothonotary of the court of queen's bench for the province of Manitoba, do hereby certify that the foregoing copy of the rule *nisi* herein and the foregoing copies of the affidavits of Daniel Coyle, the Most Reverend Robert Machray, Alexander Logan, Robert Henry Hayward, Alexander Polson, George Bryce, Edmund M. Wood, Thomas Dickey Cumberland, and Hector Mansfield Howell are true copies of the said rule *nisi* herein and of the affidavits of which they purport to be copies.

And I do further certify that the foregoing paper marked "A" attached to the copy of the affidavit of Alexander Logan is a true copy of the exhibit "A" to the said original affidavit of the said Alexander Logan being a certified copy of by-law 514 of the city of Winnipeg.

I do also certify that the pamphlet attached to the copy of the affidavit of Robert Henry Hayward is a true copy of the exhibit "B" to the affidavit of the said Robert Henry Hayward.

And I do further certify that the foregoing copies of the reasons for judgment of the honourable the chief justice of this court and of the Honourable Mr. Justice Bain are true copies of the said reasons for judgments, respectively, and that the foregoing copies of the rule absolute to quash the by-law and of the rule absolute allowing an appeal herein to her most excellent majesty the queen in council are true copies of the original rules absolute issued herein, and that the rules, affidavits, exhibits and reasons for judgments, above referred to, are the only rules, affidavits, exhibits, or other material or reasons for judgments made, filed or given in connection with the said application and constitute the complete record of all the proceedings upon said application.

In testimony whereof I have hereunto set my hand and affixed the seal of the said court of queen's bench for the province of Manitoba, this 28th day of January, A.D. 1892.

G. H. WALKER,
Prothonotary.

www.ingramcontent.com/pod-product-compliance
Lightning Source LLC
Chambersburg PA
CBHW030838270326
41928CB00007B/1104

* 9 7 8 3 3 3 7 3 0 1 5 9 0 *